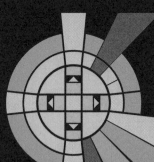

CREDITS

1732011

191984

221084

AUX SYS

SYSTEM DESIGN
NATHAN DOWDELL

LINE DEVELOPMENT
SAM WEBB

WRITING
MARCO RAFALÁ, FRED LOVE,
ANDREW PEREGRINE, ANTHONY JENNINGS,
DARREN WATTS, ALASDAIR STUART,
JOE RIXMAN, OLI PALMER, AND JIM JOHNSON

EDITING
SCOTT PEARSON, SAM WEBB,
JIM JOHNSON, AND RICHARD L. GALE

PROOFREADING
ARIC WIEDER

COVER ARTWORK
TOBIAS RICHTER

INTERNAL ARTWORK
RODRIGO GONZALEZ, TOBIAS RICHTER,
CONNOR MAGILL, JOSEPH DIAZ,
DAVID METLESITS, NICK GREENWOOD,
JOSHUA CALLOWAY, MICHELE FRIGO,
GRZEGORZ PEDRYCZ, WAYNE MILLER

ART DIRECTION
SAM WEBB

GRAPHIC DESIGN
MATTHEW COMBEN

LAYOUT
MICHAL E. CROSS AND RICHARD L. GALE

PRODUCED BY
CHRIS BIRCH

PUBLISHING ASSISTANT
SALWA AZAR

OPERATIONS MANAGER
GARRY HARPER

PRODUCTION MANAGER
STEVE DALDRY

COMMUNITY SUPPORT
LLOYD GYAN

FOR CBS STUDIOS
JOHN VAN CITTERS, MARIAN CORDRY,
VERONICA HART, AND KEITH LOWENADLER

MŌDIPHIÜS™
ENTERTAINMENT
2D20™

Published by Modiphius Entertainment Ltd.
2nd Floor, 39 Harwood Road, London, SW6 4QP, England.
Printed by SKN Druck und Verlag GmbH & Co. KG

INFO@MODIPHIUS.COM
WWW.MODIPHIUS.COM
STARTREK.COM

Modiphius Entertainment Product Number: MUH051062
ISBN: 978-1-910132-86-9

CONTENTS

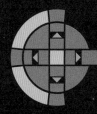

3441A

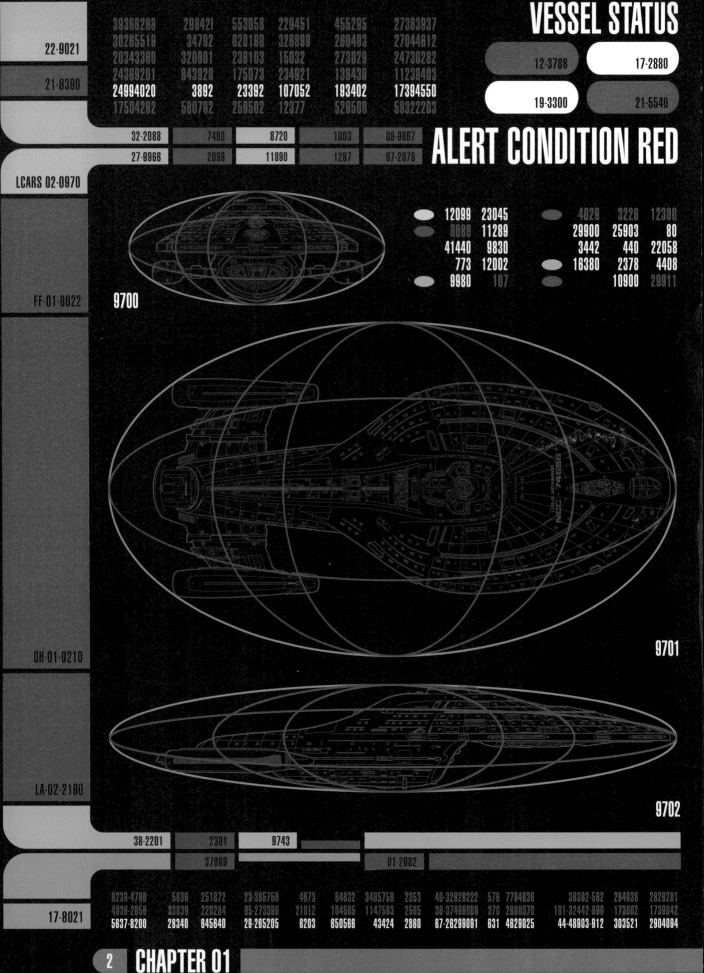

VESSEL STATUS

22-9021

39366298	298421	553058	229451	455295	27383937
30265519	34792	620198	326898	260483	27044812
20343380	320901	236103	15032	273029	24730282
24369201	843920	175073	234921	138430	11239403
24994020	**3892**	**23392**	**107052**	**193402**	**17394550**
17504262	580792	259502	12377	529500	59322203

21-8390

12-3788   17-2880

19-3300   21-5540

ALERT CONDITION RED

LCARS 02-0970

| 32-2088 | 7480 | 8720 | 1003 | 08-9667 |
| 27-9966 | 2099 | 11890 | 1287 | 07-2079 |

FF-01-8022   9700

12099	23045		4029	3226	12300
9088	11289		29900	25903	80
41440	9830		3442	440	22058
773	12002		16380	2378	4408
9980	107			10900	29911

OH-01-0210   9701

LA-02-2190   9702

| 38-2201 | 2301 | 9743 | |
| | 37889 | | 01-2082 |

17-8021

0239-4780	5836	251872	23-305750	4673	84032	3485758	2353	40-32020222	576	7704836		39382-582	264838	2828281
4936-2056	93839	220284	65-273386	21012	104585	1147593	2505	38-37499009	370	2000370		101-32442-890	173002	1738042
5637-8200	28340	645640	29-265205	6203	650566	43424	2860	67-26299091	631	4629025		44-48903-912	303521	2904094

CHAPTER 01.00

INTRODUCTION

49816529318672
3021239494

INTRODUCTION
THESE ARE THE VOYAGES

"THAT MAY BE THE MOST IMPORTANT THING TO UNDERSTAND ABOUT HUMANS. IT IS THE UNKNOWN THAT DEFINES OUR EXISTENCE."

— COMMANDER BENJAMIN SISKO

Exploring the great unknown 'out there' is one of the primary tenets of the *Star Trek* setting. Equally important is exploring the known as well — what lies in the heart and mind of every living being on the countless worlds throughout the Federation and the greater Galaxy. By exploring both the known and unknown, we deepen our knowledge and grow just a little bit smarter.

This book provides you, the Gamemaster or Player of **Star Trek Adventures**, the means to further that theme of exploration. *These are the Voyages, Volume 1* contains eight full-length missions for use with the **Star Trek Adventures** roleplaying game. Each mission has been designed to provide at least 4-5 hours of gameplay for the average group of GM and players. The missions offer a range of experiences, from exploring the mysteries of a wormhole, squaring off against various adversaries, and delving into a variety of strange new worlds and meeting new life and new civilizations.

HOW TO USE THIS BOOK

Each mission may be used as the starting point of a new **Star Trek Adventures** campaign or dropped into an existing campaign with a minimum of revision. They also work well as standalone missions. None of the missions require an encyclopedic understanding of the *Star Trek* universe, and all have been designed to stand independent of any episode or movie in the *Star Trek* canon (i.e., you don't need to have watched a specific episode or movie to understand the events presented in each mission). While some of the missions were written with a specific era of play in mind, guidance is included to help you modify them for use in any era with a minimum of effort.

We hope you enjoy the missions contained within this book. We encourage you share your experiences playing these missions with us and the **Star Trek Adventures** community. And now, gather your crew, select a mission, grab some dice, and boldly go where no one has gone before!

A WORLD WITH A BLUER SUN

An automated distress call diverts the Player Characters to an M-class planet in an uncharted star system that orbits an unstable wormhole. On the surface of the planet, the Player Characters find a crashed Romulan vessel and a shuttlepod from the *NX*-class *Starship Atlantis*, which, according to history, was lost over 100 years ago during the Earth-Romulan war. Yet the pod's chronometer shows it landed only six years ago. When the wormhole inexplicably expands, the immense gravitational forces strain the players' ship's engines to the breaking point. As it attempts to leave orbit, the players' ship is caught by the anomaly. Sensors detect another vessel also trapped — the *Atlantis* with 50 life signs aboard. Players will be tested as different eras collide while the truth about the wormhole is uncovered.

BORDER DISPUTE

The *U.S.S. Nightingale*, a Nova-class Federation science vessel, has accidentally crossed into the Romulan Neutral Zone. Moments after the mistake was discovered, a Romulan warbird decloaked and opened fire. The attack took out most of the *Nightingale*'s engineering section and engineers. However, the *Nightingale* did manage to fire back and appears to have damaged the warbird. Both ships are now stuck in the Neutral Zone until they can effect repairs. Unfortunately, the Romulans are insisting they will take the *Nightingale* and her crew back to Romulus to stand trial for war crimes. But things are not as they seem. Can the players win a battle of wits with a Romulan captain and save the crew of the *Nightingale*, or will this encounter lead to war?

ENTROPY'S DEMISE

Situated near the Federation's border with the Romulan Empire, Carina VII is an idyllic world with lush forests, a pleasant climate, and abundant resources. Until recently, Morgan's Hope, the colony's capital, had thrived, but in the last year, strange events have been occurring: people residing on the planet have aged rapidly, structures that should have lasted for decades crumble in days, and crops that were planted in the morning mature overnight and are rotten before the next afternoon. Even more disturbing, the colonists are spreading rumors that Romulans have been sighted in the system. The Player Characters' ship is dispatched to Carina VII to investigate the cause of the rapid aging.

FORESTS OF THE NIGHT

The players' starship has been assigned to explore a new sector, which is filled with unusual numbers of ion storms. After weeks of cataloging supernovae, quasars, and uninhabited systems, they pick up a strange metallic object on their sensors, and realize it must be an alien ship. It's spinning slowly, moving slower than light, and emitting a strange radiation that is similar to the types of ion storms that plague this sector. However, it does seem to contain indistinct life signs. The crew soon discovers the ship contains a massive forest, inhabited by strange alien lifeforms. The Player Characters will have to deal with ghostly lights, dangerous plants, and something moving in the shadows stalking them through the terrifying terrain, in order to solve the mystery.

BIOLOGICAL CLOCK

The crew's vessel picks up unusual tetryon emissions from an unexplored planet known as Optera IV and investigating the tetryons will lead the crew to encounter giant insectoid creatures. The crew may dismiss the insectoids as unintelligent at first, but they'll quickly discover the tetryon emissions are actually a form of communication employed by the insectoids. The crew will have to decide how the Prime Directive applies as another warp capable species enters the situation.

PLAGUE OF ARIAS

The character's ship is dispatched to Starbase Hephaestus, one of Starfleet Medical's primary research centers. They are to assist in the anniversary celebrations of Doctor Elizabeth Nostrum's work on Arcturus V curing the 'Aria Plague.' The station is a hive of activity and the station's commanding officer, Captain Jenner, needs all hands on deck to assist. A vessel, *The Solid Bet*, is undergoing repairs at Hephaestus. Tulana Vulko, the captain of *The Solid Bet*, has faked the damage her ship sustained. In reality, she's at Hephaestus because of what she and Jenner have in common — a terrible secret regarding the plague Jenner's grandmother, Doctor Nostrum, cured. An investigation, battle, and chase ensue.

THAT WHICH IS UNKNOWN

The Player Characters are on routine patrol when they receive orders to travel to the Takara system, where they will observe and provide security for the field testing of a new and improved high-yield quantum torpedo. They arrive and assist the head of the project, Dr. Ja'Brenn. The prototype is delivered to a derelict craft and activated, but before it can be tested, rogue Klingon birds-of-prey attack the ship; steal the prototype, and destroy the derelict ship before breaking off and fleeing toward Romulan space. Starfleet Command orders the Player Characters to track the Klingons and retrieve the torpedo before they enter the Neutral Zone and defuse a confrontation between the Takarans and Romulans.

THE SHEPHERD

The Player Characters and their ship respond to a distress signal broadcasting from a colony on Stallas II and discover that the inhabitants are locked in conflict. The crew must rescue the civilians who sent the distress signal and get them to safety, while at the same time, investigate the cause of the revolt. The Player Characters must attempt to solve a mystery and find a way to protect the colony as well as preserve the life of a strange alien known as the Shepherd.

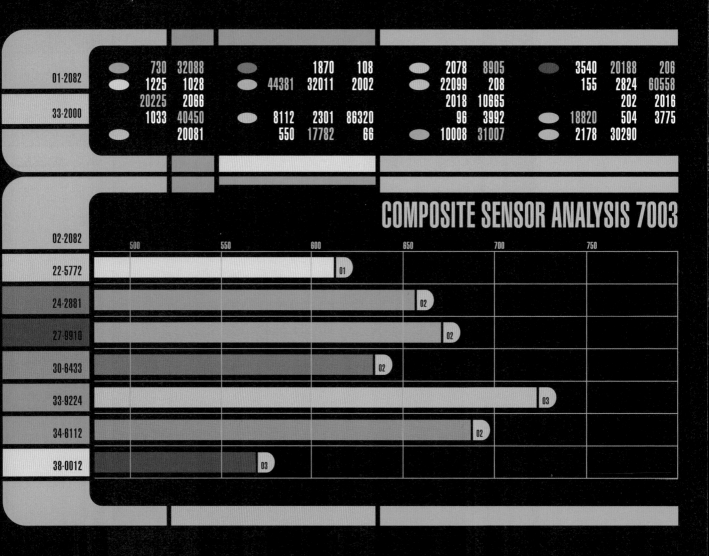

CHAPTER 02.00

A WORLD WITH A BLUER SUN

BY MARCO RAFALÁ

12058672803425
5498456121

A WORLD WITH A BLUER SUN

SYNOPSIS

This mission is set during The Original Series era, but can easily be adapted for use in other *Star Trek* eras (see sidebar).

The Player Characters depart Starbase 4 to begin their five-year mission of deep space exploration, but an old-style automated distress call diverts them to Class-M planet in an uncharted star system. The star system orbits an unstable wormhole, and its planets have all undergone geological disruptions in the recent past. Biosigns identify one human survivor on the Class-M planet. On the surface, the Player Characters find a crashed Romulan vessel and a shuttlepod from the *NX*-class *Starship Atlantis*, which, according to history, was lost over 100 years ago during the Earth-Romulan war, yet the pod's chronometer shows it landed only six years ago. When the wormhole inexplicably expands, the immense gravitational forces strain the ship's engines to the breaking point. As it attempts to leave orbit, the Players' ship is caught by the anomaly. Sensors detect another vessel

also trapped — the *Atlantis* with 50 life signs aboard — but the ship does not respond to hails.

The Player Characters' values will be put to the test when they beam into the middle of a conflict that has raged for two years between the *Atlantis'* pre-Federation Earth crew and an unknown creature who can assume the identity of any one of them. Unable to escape the wormhole or even trust one another, the crew's paranoia has festered into violent xenophobia. They have divided into factions, attacking and even killing shipmates to neutralize the alien threat. Unaware of the wormhole's time dilation, they believe they are still at war. The Player Characters must navigate the factions and diffuse the violence — while also uncovering the truth about the alien and the wormhole.

Hidden among the crew, the alien is a peaceful scientist from another universe who created the wormhole by accident when his prototype gravity drive malfunctioned. His lifeform

ADAPTING THIS MISSION TO OTHER ERAS

Central to adapting this mission to other eras is the *NX*-class *Starship Atlantis*. The *Atlantis* served in the Earth-Romulan War, and went missing during that conflict. How long this vessel has been missing is up to you and your group.

By the time of *The Next Generation, Deep Space Nine*, and *Voyager*, the Earth-Romulan War is in the distant past. For a mission set within this era, 200 years or more have elapsed, depending on the stardate of your game. That interstellar conflict is ancient history to Federation officers from this period. But the war may feel closer to home for officers of The Original Series era. A Player Character from that time-period may still hold onto the prejudices of the past.

For games set within the *Enterprise* era, consider the extremist group Terra Prime. Some aboard the *Atlantis* might be sympathetic to this xenophobic terrorist organization. Terra Prime might even have agents serving in key positions aboard the *Atlantis*. The conflict the Player Characters encounter could be the result of a

coup. Be sure to adjust the history of the *Atlantis* if the Earth-Romulan War has yet to occur in your game.

Regardless of the era, there is still a way to connect the Player Characters more closely to the scenario. A close friend or family member could be serving aboard the *Atlantis* for *Enterprise* era games. In later time-periods, an ancestor may have fought in the Earth-Romulan War. A distant relative may have even served aboard the *Atlantis*. A Player Character could discover this while researching the history of that vessel. What if this relative is still alive aboard the *Atlantis*? This revelation could drive interesting roleplay and add Complications when the PC's responsibilities as an officer in the Federation come into conflict with this long-lost family member.

In addition, while this mission sets Starbase 4 as the point of departure for the Players, feel free to move the starting action to another starbase or location that better suits your ongoing game narrative.

was incompatible with this universe, however, and he absorbed the *Atlantis* crewman in desperation — never intending to injure anyone. Working in secret, he's discovered that the wormhole will continue to grow and encompass countless worlds beyond this star system. The only way to stop it is to detonate the *Atlantis'* warp core at the center of the wormhole and destroy his own trapped vessel. To return the alien to his universe, and protect their own, the Player Characters will need to find him and open a dialogue. But time is running out.

DIRECTIVES

In addition to the Prime Directive, the Directives for this mission are:

- Seek Out New Life and New Civilizations
- Explore Spatial Anomalies and Unexplained Phenomena

Gamemasters begin this mission with 2 points of Threat for each Player Character in the group.

CHAPTER 02.20

A WORLD WITH A BLUER SUN
ACT 1: THE DISTRESS CALL

SCENE 1: THE AUTOMATED DISTRESS CALL

After taking on supplies and final crew assignments at Starbase 4, the Players set course for an uncharted sector of space. The sense of excitement and optimism among the crew is palpable. What will they find in the months and years ahead as they push the frontiers of space and knowledge? Several days out from the starbase, they receive an old-style automated distress call from a pre-Federation vessel and divert course to investigate. They trace the signal to a Class-M planet in an uncataloged star system orbiting an unstable wormhole, and enter a standard orbit around the planet.

INVESTIGATING FROM ORBIT

As they begin their investigation, the Player Characters will probably wish to scan the planet surface. This is a **Reason + Science Task**, assisted by the ship's **Sensors + Science**, with a Difficulty of 1. Success reveals:

- A debris field of Romulan origin. Near the crash site is an old Earth shuttlepod.

- The shuttlepod is intact, functioning in low-power mode. It is transmitting the automated emergency beacon.

- The planet harbors no indigenous intelligent lifeforms but there is one human near the crash site.

CAPTAIN'S LOG

CAPTAIN'S LOG, STARDATE 1416.4

We leave Starbase 4 ready for what's out there, for what lies beyond the edge of known space. She's a fine ship with a fine crew, one of the best in the fleet. I could not be more proud to be their captain. This five-year mission into the unknown is one we have prepared for all our lives. And I'll be honest, it promises to be a fine adventure.

CAPTAIN'S LOG, SUPPLEMENTAL

We intercepted an old-style automated distress call from a old Starfleet vessel. Could the descendants of survivors from an ancient shipwreck still be alive somewhere out there, marooned on a strange planet? I wonder. The science officer has traced the signal to its source: an M-class planet. The star system is uncataloged and unique in my experience as it orbits an unstable wormhole. In two days we will arrive and begin our investigation.

ROMULAN VESSELS AND CLOAKING DEVICES

The Original Series episode "Balance of Terror" implied that Romulan vessels of the 22nd century did not have cloaking devices and this mission operates under that assumption. The problems inherent in the vast power requirements needed to cloak an entire starship had not yet been solved. Therefore, Romulan cloaking technology of the time-period was limited to smaller objects such as mines. The Romulan vessels seen in the *Star Trek: Enterprise* episode "Minefield" could be considered prototypes that eventually failed.

However, this is your game and if your Players are keen to explore the possibility of the discovery of a 22nd century cloaking device, follow them on their course. It could make for an interesting plot thread that you can expand into several new missions for your crew.

If they spend Momentum to *Obtain Information*, the scan reveals:

- The planet's surface suffered recent tectonic plate shifts that caused worldwide earthquakes and tsunamis, suggesting the wormhole appeared near this system only recently. Ongoing volcanic activity has affected both the landscape and climate, cooling much of the world.

Any attempt to open communications with the shuttlepod, will be met with silence.

Enterprising Player Characters might also consider a *Sensor Sweep* of the wormhole. This is a **Reason + Science Task**, assisted by the ship's **Sensors + Science.** Due to strange interference from the anomalous wormhole, the Difficulty is 3. A failure should Succeed at Cost, which will increase the Difficulty by 1 the next time Player Characters use the Sensors System (see Romulan Mines in Scene 2). The Player Characters may wish to launch a probe to reduce the Sensor Sweep Task Difficulty to 1. In this case, if they Succeed at Cost, the extreme gravitational forces also crush the probe, but not before it relays information back. Success reveals:

- The wormhole is unstable at its terminus with anomalous, fluctuating gravity readings.

If they spend Momentum to *Obtain Information*, the *Sensor Sweep* reveals:

- There is an object at the center of the wormhole, perhaps a vessel of some kind.

- Readings are fluctuating: the object appears to be there and then not there in rapid succession.

- This object is at the epicentre of the strange gravity readings and may even be the source.

Note that this object is, in fact, an alien vessel from another universe (though the Player Characters will not be able to determine this). The *NX*-class *Atlantis* is also trapped by the wormhole but the tremendous power generated by the alien ship's gravity drive is wreaking havoc with sensor readings. They won't be able to detect the *Atlantis* until the gravity pulls them closer.

At this point the Player Characters will probably send a landing party to the planet's surface to investigate.

SCENE 2: THE CRASH SITE

Read aloud the following:

The Romulan vessel crashed in what appears to be a once-forested valley, now a jagged landscape where slabs of rock jut upward and limbless trees stand at unnatural angles, hanging on even as the land shifted beneath them. Fallen trees litter the uneven ground and twisted, blue-barked seedlings sprout from the carcasses. Several volcanoes smoke in the distance, filling the sky with ash. The sun is a cold yellow disk in the ash clouds. Small furry-tailed animals, each with one red eye, scurry about, while brightly-colored, beetle-like creatures the size of a human hand dart from rock crevices, their five-pronged pincers snapping.

Not much remains of the Romulan ship beyond huge chunks of charred hull, covered in a blanket of strange, blue-tinted moss — which appears to be one of the few plant species thriving. The pre-Federation shuttlepod rests nearby, its roof and sides thick with the blueish moss except around the door which has been cleared in patches as if removed by hand.

Examining the crash site will require a Task from one of the Player Characters. This could be **Reason + Science** or **Reason + Engineering**, with a Difficulty of 2.

- A success determines that the ship was heavily damaged in battle. There is evidence of radiation consistent with the atomic weaponry and phase-modulated energy canons of the Earth-Romulan War.

- Should a Player spend Momentum to get more information, their tricorder readings will date the debris at just six years old, though the make of the vessel places it firmly within the 22nd century.

THE SHUTTLEPOD

The shuttlepod's registry reveals that it belongs to the *Starship Atlantis,* an *NX*-class vessel believed lost with all hands during the Earth-Romulan war. No Task is required to examine the shuttlepod's systems. Its energy reserves are almost depleted. The shuttlepod's logs show that the craft landed 110 years ago but the chronometer reads that only six years have elapsed.

ENCOUNTER: THE HUMAN SURVIVOR

Tricorder readings show that the survivor is not far from the shuttlepod. In fact, Lieutenant Kearney is watching the Player Characters from behind a large boulder. His uniform, what is left of it, is ragged and torn and provides only modest coverage. His hair and beard are long and tangled in mangy knots.

Six years alone on this strange planet have taken their toll on the man's psyche. To assess his condition, the Player Characters will need to perform a scan with a medical

tricorder. This is a **Reason + Medicine Task** with a Difficulty of 1. A success reveals he is under the influence of a potent substance with psychotropic effects that has altered his perception and mood. His extreme agitated and paranoid state is a direct result of this compound.

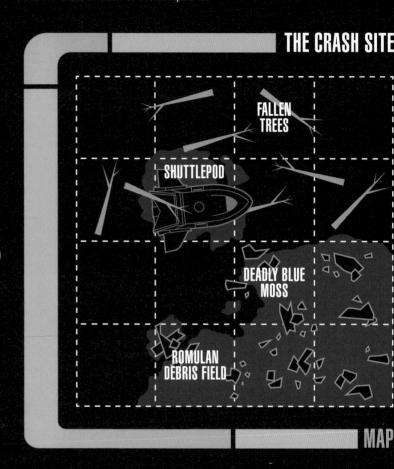

THE CRASH SITE

FALLEN TREES

SHUTTLEPOD

DEADLY BLUE MOSS

ROMULAN DEBRIS FIELD

MAP

LIEUTENANT JOHN KEARNEY, ARMORY OFFICER [NOTABLE NPC]

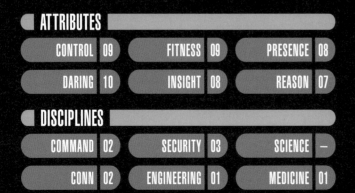

TRAITS: Human, Crazed (until his condition is successfully treated), Loyal (after he has recovered)

VALUE: My Crew is My Family

ATTRIBUTES

CONTROL	09	FITNESS	09	PRESENCE	08
DARING	10	INSIGHT	08	REASON	07

DISCIPLINES

COMMAND	02	SECURITY	03	SCIENCE	–
CONN	02	ENGINEERING	01	MEDICINE	01

FOCUSES: Shipboard Tactical Systems, Survival, Hand-to-hand Combat

STRESS: 12   **RESISTANCE:** 0

ATTACKS:
- Bow (Ranged, 4▲ Piercing 1, Size 2H)
- Unarmed Strike (Melee, 4▲ Knockdown, Size 1H, Non-lethal)

SPECIAL RULES:
- **Weapon-improvisation:** Lieutenant Kearney can improvise a weapon out of even the most innocuous objects. When using an improvised weapon he may re-roll one ▲.
- **Sure Shot:** When using the *Aim* Minor Action, Kearney may re-roll two d20s, instead of the usual one d20, on an attack before the start of his next Turn.

PERSONAL LOG, SUPPLEMENTAL

The Romulan bird-of-prey crashed before her crew could enable the self-destruct mechanism. A cheer went up among the crew in the torpedo bay as huge sections of the enemy vessel burned up in the atmosphere. I don't blame the crew for cheering death. We spent weeks playing a deadly game of cat-and-mouse through a nearby asteroid field until we finally got the jump on them in this uncharted star system.

Scans of the planet revealed that whole segments of the hull went down intact and were strewn across a debris field over 100 kilometers long. Captain Suarez sent us to the planet surface to salvage the wreckage for technology that might help the war effort.

PERSONAL LOG, SUPPLEMENTAL

After a thorough investigation of the Romulan vessel we found no salvageable technology. As we returned to our shuttle, the ground began to quake and one of the distant volcanoes, which we had earlier thought dormant, erupted. Its ash quickly blocked out the sun. We found our shuttle on its side, thrusters damaged. We retreated inside to transmit our report to the *Atlantis* crew and request immediate assistance, but received no answer. We have spent the night holed up here, battered by violent weather, eruptions, and more quakes. None of us have slept. Though at least the night righted the shuttle.

From what we can surmise, the *Atlantis* has disappeared. If she had to break orbit, the captain would have found a way to let us know. Has she been destroyed by another Romulan bird-of-prey in a surprise attack, stranding us here? Ensign Bowman thinks he can repair the shuttle's thrusters, and that we should return to orbit in hopes of finding answers.

PERSONAL LOG, SUPPLEMENTAL

Ensign Bowman is dead. He worked through the night on the thrusters. We found him outside in the grey morning, covered in a strange blueish moss, which seemed to be eating him alive. There was nothing we could do to save him.

The shuttlepod can't leave the planet surface, even if we could repair the thrusters. The moss has infiltrated the engine exhaust ports and drained the power system. It must feed on energy. We are putting the shuttle in low-power mode and setting an emergency distress beacon in hopes of rescue. Using gloves from our EVA suits, Ensign Crane and I will be taking shifts clearing the moss from the door. The ground continues to quake daily.

PERSONAL LOG, SUPPLEMENTAL

Two weeks and the moss regrows each day, almost as fast as it can be cleared. Even rationing, our supplies are nearly gone. We will hold out as long as we can. The weather grows cold. Except for the moss, it seems all other plant life is dying.

PERSONAL LOG, SUPPLEMENTAL

There was an accident. Crane cut his arm while hunting the single-eyed rodent-like animals we have been subsisting on. The moss must have gotten in the wound. It ate him from the inside out, like a flesh-eating bacterial disease. This will be my last entry. No one is coming. I am alone here now.

To determine the source requires a **Reason + Science Task** with a Difficulty of 2. A success reveals:

- A nearby river containing a chemical compound that acts like a powerful psychotropic drug on the human mind.

- If the Player Characters collect a sample of the compound, this creates an Advantage for Kearney's medical treatment aboard the ship (see Dealing with Lieutenant Kearney in Act 2).

During the survivor's time marooned here, he has used up the shuttlepod's stores of weaponry. He has since fashioned a bow and arrow and will attack the Player Characters as they examine the craft. The combat shouldn't last long. A well-placed phaser, set to stun, should subdue Kearney.

Once Kearney is subdued, the Player Characters will receive a frantic call from their ship.

SCENE 3: A CALL FROM THE SHIP

The wormhole has inexplicably grown. This threatening circumstance automatically adds 2 points to the **Threat Pool**. The immense gravitational forces generated by the anomaly have begun to pull the Players' ship out of orbit. Remaining in orbit is placing an excessive strain on the engines. From this point on, staying in this system is a drain on the ship's Power.

- Spend any Threat accumulated to remove 1 Power from the ship for every point of Threat spent.

The wormhole's gravitational forces, coupled with its subspace and temporal distortions, place an enormous strain on the ship. Due to the ongoing effects of the phenomenon, the ship will not be able to generate its full capacity of Power at the start of each scene. It will only be able to generate 1 point of Power.

Power Management Tasks that reroute power from the backup reserves can Succeed at Cost, increasing the Difficulty of Tasks that rely on these and other ship functions.

Without Full Power, basic ship functions are operating on battery reserves. Under these conditions, there is little hope of breaking free without placing an enormous strain on the engines, risking an overload. Should the Power reach 0, the ship suffers an Engine Complication. The engines overload, fusing the dilithium crystal converter assembly. If this happens, the ship cannot generate more Power and warp drive becomes impossible until replacement crystals are found and installed.

At this point, the landing party will probably beam back aboard the ship with Lieutenant Kearney and attempt to break orbit. This is a **Control + Engineering Task** assisted by the ship's **Sensors + Engineering**. Due to the Power problems created by the wormhole, the Difficulty is increased

to 2. The ship should have at least 1 Power available for the transporters but if the Player Characters find themselves without available Power, they have two options:

- Send a shuttle down to the planet to retrieve the landing party. Considering the growing gravitational forces at the heart of the wormhole, this should be a Challenge with simple Tasks, with a Complication Range of 2:

    - **Navigating to the Surface:** This requires a **Daring** or **Control + Conn Task** with a Difficulty of 2.

    - **Landing:** To land the shuttle on the treacherous terrain requires a **Reason + Science Task** with a Difficulty of 2. If the Task fails, the Players may be allowed to Succeed at Cost, adding a Complication such as a Player Character being injured due to a rough landing or the pilot landing the shuttle in the middle of an earthquake.

    - **Return Trip:** Returning to the ship requires another **Daring** or **Control + Conn Task** with a Difficulty of 2.

- Reroute Power to the transporters. See **Beaming over to the *Atlantis*** in Act 2 for an example of how this Challenge might be addressed.

A WORLD WITH A BLUER SUN
ACT 2: THE WORMHOLE

SCENE 1: BACK ON BOARD

When the Player Characters beam back aboard their ship, the gravitational forces wrench the ship from orbit. The vessel begins its slow, inexorable slide toward the wormhole. Intermittent sensor readings now detect the *Starship Atlantis* similarly trapped with 50 human life signs aboard — all that remains of her full crew compliment of 83. Many of the ship's non-essential systems are off-line, including the transporters. Structural integrity is barely holding. Estimated time to full structural collapse: a matter of hours.

Any attempt at opening communications with the *Atlantis* is met with static. This scene moves between the newly discovered *Atlantis*, the dangers posed by the wormhole, and Lieutenant Kearney who requires medical attention.

DEALING WITH LIEUTENANT KEARNEY

It might be wise to restrain him because once Lieutenant Kearney regains consciousness — assuming he was stunned — he will attempt to escape, believing himself captured by Romulans. If the Player Characters don't announce that they have placed Kearney in restraints, allow them to learn this lesson the hard way.

If the PCs didn't examine him on the planet surface, then a medical examination in sickbay is a Difficulty 0 Task. This will determine that Lieutenant Kearney has ingested a substance with psychotropic effects, altering his perception and mood and resulting in his extreme agitation and paranoid state. He should be kept under constant care and observation.

Should the Player Characters wish to speak with Lieutenant Kearney, they will need to address his mental state, most likely by administering a pacifying agent with a hypospray. Calming Kearney down long enough to learn anything will require an **Insight + Medicine Task** with a Difficulty of 1. If he is awake and resists this attempt, make this an Opposed Task, with Kearney using whichever Attribute + Discipline combination that most applies. Should the Task succeed, he will become pacified and appear drowsy. In this state, they will be able to question him just long enough to learn his name, rank, and serial number along with the following details:

- He is an armory officer serving aboard the *Atlantis*.

- His commanding officer is Captain Reinhardt Suarez.

Other information he may provide can be found in his personal logs. He will soon fall unconscious and may be stirred again if a stimulant is used instead of the pacifying agent. Each time the Player Characters do this, they risk harming the Lieutenant. Knowing this is a Difficulty 0 Task, with the Complication range increasing by one after every stimulant, the ship's doctor may advise against it. Eventually, it will become obvious that they will not learn anything useful from the Lieutenant in his current state. Generating a Complication, the characters may injure Kearney, or worse.

Determining the best treatment for Lieutenant Kearney is a Linear Challenge. Since the cause has already been identified above, this will require three Tasks to complete in order:

- **Study the Patient:** A Player Character must study the patient to learn more about what ails him. This is a **Control + Medicine Task** with a Difficulty of 2, assisted by the ship's **Sensors + Medicine**. However, increase the Difficulty by 1 for each time the Player Characters used a stimulant to interrogate Kearney. A success reduces the Difficulty of the next step by one.

- **Find a Treatment:** Using the knowledge obtained from studying the patient and the effects of the psychotropic compound in his system, the Player Character may now formulate a treatment regimen. But Lieutenant Kearney spent years ingesting this compound and that will make finding a way to treat him more difficult. This could be accomplished with a **Control** or **Reason + Medicine Task**, with a Difficulty of 4 (or 3 if the previous step was successful), assisted by the ship's **Computers + Medicine**. If the Player Characters created Advantage by obtaining a sample of the chemical compound, reduce the Difficulty by 1. Once this Task is completed successfully, the Player may now provide relief to the patient.

- **Administer the Treatment:** Using a hypospray, the Player may now administer the treatment to counteract the psychotropic substance and begin to heal the damage caused to his nervous system. However, determining the correct dosage will require an **Insight + Medicine Task** with a Difficulty of 3. A failure means that Kearney has received too high of a dosage, and may be in a coma for days or even weeks. A Success at Cost will result in a Complication (see below).

If the Challenge is completed successfully, Lieutenant Kearney will begin to recover and may even be of help to the Player Characters later in the mission.

Complications on any of these Tasks will slow down Lieutenant Kearney's recovery time. His recovery will take days and he will not be well enough to aid the PCs.

THE WORMHOLE AND COMPLICATIONS

While the ship's doctor examines his patient, the bridge, engine room, and other key systems are bustling with activity. If the Player Characters learned that the object at the heart of the wormhole is the source of the strange gravity readings, they may attempt to destroy it.

Phasers have no effect on the object. A photon torpedo blast registers a miniscule reduction in the gravitational output. The reason: the object is constructed from a completely unknown material — a metal not even on the periodic table — though the Players will be unable to detect this due to spatial and temporal disruptions from the anomaly interfering with sensor readings. These disruptions are a direct result of the object being trapped in a state of both exploding and imploding.

A **Reason + Science Task**, assisted by the ship's **Sensors + Science** with a Difficulty of 0, does enable the Player Characters to deduce that the photon torpedoes only have an effect because they are tactical matter/antimatter weapons. They also learn that even the entire ship's compliment of torpedoes would not be enough to destroy the object. Spending Momentum to gain more information reveals the yield needed:

- The fusion-triggered detonation of a starship's matter/antimatter engine.

TIME DILATION

The gravity drive at the center of the wormhole is causing the entire star system to experience the effects of time dilation. The closer to the phenomenon, the faster the dilation. For the crew of the *Starship Atlantis*, trapped in the anomaly over 100 years, only two years have passed. Six years have gone by for the *Atlantis'* armory officer, marooned on the planet surface. The Player Characters will soon discover that these effects are growing and if left unchecked, they will encompass countless worlds in nearby star systems.

ROMULAN MINES

Complicating matters for the Player Characters are the four 22nd century Romulan mines cloaked in this system. There is

an opportunity, however slim, for the ship to detect this threat just in the nick of time and minimize the impact of the mines, or even avoid them entirely. The Player Characters might see the mines as blips on their scanners, or they may perceive them as curious sensor echoes.

- This is a **Reason + Science Task** with assistance from the ship's **Sensors + Science.** The cloaked mines possess the Hidden 1 Quality so the Difficulty for this Task is increased from 3 to 4.

If the Player Characters succeed in detecting the cloaked mines, the helm will need to take emergency evasive action.

- Evasive Action is a **Daring + Conn Task** with assistance from the ship's **Engines + Conn**. The Difficulty for this Task is 2.

If the evasive maneuvers succeed, the ship successfully avoids detonating the mines. Should the Player Characters fail the detection Task or *Evasive Action* helm action, their vessel will be struck.

- Romulan Mine (Range C, Damage 4⚔ Piercing 3, Persistent 3, Hidden 1, Devastating)

BEAMING OVER TO THE ATLANTIS

If the Players' ship is at 0 Power, then they will need to reroute emergency systems to free up one Power to use the transporters. Transporting a landing party to the *Atlantis* is a Challenge that will require two Tasks to complete in order. It may be beneficial for the Player who performs this Challenge to have a Focus in Transporters.

- **Reroute Power to the Transporter:** This a **Reason + Engineering Task** with a Difficulty of 2. Performing this Task in main engineering reduces the Difficulty by 1. This Task can Succeed at Cost since the engineer is removing power from other key systems: increase the Difficulty and Complication Range by 1 for future Tasks that depend on those systems.

  Once Power has been rerouted successfully, they may move on to the second step.

- **Transport the Landing Party:** With sufficient Power rerouted, the landing party may now beam aboard the *Atlantis*. As per the normal rules, this is a **Control + Engineering Task** assisted by the ship's **Sensors + Engineering**. Due to the Threat brought on from the gravitational forces and the time dilation, the Complication Range increases to 4. The Game Master may also wish to spend Threat to increase the Difficulty.

  In addition, remember to increase the Difficulty by 1 if the Player Characters are not beaming over to the *Atlantis'* transporter pad.

Complications that arise from this Challenge will mean that once the landing party has beamed over, the transporters overload and will need to be repaired before they can be used again. Alternatively, perhaps only a portion of the landing party beamed over successfully. The remainder of the personnel are still on the transporter pad as the system shorts out in a cloud of smoke and sparks. The transporters will need to be repaired before they can be used again.

Should the Task to transport the landing party fail without Complications, then the system has lost power prior to the beam out and the Player Characters must begin again at the first step in the Challenge.

The Player Characters might approach this Challenge with a creative "*It's so crazy it might work,*" plan like attempting to sync the two vessels' transporters together to boost the signal and increase the chances of a successful transport. This would be the second step in the Challenge after successfully Rerouting Power to the transporter. The Attributes and Disciplines involved in this Task could be **Daring + Engineering** or **Reason + Engineering**, assisted by the ship. This is an unusual approach not without danger and so the Difficulty should be set to 4. If they come up with such a plan and execute it successfully, feel free to reduce the Difficulty or Complication Range when transporting the landing party to the *Atlantis*. A failure here could knock out their Transporters, making repairs almost impossible. They may even be forced to attempt to board the *Atlantis* using a shuttle. But piloting a shuttle through the extreme gravitational forces of the anomalous wormhole would be an extraordinarily dangerous endeavor.

SCENE 2: THE ATLANTIS CREW

This scene assumes that the Player Characters have chosen to beam aboard the *Atlantis'* transporter pad. The transporter is on D deck, a section of the ship controlled by Chief Engineer Darlene Phillips and a faction of engineering and security personnel. This faction is currently engaged in a fight against the command faction who plan to capture Phillips and subject her to a military tribunal.

Regardless of where the scene is ultimately set in your game, when the Player Characters materialize they find the ship's emergency lights on and flickering. Turbolifts are inoperable. The hull creaks under the strain from the extreme pressures of the anomalous wormhole. Echoing through the corridors, are the sounds of energy weapons fire and people shouting.

ENCOUNTER: THE BATTLE IN THE CORRIDOR

It isn't difficult for the Player Characters to locate the conflict. As they enter the corridor, Chief Engineer Phillips is stunned and dragged back toward a vertical access ladder by members of the command faction. At this point, the Player Characters must choose how to engage. Here are some likely options:

- The Player Characters take sides in the battle. When the battle ends, they must successfully explain who they are and win that faction's trust. If they helped one of the two factions, reduce the Difficulty of the Social Conflict by 1.

- The Player Characters are captured by the engineering or command faction and undergo hostile questioning. Again, they will need to convince the faction of who they are and why they should be trusted.

- The Player Characters remain hidden and let the situation play out. After the battle, they might approach either faction or move about the ship in secret, gathering information from computer terminals until they're ready to decide on a course of action. In this scenario, they may stumble upon the sciences faction or be captured by command or engineering.

The conflict ends with the chief engineer unconscious and carried up the ladder. With their leader captured, the engineering faction retreats to engineering to formulate a swift reprisal, and rescue.

If the Player Characters sided with the command faction in the initial battle or they are otherwise embedded with them, they must decide if and how to intervene to save the chief engineer's life. If they sided with the engineering faction or are otherwise embedded with that faction, they must decide if they will assist in the chief engineer's rescue. The Player Characters may be swayed to aid engineering if they hear the story of the captain's death and the first officer's suspected culpability (see **The Story of the *Atlantis* and her Crew,** p.18, for details).

Should the Player Characters decide not to get involved in the battle between the two factions, and instead remain

EMERGENCY MASS BEAMING

If the Player Characters suggest risking an emergency mass beaming of the *Atlantis* crew to their ship, most of what follows could still occur aboard their own vessel with some modifications. Assuming the transport is successful, they brought an alien aboard who can assume the identity of any one of them and a crew who have been at each other's throats for two years. In addition, they will still need to find a solution to the problem of a wormhole growing exponentially and generating inexplicable gravitational forces.

hidden this will require a **Control** or **Daring + Security Task** from each Player. This is a Difficulty 0 Task — the two factions are too busy fighting one another to notice anything out of the ordinary.

Any attempt to reason with either faction will require a **Presence** or **Insight + Command Task**. The Difficulty of any social interaction should be set at 3 and modified, either up or down to reflect the situation the Player Characters find themselves in.

SCENE 3: INVESTIGATING IN SECRET

If the Player Characters wish to move about the ship in secret, this action requires a **Control** or **Daring + Security Task** from each Player. Their goal should determine the Difficulty of this Task:

- Difficulty 2 for moving between locations that can reasonably be considered within Medium range. Crew quarters at the end of the long corridor they find themselves in, for example.

- Difficulty 3 for moving between locations within the same deck but requiring several connecting corridors to traverse. Moving from the transporter room to engineering, for example.

- Difficulty 4 for moving between decks.

The *Atlantis* crew always move about the ship in pairs. Security personnel for the command and engineering factions routinely patrol sensitive areas of the ship under their control. Members of the sciences faction, while not skilled security officers, perform the same duties in their respective domains. In fact, the Player Characters may happen upon crewmen chasing, assaulting, or even killing another shipmate suspected of being the alien.

Complications that arise from moving about the ship in secret might include the following:

- Increase the Difficulty by 1 the next time the Player Characters try to move while they wish to remain hidden. This could represent several issues, including the fact that they have appeared on the ship's security monitors.

- The Player Characters have reached their intended destination but are intercepted by two *Atlantis* crewmembers on patrol.

GAINING ACCESS TO A COMPUTER STATION

Should the Player Characters gain access to a computer station, they could learn about what happened to the *Atlantis* (see **The Story of the *Atlantis* and her Crew**, p.18).

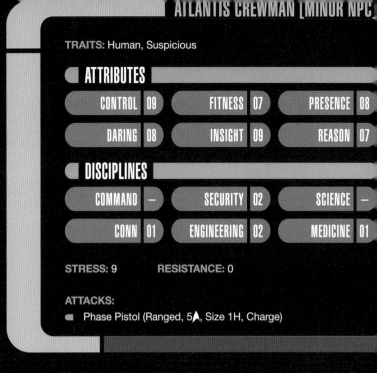

ATLANTIS CREWMAN [MINOR NPC]

TRAITS: Human, Suspicious

ATTRIBUTES

| CONTROL | 09 | FITNESS | 07 | PRESENCE | 08 |
| DARING | 08 | INSIGHT | 09 | REASON | 07 |

DISCIPLINES

| COMMAND | – | SECURITY | 02 | SCIENCE | – |
| CONN | 01 | ENGINEERING | 02 | MEDICINE | 01 |

STRESS: 9   **RESISTANCE:** 0

ATTACKS:
- Phase Pistol (Ranged, 5⚔, Size 1H, Charge)

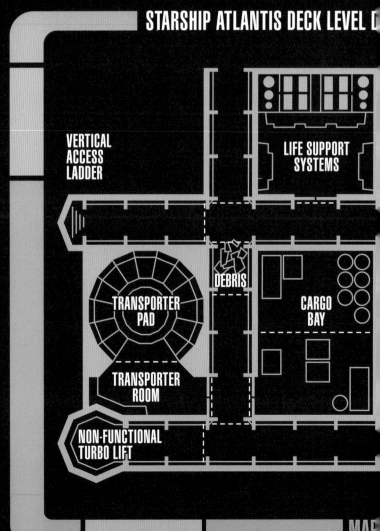

STARSHIP ATLANTIS DECK LEVEL [

VERTICAL ACCESS LADDER

LIFE SUPPORT SYSTEMS

DEBRIS

TRANSPORTER PAD

CARGO BAY

TRANSPORTER ROOM

NON-FUNCTIONAL TURBO LIFT

MAP

It might also be helpful to remind them of the *Atlantis'* condition with a simple, Difficulty 0 Task:

- Many of the *Atlantis'* non-essential systems are off-line to conserve power for the engines and life support.

- The crew maintains a polarized hull plating to strengthen the vessel's structural integrity against the gravitational forces, but this is not a permanent solution.

- Numerous fissures in the hull have formed, forcing the crew to seal off whole decks and the outer areas of decks that have not yet decompressed. Structural integrity collapse is unavoidable. In a matter of hours, the *Atlantis* will be crushed by the anomaly's gravity.

In addition to the above information, Player Characters may uncover a clue to who rerouted the *Atlantis'* Power to the transporter. To do this they must search through the ship's computer files with the intent to find this information. The individual covered his tracks so the Difficulty for such a Task is 4. The appropriate skill for this Task is **Conn**, while the Attribute could be **Daring** or **Reason**. A success at this Task means the Player could trace the action to a specific terminal in engineering. A Complication that might arise from this action means that someone discovered the Player Character snooping around in the log files of that terminal. If this happens, their location has been compromised and a security detail have been dispatched to find them. The Player Characters may spend Momentum to mask their presence in the system, or hide their true location.

THE STORY OF THE ATLANTIS AND HER CREW

The battle-hardened crew of the *NX*-class *Atlantis*, under the command of Captain Reinhardt Suarez, had already seen their fair share of sorrows in the Earth-Romulan war. They had all lost friends and family to this violent conflict, and found themselves hating their faceless enemy. Two years ago, while coming to the aid of Earth Colony III, the *Atlantis* drove off two birds-of-prey. They destroyed one of the vessels and chased the other into an asteroid field before shooting her down in an uncharted star system. Shortly after sending a shuttlepod down to the surface, however, an anomalous wormhole suddenly appeared. It generated an enormous amount of fluctuating gravity. Fighting against that strange gravity sapped the *Atlantis* of her power and trapped the starship.

When the crew detected an alien lifeboat also caught by the wormhole, they brought it into the launch bay. An armed security detail opened the lifeboat and a creature lunged out and instantly absorbed one of the crewmen. It happened so fast that no one there could even describe what the alien looked like before it took the shape of their shipmate. Horrified, they opened fire and the alien fled into the bowels of the ship. The hunt began.

Suspicion and rumors spread like wildfire throughout the crew. Was this a Romulan? No one had ever seen one before. Was the enemy now among them or something more insidious? Trapped aboard the *Atlantis* with systems failing and unable to trust one another, the crew's paranoia festered and violence broke out. Trying to calm a fight between First Officer Caitlyn Mallory and Chief Engineer Darlene Phillips — and the crewmembers that followed each of them — Captain Suarez was killed. Many blamed Mallory — believing she saw an opportunity to take command by killing the captain. Following the Captain's death, Mallory's first official act was to launch an inquisition that only further drove the crew into opposing factions.

NAVIGATING THE ATLANTIS FACTIONS

ENGINEERING FACTION

The engineering faction is controlled by Chief Engineer Darlene Phillips. The largest and most powerful of the three factions, she commands the ship's engineering team and most of the security personnel. They have effectively commandeered the *Atlantis* from their position in main engineering, shutting down all protein resequencers except for those on D deck, and bartering reserve power for fresh vegetables from the sciences faction who maintain the hydroponics bay on E deck.

- **Areas of the ship controlled:** All of D deck is under their control — this houses main engineering, life support, the transporter room, cargo bays, and several quarters for junior officers and enlisted crew.

- **What they believe:** Engineering blames the first officer for the captain's death. Some wonder aloud if she didn't murder Suarez herself in a coup to seize command. They believe the alien is a hostile invader, perhaps a vanguard to an invasion force that is taking advantage of Earth's conflict with the Romulan Star Empire. There could be more aliens out there on other ships in the fleet, perhaps even on Earth, taking over key personnel to compromise their command structure. This faction wants to find and kill the alien — and if half the *Atlantis* crew must be sacrificed in the process, then so be it. This is war.

KEY NPCS
- **Chief Engineer Darlene Phillips** is ruthless, perhaps more ruthless than the first officer. She has been known to cut off life-support to sections of the ship if she thinks the alien is in that area. In this way, she has killed many of her fellow crewmen. She rationalizes these murders by telling herself that difficult choices must be made in wartime for the greater good.

TRAITS: Human, Callous

VALUE: Hesitation Can Be Deadly

ATTRIBUTES

CONTROL 10	FITNESS 09	PRESENCE 08
DARING 11	INSIGHT 07	REASON 09

DISCIPLINES

COMMAND 02	SECURITY 01	SCIENCE 01
CONN 02	ENGINEERING 03	MEDICINE —

FOCUSES: Warp Field Dynamics, Electro-Plasma Power Distribution

STRESS: 10   **RESISTANCE:** 0

ATTACKS:
- Phase Pistol (Ranged, 4▲ Size 1H)

SPECIAL RULES:
- **Engineer's Instinct:** When attempting a Task related to the Engineering Discipline, Phillips gains one bonus d20.
- **Cunning:** During combat, if Phillips spends two Momentum from a successful Task to attempt a second Task, she may re-roll one d20. The Difficulty of the second Task increases by one per the normal rules.

A peaceful scientist from another universe, the alien seeks only to undo the damage he unwittingly caused when his prototype gravity drive malfunctioned. He is plagued with guilt about all that has transpired — and is desperate to prevent the further devastation the unstable wormhole will cause if it is not sealed.

SPECIES: Unknown

TRAITS: Curiosity, Objectivity, Skepticism, Empathetic

VALUES:
- I Will Not Let Countless Species in Both Universes Die because of My Mistake
- Humans Fear What They Do Not Understand.
- Scientific Knowledge Is an Enabling Power that Must Be Used Wisely, and Only for the Common Good
- With More Knowledge Comes More Wonderful Questions, Illuminating the Deepest Mysteries of Creation

ATTRIBUTES

CONTROL 12	FITNESS 08	PRESENCE 08
DARING 07	INSIGHT 10	REASON 12

DISCIPLINES

COMMAND 01	SECURITY 03	SCIENCE 05
CONN 02	ENGINEERING 04	MEDICINE 01

FOCUSES: Astrophysics, Astronavigation, Spatial Phenomena, Physics, Small Craft, Gravity Drive Propulsion, Quantum Mechanics

STRESS: 11   **RESISTANCE:** 2

ATTACKS:
Phase Pistol (Ranged, 6▲ Size 1H)

SPECIAL RULES:
- **Host Form:** When the alien absorbs a sentient lifeform, he not only assumes its shape but he retains the knowledge and memories of his new host body.
- **Inconspicuous:** In his host form, the alien can remain unnoticed or give off the appearance of being non-threatening. Whenever suspicion of his true nature is aroused he may spend one Threat to increase the Difficulty of enemy Tasks by one.
- **Fast Recovery 2:** The alien regains 2 Stress, up to his normal maximum, at the start of each of its turns. If injured, the alien may spend two Threat to remove the injury.
- **Extraordinary Insight 2:** The alien possesses exceptional powers of Insight. Add 2 automatic successes on Tasks using that Attribute.

FIRST OFFICER CAITLIN MALLORY (ACTING CAPTAIN) [MAJOR NPC]

Hardened by the Earth-Romulan war, Mallory has become increasingly ruthless during the Atlantis' current ordeal. She rationalizes her cruel actions with the belief that only she knows what is best for the crew. A charismatic and manipulative leader, her subordinates both admire her strength and fear her wrath.

SPECIES: Human

TRAITS: Manipulative, Overconfident, Single-minded

VALUES:
- I Must Protect the Crew — Even from Itself
- Interstellar War Demands We Set Aside Our Humanity to Safeguard Humanity
- Kindness Doesn't Win Wars
- If I Must I Will Use My Crew's Beliefs against Them to Achieve Victory over Our Enemy

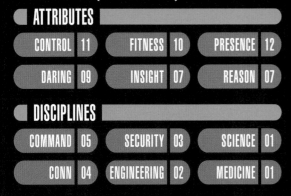

ATTRIBUTES

| CONTROL | 11 | FITNESS | 10 | PRESENCE | 12 |
| DARING | 09 | INSIGHT | 07 | REASON | 07 |

DISCIPLINES

| COMMAND | 05 | SECURITY | 03 | SCIENCE | 01 |
| CONN | 04 | ENGINEERING | 02 | MEDICINE | 01 |

FOCUSES: Helm Operations, Persuasion, Astronavigation, Interrogation, Phase Pistols, Hand-to-hand Combat

STRESS: 13   **RESISTANCE:** 0

ATTACKS:
- Phase Pistol (Ranged, 6▲, Deadly, Size 1H)

SPECIAL RULES:
- **Fearless:** Mallory cannot be easily intimidated. In all Social Conflicts where a character uses threats or other forms of coercion against her she may re-roll two d20s.
- **Resilience:** War has hardened Mallory in both the mind and the body. She suffers one less point of Stress from any damage inflicted upon her.
- **Commanding Presence:** When using the Direct Task to assist one of her subordinates, that individual may re-roll one d20.
- **Exploit:** When using the Exploit Task, Mallory may re-roll any number of d20s.

Ensign Lou Mendola oversees security for the chief engineer. He has never been in a command position before and feels uneasy about the role. He fears Phillips and that fear keeps him in line. He never questions her orders. His proximity to engineering made him the perfect candidate for the alien. The alien absorbed Ensign Mendola several days before the Player Characters arrived. He will soon complete modifications to the ship that will enable him to take control of the vessel from the command center.

COMMAND FACTION

The command faction is run by the first officer and ship's helmsman, Lieutenant Commander Caitlin Mallory. She commands the remaining bridge crew and less than half of the security forces.

LIEUTENANT ED PARISH (ACTING ARMORY OFFICER) [NOTABLE NPC]

TRAITS: Human, Optimistic

VALUE: Hope for the Best, but Prepare or the Worst

ATTRIBUTES

| CONTROL | 08 | FITNESS | 09 | PRESENCE | 07 |
| DARING | 10 | INSIGHT | 09 | REASON | 08 |

DISCIPLINES

| COMMAND | 01 | SECURITY | 03 | SCIENCE | — |
| CONN | 02 | ENGINEERING | 02 | MEDICINE | 01 |

FOCUSES: Phase Pistols, Shipboard Tactical Systems

STRESS: 12   **RESISTANCE:** 0

ATTACKS:
- Phase Pistol (Ranged, 6▲ Size 1H)

SPECIAL RULES:
- **Vigilant:** The Lieutenant gains one bonus d20 to detect any attempts at subterfuge or concealment made in his presence.
- **Chain of Command:** Lieutenant Parish respects the chain of command, but he fears First Officer Mallory more. If someone attempts to persuade him to disobey one of her orders, he may spend one Threat to increase the Difficulty of the Task.

- **Areas of ship controlled:** This faction occupies B deck — comprising secondary laboratories for research and astronomical studies, as well as access to the computer core — and parts of C deck, containing additional science labs, the gym and recreational facilities. Cots are set up in those later facilities as they are now being used as shared crew quarters.

- **What they believe:** The command faction believes that the alien is an experimental bioweapon deployed by the Romulans and they can't let it go free. It is their duty to destroy the bioweapon before it destroys them. Should it reach an Earth colony or other populated area, millions could die.

KEY NPCS

- **First Officer Caitlin Mallory** is known for tossing anyone remotely suspected of being the alien out the nearest airlock. In fact, her orders state that should it be known that a crewman spent any length of time alone — that is to say, not paired with another shipmate — that individual will be sentenced to death by airlock. Mallory accuses the chiefs of engineering, science and medical of mutiny and holds a personal grudge against Phillips for being the first to undermine her authority during this crisis. Because of this she suspects that Phillips might be the alien. Mallory is manipulative in nature. This is her most potent personal Trait. She can easily sway subordinates to act against their better judgement and to do things they would normally not do.

- **Lieutenant Ed Parish** was given a field promotion when his best friend and superior, Armory Officer Kearney, was left behind on the planet. Ed hopes for the best in all things, and is still optimistic that they will be able to rescue Kearney and the other two men marooned on the planet.

SCIENCES FACTION

The sciences faction is made up of the medical and sciences departments and operated jointly by Chief Medical Officer Alejandro Martinez and Chief Science Officer Shiro Takahashi. These two officers don't always see eye to eye and may have heated debates, but they rely on available facts to make most decisions. They might be considered the easiest and most rational faction for the Player Characters to deal with, but they are also the weakest in terms of strength and numbers. And they are not without their faults.

- **Areas of the ship controlled:** This faction occupies sickbay, the hydroponics bay, and the galley on E deck and the science labs on C deck. They have a truce with the first officer who allows them limited, supervised access to the astronomical labs on B deck for the express purpose of studying the anomalous wormhole.

- **What they believe:** There is a debate raging among the members of the sciences faction. They know there is an object at the heart of the wormhole and that the gravitational forces are growing exponentially. The medical and science departments both believe the object is of Romulan origin but they disagree on almost everything else. They have sent probes into the phenomenon to study the object and determine how to disrupt the gravity field long enough for the *Atlantis* to break free. To date, the intense gravitational forces have crushed each probe just as it began transmitting data. The Player Characters may be able to piece this data together from the astronomical lab.

KEY NPCS

- **Chief Science Officer Shiro Takahashi** believes the wormhole is a natural phenomenon, and that the

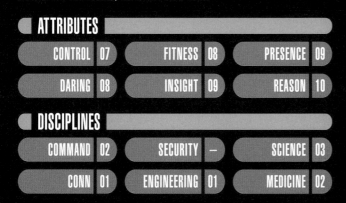

CHIEF SCIENCE OFFICER SHIRO TAKAHASHI [NOTABLE NPC]

TRAITS: Human, Obsessive

VALUE: Science Is the Most Powerful Weapon. We Must Use It to Defeat the Romulans, No Matter the Cost

ATTRIBUTES

| CONTROL | 07 | FITNESS | 08 | PRESENCE | 09 |
| DARING | 08 | INSIGHT | 09 | REASON | 10 |

DISCIPLINES

| COMMAND | 02 | SECURITY | – | SCIENCE | 03 |
| CONN | 01 | ENGINEERING | 01 | MEDICINE | 02 |

FOCUSES: Astrophysics, Spatial Phenomena

STRESS: 8   **RESISTANCE:** 0

ATTACKS:
- Phase Pistol (Ranged, 3▲ Size 1H)

SPECIAL RULES:
- **Hubris:** Shiro may re-roll any number of d20s on Tasks related to the Reason Attribute and Science Disciplines. The new results stand even if they are a worse result.
- **Troubled Conscience:** If confronted with the truth of his crimes, Shiro will push back against admitting his own culpability. In Social Conflicts, spend 1 Threat to increase the Difficulty of Persuasion Tasks against him by one.

CHIEF MEDICAL OFFICER ALEJANDRO MARTINEZ [NOTABLE NPC]

TRAITS: Human, Naive

VALUE: Humans Are Good by Nature — but Impossible Circumstances Bring Out Our Most Primitive Impulses

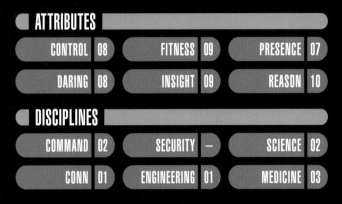

ATTRIBUTES

CONTROL	08	FITNESS	09	PRESENCE	07
DARING	08	INSIGHT	09	REASON	10

DISCIPLINES

COMMAND	02	SECURITY	—	SCIENCE	02
CONN	01	ENGINEERING	01	MEDICINE	03

FOCUSES: Medicine, Virology, Infectious Diseases

STRESS: 9   **RESISTANCE:** 0

ATTACKS:

- Phase Pistol (Ranged, 3▲ Size 1H)

SPECIAL RULES:

- **Field Medicine:** When attempting a Medicine task, ignore any increase in Difficulty for working without the proper tools or equipment.
- **Hippocratic Oath:** In a Social Conflict, if someone attempts to persuade or coerce the doctor into taking an action that goes against his physician's oath to do no harm, he may re-roll any number of d20s.

object at the heart of it is a trapped Romulan vessel that unleashed a bioweapon on the *Atlantis*. Takahashi wants to isolate and contain this bioweapon so that he can study it in depth with the goal of deploying it against the Romulan fleet. The science officer is attempting to develop a method of detecting the alien imposter. To this end, he conducts routine tests on blood and tissue samples collected from members of his faction, and on those killed in fights among the factions. Desperate to distinguish alien from human, Takahashi has graduated from testing samples and corpses to kidnapping his shipmates and conducting experiments on them. These live subjects eventually die, but he believes the results are promising. He is convinced that he will soon be able to find the doppelganger among them. When Crewman Green discovered these experiments, Takahashi murdered Green and made his death look like a suicide.

- **Chief Medical Officer Alejandro Martinez** does not believe there is an alien intruder. Reaching for a way to explain the heinous acts of his fellow crewmates, Alejandro incorrectly theorizes that the weapon traps enemy vessels in an artificial wormhole while bombarding their crews with high-frequency electromagnetic waves that heighten paranoia and violent tendencies in the human mind. His tests are benign and painless compared to the chief science officer's.

SECRET ALLIANCE

Chief Science Officer Shiro Takahashi and First Officer Caitlyn Mallory have formed a secret and uneasy alliance. Mallory has supported and encouraged Takahashi's efforts to detect the alien lifeform — going so far as to provide him with live human subjects. Though he has yet to succeed in his endeavor, Mallory cannot wait. Using Crewman Green's murder as leverage, she coerces Takahashi into agreeing to publicly declare his research a success. They plan to use his sham test to identify Chief Engineer Darlene Phillips as the alien intruder. This secret alliance could be uncovered in the physical sciences lab (see **Ship Locations** for details).

SHIP LOCATIONS

The following locations are not exhaustive but these areas offer some of the best opportunities for the Player Characters to interact with the *Atlantis'* systems and crew.

BRIDGE

The bridge is sealed off due to micro-fractures in the hull that have exposed A deck to the vacuum of space.

ENGINEERING

Located on D deck, this is where the bulk of the *Atlantis'* engineering crew can be found as they diligently care for the engines under the stress of this environment. The chief engineer and her team have slowed the *Atlantis'* inexorable slip further into the wormhole, but the engines can't take much more and they will eventually fail but not before the extreme pressures of the gravitational forces crush the hull. A Player Character can determine this using a **Reason + Engineering Task** with a Difficulty of 2. But they first must either win the trust of this faction, or somehow inspect the systems without being noticed. Similarly, if they can examine the terminal where someone rerouted Power to the transporter using a **Reason + Engineering Task** with a Difficulty of 2, they may discover the following information:

- The engines routinely experience power fluctuations and surges. The logs show that to prevent a critical overload, Ensign Mendola rerouted power to several subsystems, including ship's sensors and the transporter.

COMMAND CENTER

Located on D deck, and under the control of the engineering faction, this is where Ensign Lou Mendola spends most of his time. Stationed here with another crewman, Mendola coordinates with the chief engineer's security personnel while monitoring internal security scans to keep track of the opposing faction's movements, and locate the alien intruder. Player Characters will notice a patchwork of power cables that dangle from open panels in the wall and ceiling and connect to exposed power couplings that tie into several computer terminals. The project looks unfinished and could not be undertaken without the chief engineer's approval.

An examination by a knowledgeable Player Character, such as an engineer, might notice that these modifications, when complete, will allow control of the *Atlantis* from the command center. This requires a successful **Reason + Engineering Task** with a Difficulty of 2. Spending Momentum should reveal how these modifications will endanger the ship due to the increased risk of a cascading overload that could result in a warp core breach. If confronted with this information, Mendola will say that without a functioning bridge the risk is warranted.

TRANSPORTER ROOM

Located on D deck, the transporter has largely been ignored by the crew. Most of the crew never used it, not trusting the nascent technology, and they certainly never suspected that another vessel would come within range to beam over.

LAUNCH BAY

Located on E and F deck, the launch bay decompressed when the bay doors buckled under the strain from the gravitational forces. Player Characters will need EV suits to enter this area. Should they gain entry, they will find the alien lifeboat. A careful analysis of the craft may be able to ascertain that the vessel's point of origin is not from this universe. This could be a **Reason + Conn** or **Science + Conn Task** with a Difficulty of 4.

ASTROMETRICS

This lab is on C deck. If the Player Characters try to direct the ship's sensor array to study the anomalous wormhole, they will need to reroute Power to the Sensors. However, the engineering faction has made rerouting Power to other systems only possible from the engineering room. The Player Characters can examine data collected from previous Sensor Sweeps that are still stored in the lab's Computers. This involves a **Reason + Science Task** with a Difficulty of 3. There might be several different outcomes from a successful Task:

- If they have already visited the Launch bay and examined the alien lifeboat, then a success here means that the Player Characters have determined from the sensor readings that the object at the heart of the wormhole is constructed of the same unknown materials as the alien lifeboat.

- If the Player Characters have not yet been to the launch bay, then a success here reveals nothing that they do

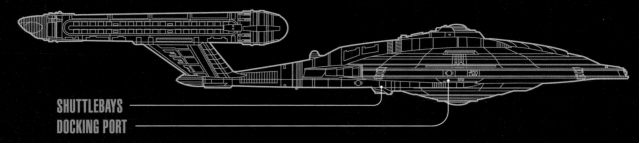

not already know from their own ship's sensor readings. They will, however, see a reference in the data files to the unknown metals of an alien craft in the launch bay.

Unless the Player Characters are here covertly, they must first gain the trust of the command faction before being allowed in the lab.

SICKBAY

Located on E deck, this is where the Player Characters will find Chief Medical Officer Alejandro Martinez performing an autopsy on a recently deceased crewman. Crewman Henry Green's suicide seems obvious from the slash marks on his wrists, but the doctor appears convinced that he will find something else. Should the Player Characters wish to assist the doctor, he will tell them how to find the crewman's quarters. Perhaps they can find something there. In his quarters, they will find a simple suicide note still up on his monitor:

We're locked in a slow dance with death, a shapeshifting Grim Reaper that stalks the corridors. If it doesn't kill us first, the ship will tear itself apart. This way is better. I'm sorry.

- If the Player Characters read Crewman Green's personal logs they will find no evidence of mental instability, or an emotional break that would lead him to the decision to take his own life. They do, however, find an encrypted log entry requiring a Difficulty 3, **Reason + Security Task** to unlock. The data file is corrupted so only some of the log is readable. A Complication might mean that decrypting the file has damaged the remaining data, rendering it unreadable. What remains of the encrypted file points to Crewman Green fearing for his life after stumbling upon the chief science officer in the physical sciences lab conducting an unethical experiment on a living crewman who had been publicly declared dead (see the entry for Chief Science Officer Shiro Takahashi, p.21).

PHYSICAL SCIENCES LAB

Located on C deck, this is mainly concerned with the study of physics, chemistry, and related subjects but the chief science officer has an unorthodox use for this lab. There are several medical scanners and devices from other branches of science that he cobbled together in his desperate attempt

to develop a method of detecting the alien imposter. As the Player Characters turn the corner to approach this lab, two crewmen exit carrying a dead body to an airlock. Then First Officer Mallory exits and Takahashi follows her into the corridor. They are having a heated dispute. Takahashi proclaims that it doesn't work yet. Mallory doesn't care if it works. She castigates the science officer, telling him that he will use the device as directed.

COMPUTER CORE

The computer core is considered neutral ground. It is located at the center of the saucer module and takes up decks B, C, and D. While in the core, Player Characters can move between these three decks using vertical access ladders. Ship's logs and other data pertaining to the *Atlantis* and her crew can be easily accessed from here. Entry points to the core are guarded, on D deck by security from the engineering faction, and on B and C decks by members of the command and sciences faction respectively.

SEALED DECKS

The following decks are sealed due to hull breaches: A deck, the aft section of E deck where the Launch Bay is located, F deck, and G deck.

THE FIRST OFFICER'S ANNOUNCEMENT

At some point, once the Player Characters have completed their investigations — whether they are still covertly on their own, took sides with one of the warring factions, or were themselves captured — read First Officer Mallory's solemn, ship-wide intercom message:

"This is Acting Captain Mallory speaking. As you may know, we now have Chief Engineer Phillips in our custody. She stands accused of mutiny, and may very well be the alien intruder which would explain a great many things about her behavior of late. A military tribunal will convene within the hour in the main conference room on B deck to determine the chief engineer's innocence or guilt. Those who wish to attend must relinquish their weapons to Lieutenant Parish upon arriving through the computer core. All other access points to this deck have been sealed. That is all."

A WORLD WITH A BLUER SUN
ACT 3: FROM A BLUER SUN

SCENE 1: MORE MONSTROUS THAN THE MONSTER

There are several ways for the Player Characters to find themselves at the military tribunal. If they aligned with command they may be attempting to influence the outcome of the proceedings from within the faction to save the chief engineer's life. If they aligned with engineering, they may be assisting that faction's plan to rescue Phillips. Any attempt to persuade this faction to use the stun setting in their plans is a daunting (Difficulty 3) Task. If the Player Characters have not taken sides in the conflict, they may be attending peacefully in a bid to talk reason. Alternately, they may be prisoners of one of the factions, forced to attend the tribunal — or even be on trial themselves.

Regardless of how they arrive, Lieutenant Parish confiscates their weapons in the computer core as they enter B deck. Attempting to persuade Parish against this is an impossible task, unless the Players use any Advantages or Traits to make the Task possible. If Lieutenant Kearney is with the Player Characters at the start of this scene, this may be possible, with a Difficulty reduced to 4. Parish will be overcome with joy and confusion at seeing his old friend alive again. Momentum spent here might even compel Parish to leave his post and join them at the tribunal. The remaining three crewmen will stay behind to guard the only way on and off the deck.

THE TRIBUNAL

Mallory is armed with a phase pistol and seated on one side of a big oval table with three crewmen loyal to her. This is the panel that will decide the chief engineer's fate. The chief engineer sits opposite the panel in restraints. Armed security guards stand on either side of her. Dozens of other crewmembers from across the factions have come to observe. They stand around the sides of the room and spill into the corridor. They appear uneasy in such a large gathering, searching the faces of their shipmates. They wonder who might be the creature and when it might strike.

Mallory gives her opening statement, accusing Chief Engineer Phillips of holding her ship hostage through control of life-support and other essential ship functions. She is charged with mutiny and the murder of dozens of her own shipmates.

Here are some key moments to consider during this scene:

- Mallory calls the first witness, Lieutenant Verga, who narrowly escaped death. He was in the Sensor Monitoring Station on G deck when the chief engineer shut off life-support and sealed the entire deck. He made it out through an access ladder before the emergency bulkheads shut behind him. In his dreams, he can still see his shipmates, gasping for air. He can still hear their cries for help as they suffocated.

- Chief Engineer Phillips interrupts: "Don't pretend you don't know the invader was on G deck that day. I did what I had to do to protect everyone. I lost two of my own crew that day."

- The crowd erupts — in both jeers and cheers. Mallory gavels the table and calls her second witness, Chief Science Officer Shiro Takahashi.

- The science officer pulls out a modified tricorder and says that he has successfully devised a way to distinguish the alien from human. Takahashi scans the

THE RETURN OF ARMORY OFFICER KEARNEY

If the Player Characters were successful in treating Lieutenant Kearney, then during his recovery aboard their ship he learns about the fate of the *Atlantis* and will insist on beaming over to help his shipmates.

Alternatively, the Player Characters might inquire about his recovery over the course of Act 2 and ask for him to be beamed over when he is well enough, believing his presence might assist them in convincing the *Atlantis* crew of their good intentions. If this is the case, Lieutenant Kearney will be happy to help those who rescued him.

Lieutenant Kearney's presence during the tribunal is an Advantage.

chief engineer with the device and declares that she is the intruder. Then Mallory commands a security detail to seize Phillips and take her to the airlock.

INTERVENING IN THE PROCEEDINGS

Player Characters can intervene in these proceedings at any time — and are encouraged to do so — by engaging in a Social Conflict. However, if they spent most their time covertly moving around the vessel, not interacting with one or more of the factions, it is unlikely they will be able to positively affect the outcome of the tribunal.

Attempting to persuade Mallory is a Difficulty 5 Persuasion Task. If the Player Characters have not cultivated a positive relationship Advantage with the first officer or her faction, then she regards them as an enemy aligned with the shapeshifting alien, possibly aliens themselves, and the Difficulty of the Task is increased by 2. With the Difficulty over 5, the Task becomes impossible.

The Player Characters may have a better chance at reasoning with the assembled crew. This is also a Difficulty 5 Persuasion Task. But past actions will affect the difficulty level:

- If any crewmember present previously had a positive interaction with the Player Characters, reduce the Difficulty by 1.

- If the Player Characters provide evidence of the chief science officer's unethical experiments, reduce the Difficulty by 2.

- If the Player Characters have uncovered Takahashi's collusion with the first officer to frame Phillips, they can attempt to appeal to the better angels of his nature. Persuading him to admit that the tricorder cannot distinguish the alien intruder from the crew is a Difficulty 3 Persuasion Task (Takahashi fears Mallory more than the Player Characters so the perceived risk to himself is significant). Forcing him to confront the ugly truth of his own culpability will weigh heavily upon his already troubled conscience so he might also respond well to Intimidation. If the Player Characters successfully induce Takahashi to admit his crimes, reduce the Difficulty of the reasoning with the assembled crew by 1.

- Lieutenant Kearney's presence will also affect the Difficulty (see sidebar). If the Player Characters did not call for Lieutenant Kearney prior to arriving at these proceedings and he has recovered, then he may beam over now.

By taking the narrative up to this point into consideration, the Gamemaster may spend Threat to create a Complication to negate an Advantage. This could come in the form of Mallory manipulating the *Atlantis* crew into believing the Player Characters are in collusion with the intruder.

RESOLUTION

Should the Player Characters successfully intervene on behalf of the chief engineer, and sway the assembled crew against the tribunal, then Mallory attempts to kill Phillips. Her phase pistol is set to Kill and contains the Deadly Quality. Spend Threat to allow Mallory to take the first turn. This is a **Control + Security Task** and the Difficulty is 3 since the Player Characters and multiple *Atlantis* crewman may be struck if a Complication is triggered.

Due to the close quarters, allow the Player Characters a chance to intervene. Here are two options for handling this situation:

SPENDING MOMENTUM

- They can *Create a Complication* for Mallory by spending Momentum to increase the Difficulty of her attack by one for every two Momentum points spent. This represents the Player Characters creating a distraction or otherwise interfering with Mallory's shot.

- They can spend Determination to create an Advantage to negate a triggered Complication. Ask the Player to describe how his or her actions prevented a crewman or fellow Player Character from being struck by the phase pistol.

OPPOSED TASK

- If a Player Character can use Determination tied to an appropriate Value, allow him to spend it in a one-on-one struggle against Mallory before she fires off a shot. This effectively becomes a melee attack with the Player Character attempting a **Daring + Security Task** opposed by Mallory's **Daring + Security Task**. The Difficulty for both is 1. If Mallory wins, then she shakes off the Player Character. Spend two Threat to attempt her attack against Phillips, and increase the Difficulty to 4. If the Player Character wins, the weapon has been knocked from Mallory's hand. If the Player Character wishes to knock her out, then he will need to inflict enough damage to incapacitate Mallory.

If the Player Character's efforts to intervene during the tribunal have failed, then the scene moves down the corridor to an airlock for the execution.

ENCOUNTER: THE ENGINEERING FACTION ATTACKS

Meanwhile, an armed force from the engineering faction overwhelms the guards in the computer core and launches their surprise attack to rescue the chief engineer. This force consists of 15 crewmen armed with phase pistols. Unless the Player Characters had persuaded them otherwise, their weapons are set to Kill. They attack the conference room if the action is still taking place there, or they will intercept the chief engineer as she is being moved to the airlock.

Allow the combat to last several rounds. Perhaps the Player Characters take advantage of the confusion and attempt to retrieve their weapons from the computer core, if they didn't already keep them thanks to Kearney's influence with Lieutenant Parish. At an appropriate moment during the combat, the ship lurches violently and knocks everyone off balance. The red alert claxon blares and the distressed voice of a young crewman crackles over the wall intercom. There is a reactor breach and he can't stop the containment collapse because all controls have been rerouted to the command center.

Make note of the outcome here, for these specifics may affect the course of the rest of the mission:

- Was Mallory successful in killing Phillips?

- Did the Player Characters restrain or stun Mallory?

- If Mallory was stunned or otherwise knocked out and left behind, she will regain consciousness and appear near the end of scene 5.

SCENE 2: ESCAPING THE WORMHOLE

The Player Characters will likely arrive outside the command center first, with ten members of the *Atlantis* crew close on their heels. Some of them are armed and many still harbor deep-seated resentments against the alien. But those who do will wait for their moment to act.

ENSIGN MENDOLA AND THE COMMAND CENTER

The door to the command center is sealed and the only way to open it is to use a phaser to cut through the correct circuits within the wall. This is a Challenge with Simple Tasks:

- Identifying the correct circuits: This is a **Reason + Engineering Task** with a Difficulty of 3. If Chief Engineer Phillips is alive, then her knowledge of the electronic schematics for this area provides an Advantage, reducing the Difficulty to 2. A success creates an Advantage for the next step, while a Complication will make successfully completing the next task more uncertain, increasing the Complication Range to 4.

- Cutting the circuits: This is a **Daring** or **Reason + Engineering Task** with a Difficulty of 4. A Complication here results in damage to the Computer systems, making future Tasks to repair the *Atlantis* more difficult.

STARFLEET ENGINEER

TRAITS: Human

ATTRIBUTES

| CONTROL | 10 | FITNESS | 09 | PRESENCE | 08 |
| DARING | 08 | INSIGHT | 09 | REASON | 10 |

DISCIPLINES

| COMMAND | 01 | SECURITY | 01 | SCIENCE | 02 |
| CONN | 01 | ENGINEERING | 02 | MEDICINE | 01 |

STRESS: 10   RESISTANCE: 0

ATTACKS:
- Unarmed Strike (Melee, 2▲, Knockdown, Size 1H, Non-lethal)
- Phase Pistol (Ranged, 4▲, Size 1H)

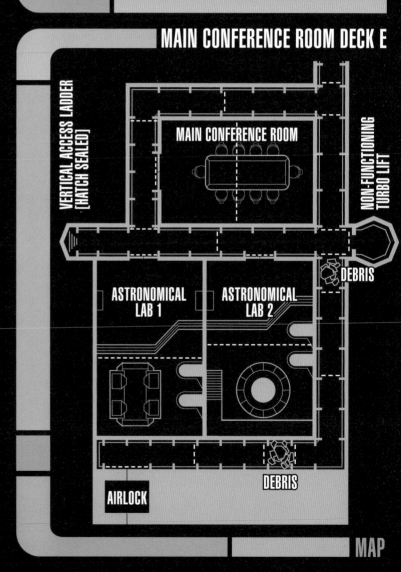

MAIN CONFERENCE ROOM DECK E

VERTICAL ACCESS LADDER [HATCH SEALED]

MAIN CONFERENCE ROOM

NON-FUNCTIONING TURBO LIFT

DEBRIS

ASTRONOMICAL LAB 1

ASTRONOMICAL LAB 2

DEBRIS

AIRLOCK

MAP

While they work to safely open the door, Ensign Mendola speaks to them through the companel on the wall:

"I am sorry but this is the only way. I never meant for any of this to happen. You must believe me. I never wanted to hurt anyone. But you humans, all you do is hurt each other and that which you do not understand. But even though you've hunted me like an animal, I harbor no hatred for your kind. I am a scientist, a peaceful explorer and if I could save your lives I would. Please take comfort in the knowledge that your sacrifice will save millions of lives on countless worlds."

The Player Characters may now wish to engage in dialogue with Mendola via the companel to find out where he came from and what his plans are. Note that if they ask him his true name, the name of his home planet, or anything that must be conveyed in his native tongue, Mendola will reply that the human vocal chords were not designed to speak his language.

If the Player Characters fail to open the door, they can attempt to persuade Mendola to let them in. See **Helping the Alien Get Home.**

GAINING ENTRY TO THE COMMAND CENTER

Once the door is open, the Player Characters must contend with a volatile *Atlantis* crew, many of whom are intent on killing the alien outright. The difficulty of protecting the alien will depend on how persuasive the Player Characters were during the tribunal, as well as the fates of Mallory and Phillips.

If Mallory was stunned at the end of the previous scene, spend Threat to bring her into this scene. She regains consciousness and quietly arrives at the opposite end of

the corridor just as the Player Characters successfully open the door. She is at Medium range with a view of Mendola inside the command center. Spend additional Threat to allow Mallory to take the first turn. She shoots Mendola with a phase pistol, set to Kill. This is a **Control + Security Task** with a Difficulty of 2 and a Complication Range increased one level. A Complication here means that Mallory has struck a terminal in the command center instead of Mendola, making future Tasks to repair the *Atlantis* more difficult.

If the Player Characters did not sway the *Atlantis* crew during the tribunal:

- Add two points to the Threat Pool and engage the assembled *Atlantis* crewmen in combat against the Player Characters. An NPC will throw the first punch, or fire the first shot. At the end of the first round, spend one Threat to add reinforcements.

If the Player Characters successfully swayed the crew during the tribunal:

- Add 1 to the Difficulty of Mallory's attack and increase the Complication Range to 3. This represents the chaos that ensues from several *Atlantis* crewmen who try to thwart her.

If Phillips is alive, she will attempt to stop Mallory and may die in the process:

- Add 1 to the Difficulty of Mallory's attack and increase the Complication Range to 4. A Complication here means that in the struggle, Phillips is struck by the phase pistol and vaporized.

NEVER AGAIN TO SEE A BLUE SUNRISE: THE ALIEN'S STORY

I created a gravity drive — the first of its kind — so that my people could finally leave the confines of their solar system. While testing the prototype, the drive malfunctioned and created this wormhole. My vessel is the beating heart of the anomaly that plagues us both, the gravity drive perpetually imploding and exploding. I abandoned ship in an escape pod and was pulled through to the other side, to your universe. I soon discovered my lifeform was incompatible with this universe. I was dying. When the *Atlantis* brought me aboard, I thought they were my saviors.

I never intended to hurt anyone. On my planet, there are two forms of life that exist in symbiosis. One is sentient, a small weak thing that would surely perish without its companion form: a strong but non-sentient animal. We merge with this creature, absorbing and taking its form, and carrying its primitive memories with us. Together, we have created civilization and have just taken our first steps off-world.

I was not in control of myself, on the verge of death, when my body acted out of self-preservation to absorb Ensign Mendola. I tried, many times, to communicate with the crew. But it quickly became apparent to me that they wanted only one thing: my death. It did not seem to matter to them that we would all soon die. The gravitational forces had already started crushing the hull. Hiding among the crew, my only goal has been to find a way to right my mistake. The wormhole is growing and will soon encompass countless worlds beyond this star system. But a detonation at the center of the wormhole of this vessel's matter/antimatter Engines will destroy my gravity drive and collapse the wormhole. I will do whatever it takes to protect your universe and my own, even if it means never again seeing the blue sunrise of home.

There are only a few ways this conflict can end:

- If Mendola survives, the Player Characters can attempt to persuade him to see past his own guilt — and work with them to find a way to close the wormhole and send him back to his universe. See **Helping the Alien Get Home**. If they fail to persuade him, they may see no other option but to allow Mendola to sacrifice himself to close the wormhole.

- If Mendola doesn't survive, and the Player Characters know his story and plan to close the wormhole, they may then choose to carry out the plan themselves, but someone will need to stay behind to pilot the *Atlantis*. If they didn't learn of his plan, then they may discover it after his death by reading his logs.

REDEMPTION FOR THE ATLANTIS CREW

In all cases, the Player Characters will likely need to convince the *Atlantis* crew to evacuate. This should be easy if the Player Characters successfully swayed the *Atlantis* crew during the tribunal. Even so, many among the war-hardened crew will feel duty-bound to go down with their ship, perhaps doing what they can to ensure hull integrity just long enough for Mendola's plan to work. The Attributes and Skills involved in this Task could be **Presence** or **Insight + Command** with a Difficulty of 3 (4 if they failed to sway the crew during the tribunal).

The degree of success in the Task above is important so the Gamemaster may want to consider encouraging the Players to buy additional d20s. If the Player Characters created Momentum while successfully persuading the crew to evacuate, they can spend it to improve the results. This will give the Player Characters the opportunity to help the *Atlantis* crew see past their short-sighted fears and hatred, helping them understand the alien never intended to hurt them — that their own actions created the violence that ensued. Should this happen, Mallory will step forward and volunteer to pilot the *Atlantis* into the wormhole, thus sacrificing herself so that Mendola can return home.

If Mallory is dead or otherwise not available, then Phillips or Takahashi will volunteer (depending on who is alive).

EVACUATING THE ATLANTIS

The Player Characters will likely need to risk an emergency mass beaming to transport themselves and the entire *Atlantis* crew to their ship, rematerializing in groups. But they will first need to route sufficient Power to the transporters (the transporters will require at least one Power to function).

- **Reroute Power to the Transporter:** This a **Reason + Engineering Task** with a Difficulty of 2 and a Complication Range of 2. Performing this task in main engineering reduces the Difficulty by 1. This Task can Succeed at Cost, increasing the Difficulty and Complication Range by 1 for future Tasks.

Once Power has been rerouted successfully, they may initiate transport.

- **Initiate Transport:** With sufficient Power rerouted, the Player Characters may now attempt an emergency mass beaming to their ship. This is a **Control + Engineering Task** assisted by the ship's **Sensors + Engineering** with a Difficulty of 2 since Player Characters and NPCS are not on a transporter pad. Due to the dangers inherit in mass beaming, the Complication Range increases to 5.

Complications that arise from this Challenge will mean that the Players' ship loses sufficient signal with each successive group rematerialized after the first. Assuming the Player Characters are in the first group, roll 2▲ to determine the number of *Atlantis* crewmen pulled back to their own vessel. Each numbered result is represented in the tens, so a result of 1 means 10 crewmen. Any Effects rolled count as a 1 and also provide an Advantage if the Player Characters attempt to re-transport the lost crewmen.

HELPING THE ALIEN GET HOME

Attempting to persuade Mendola to see past his own guilt and find another way to seal the wormhole, one that does not require his sacrifice is a Persuasion Task with a Difficulty of 3. Failure here forces the Player Characters to evacuate before the *Atlantis'* hull integrity fails. If this happens, Mendola sacrifices himself to seal the wormhole. If the Player Characters do not yet know his story, he transmits his personal logs to the Players' ship so that he will finally be understood.

If the Persuasion Task was successful, they will now need to find a way to seal the wormhole that doesn't involve Mendola's death. The Attributes and Skills involved in this Task could be **Reason + Engineering** or **Science** with a Difficulty of 4. Mendola aids the Player Characters per the normal Teamwork & Assistance rules. A successful outcome uncovers the following options:

- Set the *Atlantis* on autopilot and extend shields from the Players' ship to the *Atlantis* to protect her hull integrity long enough for the ship to reach the craft at the center of the wormhole and detonate.

  - Setting the *Atlantis* on autopilot requires a **Control + Conn Task** with a Difficulty of 0.

  - Extending shields to the *Atlantis* requires at least one Power and a **Control + Security Task**, assisted by the ship's **Structure + Engineering** with a Difficulty of 1.

- Reverse the tractor beam from the Players' ship and use it to push the *Atlantis* into the alien vessel at the center of the wormhole before it detonates. This would eliminate the need for someone to stay behind.

Reversing the tractor beam requires a **Control + Security Task**, assisted by the ship's **Weapons + Security** with a Difficulty of 3. A Complication here could mean that the *Atlantis'* hull is too fragile and crumples under the force of the tractor beam.

NAVIGATING THE WORMHOLE
The explosion of the *Atlantis'* matter/antimatter reactor destroys the alien vessel. With the gravity drive no longer in a never-ending state of exploding and imploding, the extreme gravitational forces quickly dissipate. The wormhole will recede in a matter of minutes until it too is gone. If the Player Characters convinced Mendola of a better way, he now has a chance to return home in a shuttle. However, the terminus of the wormhole periodically fluctuates between multiple universes so they

will need to conduct a Sensor Sweep to determine the exact moment when the passage opens into the alien's home universe.

With the interference from the alien gravity drive negated, this a simple **Reason + Science Task**, assisted by the ship's **Sensors + Science** with a Difficulty of 0. A successful scan reveals the pattern in the fluctuations at the terminus allowing Mendola to pilot a shuttle home.

As Mendola traverses the wormhole, the Sensors from the Players' ship detect an alien vessel on the other side ready to receive the shuttlecraft. Moments later, as the wormhole closes for good, a message signals through from the other universe. Though his human form could not survive long, his people provided him with a new form to absorb.

A WORLD WITH A BLUER SUN
CONCLUSION

ALTERNATIVE ENDING

If Mendola died and the Player Characters never learned his story, their choices and actions may be constrained. They will still need to evacuate before the *Atlantis'* warp core goes critical or the gravitational forces destroy the ship. In this case, the *Atlantis* will not be close enough to the alien vessel to destroy it but the explosion will disrupt the gravity drive long enough for the Players' ship to break free at warp. This requires at least warp factor three (moving three zones away from the wormhole). If their warp drive is down, the Player Characters may choose instead to avert the *Atlantis'* containment collapse and take the dilithium crystals back to their own ship. Once aboard with the crystals, they will be able to restore their own Engines. Though the power drain is still a threat, they might have sufficient power to jump to warp and escape the gravitational forces. However, the wormhole continues growing and over time will become a problem that the Player Characters may have to deal with in a future mission.

Once the debilitating effects of the alien's gravity drive are dealt with, full power gradually returns to the Players' ship. If some of the *Atlantis* crew survived, Starfleet will court-martial them for their actions. Members of the *Atlantis* crew who did not directly commit atrocities will be pardoned, but will need long-term psychological support.

If the Player Characters were successful at redeeming certain NPCs during the mission, they may wish to send a statement in support of leniency for the sentencing of those individuals. Such an action, however, is not without moral considerations. Starfleet might encourage Player Characters to weigh the severity of the crimes committed against the assistance those individuals provided. There is no easy answer.

CONTINUING VOYAGES...

Depending on the nature of the damages to their ship, the Player Characters may need to make repairs. The starship might even be forced to make the trip under impulse power. But it won't be long until they are under way again, setting course for the deep reaches of unexplored space…

CHAPTER 03.00

BORDER DISPUTE

BY ANDREW PEREGRINE

23987239798238
2937522398

CHAPTER 03.10

BORDER DISPUTE
INTRODUCTION

Border Dispute is an investigative mission involving a cunning Romulan plot. The Player Characters are ordered to the edge of the Romulan Neutral Zone with all due haste. A Federation science vessel has entered the zone and been fired upon by a Romulan Warbird. Can the Player Characters resolve the situation, or will it escalate into war between the Federation and the Romulan Star Empire?

The *U.S.S. Nightingale*, a *Nova*-class Federation science vessel, has accidentally crossed into the Romulan Neutral Zone. They believe it is due to a failure of their navigation array, but according to the Romulan treaty, this may be considered an act of war. Moments after the mistake was discovered a Romulan warbird decloaked and opened fire. The attack took out most

of the *Nightingale*'s engineering section and engineers. However, the *Nightingale* did manage to fire back and appears to have damaged the warbird. Both ships are now stuck in the Neutral Zone until they can effect repairs. Unfortunately the Romulans are insisting they will take the *Nightingale* and her crew back to Romulus to stand trial for war crimes once their ship can leave.

But, as you might expect with the Romulans, things are not as they seem. The whole encounter is a plot to reclaim a deep cover agent they have aboard the *Nightingale*. The agent was meant to 'die' in the attack and secretly beam to the Romulan ship with a large amount of data the agent planned to steal about the Federation forces along the

OTHER ERAS OF PLAY

For those Gamemasters from the *Enterprise* and Original Series eras, there are a wide variety of options you can use to make your games compatible with a *Next Generation* era game. The important thing to remember is to have fun with it and use whatever options you think will work. Here are a couple of suggestions you can use for your players:

- For *Enterprise* era Players, it is rather tricky to adapt this mission as the Romulans are still an unknown quantity. However, while there is no Neutral Zone, there is still a border, as Captain Archer knows only too well. So this mission should take place after the episode "Minefield" where the Romulans have decided they need to know more about humans, and have sent an agent into Federation space. In this case the Nightingale is keeping an eye on the border as part of its survey. The agent will have an easier time of things, as the Federation doesn't know what a Romulan looks like. But their problems are the same as they need to escape without the Federation discovering this fact. As before the Nightingale crosses the Romulan border (instead of the Neutral Zone), and the Romulans decide to claim it. The Player Characters are unable to enter Romulan space but can beam aboard the Nightingale and the mission can continue much as it is written. However, the

Romulans will only communicate using audio transmissions and will not beam aboard the Nightingale for any reason to preserve their identity. In this era the Nightingale is possibly an old Neptune class survey vessel. The Romulans will use an old style bird-of-prey but intimate more are cloaked nearby. If the Gamemaster is feeling especially vindictive, they might decide that the events of this mission actually trigger the Romulan War, no matter how well the Player Characters do!

- For Original Series era Players, this mission is reasonably simple to adjust. However, it should take place after "Balance of Terror" when the Federation are more aware of what Romulans look like. The plot of the mission remains the same, but some of the starship classes will have to change to suit the era, such as the Romulans using a D7 battle cruiser instead of a *D'deridex* warbird. As we have fewer Federation ship classes for this era, the Nightingale could be *Constellation*-class, but one refitted for scientific missions. It will therefore have improved scanners, but fewer weapons. While there is no war with the Dominion, the Romulans may still be upset over the recent theft of a cloaking device in "The Enterprise Incident" episode and so the Federation is eager not to push them any further.

Neutral Zone. Unfortunately, the captain of the *Nightingale* managed to encrypt the main computer before the agent could get to the data. So now the Romulans are waiting for their agent to reclaim the data before they leave, hoping that their sabre rattling will keep the Federation on the back foot.

The Player Characters arrive to assist the *Nightingale* and try to mollify the Romulans. While they help to repair the *Nightingale*, can they uncover the Romulan agent on the crew? Can they win a battle of wits with a Romulan captain and save the crew of the *Nightingale*, or will this encounter lead to war?

DIRECTIVES

In addition to the Prime Directive, the Directives for this mission are:

- Ensure the Romulans Have No Excuse to Declare War on the Federation
- Save as many of the Nightingale Crew as Possible
- Do Not Allow Federation Technology to Fall to the Romulans

Gamemasters begin this mission with 2 points of Threat for each Player Character in the group.

CHAPTER 03.20

BORDER DISPUTE
ACT 1: THE NIGHTINGALE

The mission begins in the briefing room of the Player Character's ship, which is en route to the Romulan Neutral Zone and due to arrive within the hour. This is an opportunity for new characters to introduce themselves and for the players to ask the Gamemaster about the mission in character, as part of the captain's briefing. It is also an opportunity to formulate a plan, or at least prioritise a few objectives for their mission.

CAPTAIN'S LOG

STARDATE 48326.3

We are en route to the Romulan Neutral Zone after receiving a sub-space transmission from Admiral Moss at Starfleet Headquarters. It appears that one of our ships, the *U.S.S. Nightingale* has suffered a navigational error and entered the Romulan Neutral Zone. By the terms of the treaty made after years of conflict with the Romulans, this may be considered an act of war. The Romulans have already fired on the *Nightingale*, crippling her on the wrong side of the border, and claim the crew are now prisoners of war. As the nearest ship to this critical situation, we have been ordered to assist the *Nightingale*

and defuse the situation whatever way we can. But it is going to be difficult as Admiral Moss was clear that we are not to enter the Neutral Zone ourselves unless it is a dire emergency. I will have to hope the Romulans are feeling charitable enough to let us beam over to the *Nightingale*.

This couldn't have come at a worse time, diplomatically. The Federation badly needs the Romulans to come to their aid in the war with the Dominion. Unfortunately the Romulans will know they have the upper hand in any negotiations and will make use of that. But our main concern is to avoid another war, and to protect the lives of the *Nightingale* crew. What worries me is that this is an aggressive stance for the Romulans. Are they gunning for another conflict with the Federation, or is there more to this situation than meets the eye?

Admiral Moss sent a series of files in his transmission that detail the *Nightingale* and her crew, including several personnel files and detail on *Nova* class ships in general. The Gamemaster can give out as much of this detail as the Player Characters require. There is also a copy of the

USS NIGHTINGALE [FEDERATION NOVA-CLASS SCIENCE VESSEL]

The *Nova* class is a relatively new class of ship (commissioned 2368) designed for extended science missions in Federation space. It is not well suited for combat, but can handle herself if things get tough. While it isn't designed for long-term deep space missions it has ample supplies and storage and can manage without starbase support for much longer than most vessels of a similar class.

The *Nightingale* has been assigned to planetary surveys along the edge of the Romulan Neutral Zone. While they are keeping an eye out for anything suspicious from the Romulans, they are absolutely not engaged in any espionage, quite the opposite in fact. With the Federation hoping the Romulans will join them in the war against the Dominion, they don't want anything upsetting them.

In command of the *Nightingale* is Captain Laura Blake, an experienced officer with a strong military background, who has crossed swords with Romulans on many occasions. Her first officer is Commander Alison Lewis, who is much younger with a more scientific background. Together they have made an excellent team, and Captain Blake intends to retire and leave the *Nightingale* in Commander Lewis' hands quite soon.

MISSION PROFILE: Scientific and Survey Operations

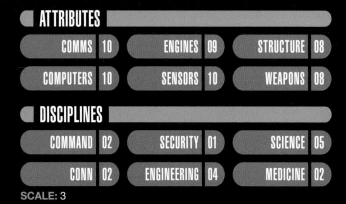

ATTRIBUTES

COMMS	10	ENGINES	09	STRUCTURE	08
COMPUTERS	10	SENSORS	10	WEAPONS	08

DISCIPLINES

COMMAND	02	SECURITY	01	SCIENCE	05
CONN	02	ENGINEERING	04	MEDICINE	02

SCALE: 3

ATTACKS:
- Phaser Arrays
- Photon Torpedoes
- Tractor Beam (Strength 2)

SPECIAL RULES:
- **Advanced Senso Suites** (Talent)
- **High Resolution Sensors** (Talent)

transmission Starfleet received from the *Nightingale's* first officer. It shows a disheveled Commander Lewis, the *Nightingale's* first officer, on a badly damaged bridge, surrounded by chaos, and she says:

"This is Commander Alison Lewis of the Federation starship Nightingale. A navigational error has caused us to enter the Neutral Zone and we have exchanged fire with a Romulan warbird. Captain Blake was killed in the attack and we have lost main power. Warp drive is offline and ships systems are down but life support is good and holding. Repairs are underway but we have lost most of our engineering crew. The Romulans are claiming we are now prisoners of war and insist they will take us to Romulus for trial once their ship is repaired. We don't want to give in to their demands, but we also don't want to start another war. Starfleet, please advise."

SCENE 1: THE EDGE OF THE NEUTRAL ZONE

Arriving at the edge of the Neutral Zone, the Player Character's ship will be hailed by the *Nightingale*. In command is a human woman they will recognise from the previous distress call as Commander Lewis. The *Nightingale* still appears badly damaged and a scan will show they have no warp power, weapons or shields. Commander Lewis will be glad of their help. The situation is grave. Captain Blake is dead and most of the engineering crew are dead or injured as the Romulans targeted the engineering section of the *Nightingale*. Commander Lewis is now the acting captain and badly in need of engineering teams from the Player Characters' ship to help with repairs. But they will need to talk to the Romulans about beaming over.

As if on cue, the Romulan ship will also hail the Player Characters. The Romulan captain is Commander Mheven, who initially takes a very aggressive posture. She reminds the Player Characters that entering the Neutral Zone will be considered an act of war and that the *Nightingale* and her crew are now prisoners of the Romulan Star Empire. While firing on the *Nightingale* was rather aggressive, Mheven is within her rights to have done so under the terms of the treaty.

The Player Characters will need to negotiate to be allowed to beam over to the *Nightingale*. Beaming over without permission will not actually provoke much of a response from the Romulans, but it will weaken the Player Characters' position if they need anything else. In fact, Mheven may decide such an action justifies her beaming some of her troops aboard. Even captured, a federation vessel is still 'sovereign territory', even more so having unconditionally surrendered. So it is legal, but diplomatically very aggressive for the Romulans to send over armed troops. It will make it harder to claim they are the good guys. However, the real reason is that it will make it trickier to make a swift getaway if Mheven can get what she wants.

TRAITS: Romulan, Disguised, Fearful of Superiors

VALUE: I Will Not Fail in My Duty to the Empire

ATTRIBUTES

CONTROL 12	FITNESS 09	PRESENCE 09
DARING 10	INSIGHT 11	REASON 09

DISCIPLINES

COMMAND 04	SECURITY 03	SCIENCE 02
CONN 02	ENGINEERING 01	MEDICINE 01

FOCUSES: Diplomacy, Intimidation

STRESS: 12 **RESISTANCE:** 0

ATTACKS:
- Unarmed Strike (Melee, 4🗡 Knockdown, Size 1H, Non-lethal)
- Dagger (Melee, 4🗡 Vicious 1, Size 1H)
- Disruptor Pistol (Ranged, 6🗡 Vicious 1, Size 1H)
- **Escalation** Disruptor Rifle (Ranged, 7🗡 Vicious 1, Size 2H, Accurate)

SPECIAL RULES:
- **Guile and Cunning:** When attempting to remain hidden or unnoticed, a Romulan may spend one Threat to increase the Difficulty of enemy Tasks to detect them by one.
- **Wary:** Whenever a Romulan attempts a Task to notice or detect an enemy or hazard, they may re-roll one d20.

While Commander Mheven will make the Player Characters work for it, she has every intention of allowing them to beam over. She knows the Romulan agent must need help to get the computer system on the *Nightingale* working. This interaction should be mainly just a role-playing encounter. However, the Player Character negotiating should make an **Insight + Command Task**. The Difficulty is only 1, but failure means the Player Characters will have to offer Mheven something to get permission to beam over. This is most likely to take the form of assurances they will behave (granting a Diplomatic Advantage if they don't), or that the Romulans can beam a small group of their people over.

Momentum can be spent to *Obtain Information* more about Mheven:

- Mheven is more nervous than someone in her position should be.

- Mheven constantly seems to play for time, drawing out any negotiation with slow decisions and pedantic clarifications.

- Mheven's nervousness seems to be a concern about how her superiors may judge her actions in this encounter.

At this point, Mheven is desperately trying to think ahead and figure out a new plan. She wants to buy more time in the hope that the Romulan agent can get what he needs, she has a better idea, or the Federation makes a mistake she can use. The original plan was to reclaim the agent and then allow the *Nightingale* to go. The Romulans would have then got what they wanted and appeared to be magnanimous and merciful. But now, getting the data is more important than good relations with the Federation.

IRW T'VAREN [ROMULAN D'DERIDEX-CLASS WARBIRD]

TRAITS: Romulan Warbird

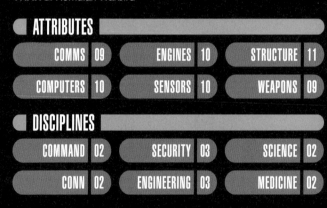

ATTRIBUTES

COMMS 09	ENGINES 10	STRUCTURE 11
COMPUTERS 10	SENSORS 10	WEAPONS 09

DISCIPLINES

COMMAND 02	SECURITY 03	SCIENCE 02
CONN 02	ENGINEERING 03	MEDICINE 02

POWER: 10 **SCALE:** 6

SHIELDS: 14 **RESISTANCE:** 6

CREW: Talented (Attribute 10, Discipline 3)

ATTACKS:
- Disruptor Banks (Energy, Range Medium, 10🗡 Vicious 1)
- Plasma Torpedoes (Torpedo, Range Long, 6🗡 Persistent 8, Calibration)
- Tractor Beam (Strength 5)

SPECIAL RULES:
- **Cloaking Device**

COMMANDER ALISON LEWIS
(FEMALE HUMAN FIRST OFFICER) [MAJOR NPC]

TRAITS: Human, Young, Dedicated

ATTRIBUTES

CONTROL 09	FITNESS 08	PRESENCE 10
DARING 09	INSIGHT 10	REASON 10

DISCIPLINES

COMMAND 04	SECURITY 02	SCIENCE 04
CONN 02	ENGINEERING 02	MEDICINE 02

FOCUSES: Astrophysics, Spatial Phenomena

STRESS: 10   **RESISTANCE:** 1

ATTACKS:
- Unarmed Strike (Melee, 3▲ Knockdown, Size 1H, Non-lethal)
- Phaser type-1 (Ranged, 4▲, Size 1H, Charge, Hidden 1)
- **Escalation** Phaser type-2 (Ranged, 5▲, Size 1H, Charge)

If she doesn't get the agent and the data, she may be forced to try and claim the *Nightingale* and her crew so she doesn't come home empty handed.

SCENE 2: BEAMING ABOARD

Having gained permission to beam a team across the Player Characters can meet up with Commander Lewis, assess the *Nightingale* and find out what really happened. Commander Lewis will be more than happy to hear any thoughts they have as she is very worried for her crew, and that their actions might start a war.

The events, as far as the *Nightingale* crew know, are the following:

- Commander Lewis was on duty, and Captain Blake was in her quarters. Everything was fine and no problems had been reported with the ship. Their course was to travel along the Federation side of the Neutral Zone to their next survey assignment.

- During a routine course check, the navigator realised the ship had gone off course. While the navigation systems showed they were on course, a more detailed position check proved they had slid into the Neutral Zone.

- Before they could change course, the Romulan *D'deridex*-class warbird decloaked and opened fire. The *Nightingale* returned fire but the next Romulan salvo took out their shields and made a direct hit on engineering. The *Nightingale* is no match for the warbird, so Lewis is surprised they inflicted as much damage as the Romulans say they did.

- Having disabled the *Nightingale*, the Romulans opened a channel to demand surrender. Lewis surrendered on the condition they were allowed to apprise Starfleet of the incident. It was at this point she sent the distress call.

- Out of the *Nightingale*'s crew compliment of 80, at least 40 people have been either killed or injured in the attack. Almost all the engineering team are incapacitated. While most of the crew are scientists, many have proved competent engineers and are working on repairs.

- Among the dead is Captain Blake. She was found dead in her quarters having activated the 'Romulan Protocol.' It is thought she was hurt trying to get to the bridge, but made it back to her quarters to activate the protocol.

- The 'Romulan Protocol' is an emergency procedure to ensure that an enemy cannot claim too much Federation data should they capture the ship. On the command of the Captain, it locks out and encrypts all data in the computer system. This means the computer is shut down and locked, although it will maintain life support and manual systems. It can be undone given time and/or a Federation computer lab.

There are a few things that don't add up though:

- The failure of the navigation systems might be a fault, but could potentially be sabotage.

- The Romulans arrived very quickly. They may have been cloaked in the Neutral Zone already. But if not they were on the border and able to speed over in double quick time. The Romulans will probably claim the latter if challenged ("a lucky coincidence"). Either way it is either against the terms of the treaty or a galaxy sized coincidence.

- The Romulans claim the *Nightingale* damaged their own warp systems. This may be true as they got in a solid hit. It seems the Romulan shields were down. While this isn't unusual after coming out of a cloak, it is odd that a trained Romulan crew didn't manage to get the shields up before the *Nightingale* fired.

While Commander Lewis wants to get to the bottom of what is going on, she really needs to look to the safety of her ship and crew. She is happy for the Player Characters to investigate, but the *Nightingale* really needs help in terms of repairs and seeing to the wounded.

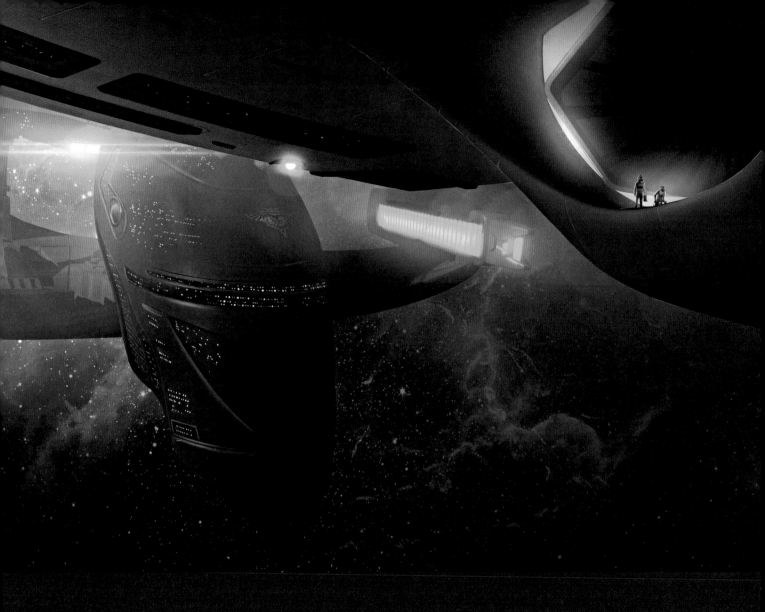

"LET'S JUST BEAM UP THE CREW!"

Enterprising characters might decide that beaming the *Nightingale* crew aboard their own ship will solve the problem. Sadly it won't, and may actually hand the situation to the Romulans.

The main problem is that the Player Character's ship can't beam everyone up in one go, and even if it could there are several wounded that will need to be prepped for beaming before they can be moved. Additionally, the Romulans will notice. The warbird will easily detect any

beaming, and know roughly how many people. It will be pretty simple to determine an evacuation is in progress.

The Romulan's reaction is a simple one, put a tractor beam on the *Nightingale* and tow it further into the Neutral Zone. This will reveal that their engines work, but they can always say they were repaired just in time. From outside the Neutral Zone the Player Character's ship is on the edge of beaming range, and way out of weapon's range.

Remember that at any point the Romulans find the Player Characters especially trying, they might choose to send troops the Nightingale. This means everything the Player Characters try to do will be under Romulan supervision.

BORDER DISPUTE

ACT 2: INVESTIGATIONS AND REPAIRS

In this act, the Player Characters should investigate the situation aboard the *Nightingale* while they work to repair it. There are a variety of paths the Player Characters might take. So they should spread out across the ship doing different jobs to gain more clues to what is going on as they help with repairs. With several engineering crews needed aboard the *Nightingale*, players might take the opportunity to create secondary characters to play. However, there are plenty of tasks that anyone with the training of a Starfleet officer will be able to take on.

These acts will introduce quite a few NPCs from the *Nightingale*, which is intentional. When the players begin to suspect a saboteur is aboard they will tend to make a shortlist based on which NPCs have names rather than following the clues. So, introducing as many new faces as possible will force them to figure out what is going on rather than metagame the situation. In fact, once the sabotage becomes clear, the Gamemaster should take any opportunity to enhance their paranoia. Who they decide to trust (if anyone) might prove extremely important in how the final events play out. Ironically, if they are too secretive, Commander Lewis might begin to suspect them of working with the Romulans!

SCENE 1: REPAIRS AND MAIN ENGINEERING

Most of the damage to the *Nightingale* is due to the strike on main engineering. The damage is extensive, and the warp core is offline for safety reasons. It has been shut down as the systems that keep it in check are in bad need of repair. The damage also caused power surges across the ship that have blown out power conduits and impacted on several secondary systems. Luckily, the life support systems are in no danger, but power reserves are low across the ship.

The mood in main engineering is a sombre one. The remaining engineering staff is mostly here and all of them have lost many of their crewmates. While most people on the *Nightingale* have lost friends today, the engineers have

lost more than most. With the chief engineer dead and no clear successor among the remaining engineers, no one is really in charge of the operation. The remaining engineers have gathered teams of mostly scientists and each taken on certain areas to fix separately. If one of the Player Character engineers wants to take charge, they can coordinate the operation more effectively. But this will take a **Presence + Engineering Task** with a Difficulty of 2 to take on the role of temporary chief engineer.

While there are repair teams working on the ship, none of them have much engineering experience beyond basic training. This means any Player Character with an Engineering Discipline of 3 is more qualified to lead any team. While other Player Characters can assist, the Gamemaster should try to find a way to make them repair team leaders, they are the heroes of the mission after all! If some Player Characters only have a low Engineering Discipline, they might be assigned to a less important system, where the rest of their team know less than they do. There are not enough engineers on the *Nightingale* for every team to have one!

Once assigned to a team, the leader will have to make an assessment of the work. They should make a **Reason + Engineering Task** with a Difficulty of 1. Any Momentum they gain will be useful in effecting repairs. If the team leader wishes, they may also attempt to motivate their team with a **Presence + Command Task** with a Difficulty of 2. If they succeed, they might also gain more Momentum to use on repairs. But if they fail, their team becomes despondent and the Complication range for any repair work increases by 1.

Repairing any system might take the repair crew across the ship. While most of the damage is in engineering, power surges have taken out several EPS conduits. This means that Player Characters who want to find an excuse to catch up with a particular NPC or investigate another area of the ship will have an adequate excuse to do so. The Gamemaster might wish to pepper any exploration of the *Nightingale* with additional encounters, such as wounded or trapped personnel, or additional damage that hasn't been discovered.

Repairing each system is an Extended Task. Luckily each Task has a Resistance of 0 as the crew have the right tools and training. The team leaders for each repair will need to attempt a Task, but as they can assemble a team they could also have 4 Crew Support to use during the repair. If a Player Character is not leading a team, they might assist their team leader.

The repairs are a race against time, as the ship needs to be operational if it is to escape the Neutral Zone. Unknown to the Player Characters, they also need to fix the ship before the computer is unlocked. Each Interval of the Extended Task is 15 minutes, with each Task attempt taking 2 Intervals. So if the repair team do well the system will be repaired quickly. Once a system is repaired, that repair team will be free to move on to another task or assist another team.

The different systems that are in need of repair are listed below. The Gamemaster might add more to reflect a particular Focus a Player Character has. In addition to detailing the appropriate Task, magnitude and Work track, we have also added the name of a *Nightingale* officer who might be leading or working on the team that the Gamemaster can characterise to expand the *Nightingale* crew:

WARP CORE SAFETY SYSTEMS [LT N'VOL – MALE VULCAN]
Insight + Engineering (Focus Warp systems)
MAGNITUDE: 2 **WORK: 8** **DIFFICULTY: 2**

Making this repair allows work on the warp core to proceed without fear of a breach. It can be skipped if the Captain agrees, but if so all work on the warp core will raise the Complication range by 3!

EXTERIOR HULL PLATING [LT SAVREK – FEMALE ANDORIAN]
Daring + Engineering
MAGNITUDE: 3 **WORK: 9** **DIFFICULTY: 3**

This job involves going outside the ship in an environmental suit to seal plating across any breaches in the hull. This job is quite simple in that the plates need to be bolted to the hull and surrounded with sealant. But working in an EV suit, under the shadow of a Romulan warship is a little unnerving and clumsy.

Repairs to the hull will allow the emergency force fields to be disengaged, freeing more power. These repairs can be left undone. But until they are fixed the drain on the power systems made by the emergency force fields means any use of a ship's system incurs an increase in Difficulty by 1.

WARP CORE REPAIR [LT MORROW – FEMALE TELLERITE]
Control + Engineering (Focus Warp systems)
MAGNITUDE: 2 **WORK: 14** **DIFFICULTY: 1**

Repairing the warp core is not especially difficult, but it is time consuming and needs to be done very carefully. At the first Breakthrough, partial power can be restored, granting

It is quite possible the Player Characters won't be able to work on every system that needs their help. In which case the following timetable gives the Gamemaster an idea of what will be repaired and when if left to the NPCs. The Player Character's work on complimentary systems might speed up some of the following if the Gamemaster allows.

The options the Player Characters will have may well depend on the state of the *Nightingale* as the various crews attempt repairs. The following is a timeline of what systems will be repaired and when as time goes on:

- **0 Hours:** Player Character crew arrives.

- **2 hours:** Exterior plating repaired*, shield and propulsion systems made safe

- **3 Hours:** Computer repaired to the point file extraction possible*, weapons and secondary systems made safe.

- **4 hours:** Warp core online. Main power partially restored. Impulse engines restored. Minimal shields possible. No phaser power but ship may fire torpedoes.

- **5 hours:** computer repaired and unencrypted.

- **6 hours:** Warp drive restored and online, all weapons and shields online.

*Until this is repaired, all use of a powered ship's system needs an extra success as the emergency force fields drain the supply and make equipment unreliable. Complication range of such Tests is also increased by 2.

*At 3 hours it is possible to differentiate the various files within the computer. While they remain heavily encrypted, they might be downloaded. The Romulan agent will do this and make a getaway if his position is unsecure.

minimal shields and impulse drive. Several minor systems can also be powered if the hull plating has been fixed; this includes internal scanning systems and replicators. Once the second Breakthrough is achieved, full power is restored to the ship as well as warp drive, full shields and weapons.

GENERAL SHIPS SYSTEMS
Reason + Engineering
MAGNITUDE: 1 **WORK: 6** **DIFFICULTY: 1**

There are several ship's systems that need to be checked over and secured before they can receive power safely.

Each system listed below is a separate repair task, but they all have the same Magnitude and Work track as they all involve much the same effort. If the warp core is repaired and powered up, these systems can be given power without any work being done. But the Difficulty to use them will be +1 and the Complication range is increased by +2. The various systems in need of a safety check and repair are:

- **Propulsion systems:** Warp and impulse drive (Ensign Costallan — Female Human)

- **Shield systems:** All forms of defensive shields (Lt Tyrell — Male Andorian)

- **Weapon systems:** All phaser banks and torpedo launchers (Ensign Collin — Female Human)

- **Secondary systems:** Lighting, Replicators, Internal scanners and many other minor systems (Lt Carial — Male Tellerite)

COMPUTER REPAIR
Reason + Engineering (Computers)

MAGNITUDE: 3	WORK: 12	DIFFICULTY: 2

Repairing the computer is difficult but once the code is cracked will move along quickly. Once two Breakthroughs have been made, the various file headings and system sections will become available. While they will still be encrypted, they might be copied or moved. Once three Breakthroughs are made, the computer system will be fully restored. There are more complexities around repairing the computer core though, which we detail further on.

SCENE 2: THE WOUNDED AND SICKBAY

Another Task that will allow the Player Characters to explore the *Nightingale* is to look for wounded. There are plenty of people unaccounted for. They might be trapped in rooms, or under beams or bulkheads. Some might have been knocked unconscious since the attack. Any Player Characters who set off to search for wounded will find some. It is up to the Gamemaster to decide the circumstances they are found in. Any that are found should be brought to sickbay.

Any Player Characters with medical training will be badly needed in sickbay. Nearly half the crew is either dead or injured. While the sickbay is undamaged, it is overrun with wounded from all over the ship. The medical team is still working to triage the incoming wounded and stabilise the worse cases. Walking wounded line the corridor outside the sickbay, and several nurses move along the line offering emergency aid.

There are eight full time medical staff on the *Nightingale*, and several biologists have been deputised as medics. The team is led by the chief medical officer, Lieutenant Commander G'Trel, a stern Vulcan. There is no power to run the Emergency Medical Hologram. With no computer the medical team have no access to medical records. While the medics know the crew very well the Complication range for any Medicine Tasks is increased by 2. The surgical systems all work, but with automation gone, scans have to be done more carefully. Surgical space is at a premium as there aren't enough surgical beds to cope with demand.

MAKESHIFT MORGUE
Many of the crew, including the captain, have lost their lives. There has been no time to do any autopsies or properly determine the cause of death for most losses. The medical team simply doesn't have the time and the dead aren't going anywhere. All the medical teams have been doing is establishing if a patient is living or dead. If they are alive they can heal them, if they are dead there is nothing they can do. The Player Characters will be told this by any of the medical team if they ask. But with the focus very much on the living at the moment they won't think to mention it unbidden.

A nearby cargo bay has been turned into a makeshift morgue (with an adjustment of the temperature controls for the room). The dead are laid out in rows and tagged for identification. Each body is covered with a sheet out of respect. If the Player Characters want to investigate the dead, no one will

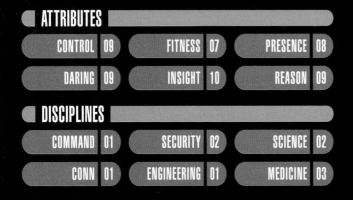

LIEUTENANT COMMANDER G'TREL
(MALE VULCAN MEDICAL OFFICER) [NOTABLE NPC]

TRAITS: Vulcan, Encyclopedic Medical Knowledge

ATTRIBUTES

CONTROL	09	FITNESS	07	PRESENCE	08
DARING	09	INSIGHT	10	REASON	09

DISCIPLINES

COMMAND	01	SECURITY	02	SCIENCE	02
CONN	01	ENGINEERING	01	MEDICINE	03

FOCUSES: Trauma Surgery

STRESS: 9   **RESISTANCE:** 1

ATTACKS:
- Unarmed Strike (Melee, 3⚔ Knockdown, Size 1H, Non-lethal)
- Phaser type-1 (Ranged, 4⚔, Size 1H, Charge, Hidden 1)
- **Escalation** Phaser type-2 (Ranged, 5⚔, Size 1H, Charge)

really mind. However, as far as the *Nightingale* crew are concerned, there are far better things they could be doing with their time. Even so, there are valuable clues here.

It takes about ten minutes to fully autopsy any of the bodies (using a tricorder). In most cases the cause of death will be asphyxiation from exposure to vacuum, physical trauma from falling wreckage, or burns from a nearby explosion. All of these wounds are consistent with what the Player Characters have been told of the attack.

The most interesting body is that of Captain Blake. It is believed she was badly injured when a bulkhead fell on her, although she just made it to her quarters to activate the Romulan Protocol before the wound killed her. A cursory investigation shows a nasty wound on her head. But a proper autopsy reveals something else. The actual cause of death was asphyxiation, and marks on her neck are consistent with strangulation. Many of her wounds might also have been caused by physical combat. It is clear her death was not an accident; there is a murderer on board!

CAPTAIN BLAKE

When the warbird attacked, Captain Blake went to activate the Romulan Protocol. The Romulan agent did his best to stop her and they fought brutally while the attack rocked the ship. The agent eventually tried to strangle her to stop her giving the final command sequence, but it wasn't enough. Captain Blake died knowing she had done all she could. After this the Romulan tried to cover his tracks, and explained his injuries as wounds from a nearby explosion in a power conduit.

SCENE 3: THE NAVIGATION ARRAY

Given that this situation began with a navigation error, the Player Characters may want to investigate the navigation systems. There is a rough record of the navigational readings available from the navigation station on the bridge. Given the computer may still be offline; there is not much to go on. But what information there is confirms the ship was on course, even though that course shouldn't have taken it into the Neutral Zone. If they investigate the navigation station, a **Reason + Conn Task** with a Difficulty of 1 will show there is no fault with the console. There are two other possibilities: that the officer on duty is to blame (accidentally or purposefully) or that the navigational sensor array itself is somehow faulty.

LIEUTENANT DALLON (MALE UNJOINED TRILL NAVIGATION OFFICER) [MINOR NPC]

TRAITS: Trill, Unjoined, Feeling Guilty

ATTRIBUTES

| CONTROL | 11 | FITNESS | 08 | PRESENCE | 10 |
| DARING | 09 | INSIGHT | 07 | REASON | 09 |

DISCIPLINES

| COMMAND | 01 | SECURITY | 01 | SCIENCE | 01 |
| CONN | 03 | ENGINEERING | 02 | MEDICINE | 01 |

STRESS: 9   **RESISTANCE:** 0

ATTACKS:
- Unarmed Strike (Melee, 2▲ Knockdown, Size 1H, Non-lethal)
- Phaser type-1 (Ranged, 3▲, Size 1H, Charge, Hidden 1)
- **Escalation** Phaser type-2 (Ranged, 4▲, Size 1H, Charge)

If they wish to question the navigation officer, Lieutenant Dallon (a male unjoined Trill) was on duty during the incident. He will answer any questions as he feels responsible for the mistake and the loss of so many of the crew. Dallion is deeply upset, blaming himself for the navigation error that has caused the death of his crewmates. Actually, his forethought to make a position check may have given the *Nightingale* precious moments to prepare before the warbird decloaked. Even so, he is taking it very badly.

While not an especially important character, Dallon is an easy stooge for the blame. Was it sabotage or is he a Romulan agent who steered them badly on purpose? Is his grief just a clever mask? He might be too upset to talk to the Player Characters, making them suspicious he is avoiding them. The Gamemaster should use Dallon as a red herring, either to make the Player Characters suspect a Federation spy, or just to make them more paranoid.

If the Player Characters want to investigate the navigation sensors, they will have to go outside the ship. The array is located a little above the main deflector dish and will need EV suits to get to it. This array is essentially a junction box for several scanning systems across the ship. It also contains several isolinear chips to adjust the scan cycle, sensitivity and coverage of the navigational sensors. It is easy to access once you get to it, as long as you don't mind taking a walk along the hull.

should attempt an **Insight + Engineering** (Focus: Sensors or Navigation) **Task** with a Difficulty of 1. If they succeed, it is clear someone has sabotaged the array. Several isolinear chips have been rearranged to cause the malfunction. This is clear evidence of deliberate sabotage, which is a vital clue.

If the Task generates Momentum, the Player Characters might wish to spend a point to *Obtain Information* about what the sabotage was intended to do. If they do they can tell the sabotage is an expert job. Instead of causing a failure of the array, it has lengthened its scan cycle. This means the system is only checking its position once in a while rather than constantly. As nothing was actually wrong, the fault remained undetected. But this fault will have had to be carefully timed. Only at this point on the Neutral Zone border would the sabotage have caused the ship to cross over, traveling straight ahead instead of making a vital course correction. So the saboteur must have carried out their work just an hour or so before the attack, and must therefore still be aboard the *Nightingale*!

Normally the computer would keep a record of any environmental suit use or access to the navigation array. While this data may be in the computer, those records will be unavailable until the computer is decrypted. This might make the Player Characters prioritise reinstating the computer, which ironically plays into the saboteur's hands.

SCENE 4: SCANNING THE ROMULANS

Cynical Player Characters might not trust the Romulans' report of the damage to their ship. There is only really one way to confirm their story (or lies) and that is to do a scan of their ship. While considered rude, such a scan is not considered an act of aggression. Scanning takes very little power, and as a science vessel, the *Nightingale* has extremely advanced scanners. Not only can it scan the Romulan ship, it is possible to do so without the Romulans detecting the scanning beam.

To complete a scan the Player Characters will have to be on the bridge, and so get the permission of acting Captain Lewis. This will require a **Presence + Command Task** with a Difficulty of 2 (Lewis really doesn't want the Romulans upset!). If the Player Characters ask the Romulans if they mind, they most certainly do! They will suggest they will consider it more than just rude. It will then be impossible to scan the warbird undetected as the Romulans will be looking for such duplicity.

Making the scan will require a **Daring + Conn Task** with a Difficulty of 1. However, the Complication range for the roll is increased to 16-20 if the Player Characters are trying to narrow the bandwidth to mask the signal. Rolling a Complication will mean the Romulans detect the scan. If the

Player Characters don't narrow the bandwidth, the Romulans will detect the scan automatically.

A successful scan will reveal the warbird is barely damaged at all. It took a certain amount of hull damage, but its armor stopped most of the attack. It was certainly not damaged as badly as they said. However, it is also clear they got their shields up very late. What the Player Characters can't tell is that this was actually because they were hoping to beam up the agent (which they can't do with shields up). Without a doubt, whatever damage the Romulans took in the attack, their ship is easily capable of warp and taking the *Nightingale* back to Romulus. So the question is why haven't they?

If the Player Characters challenge the Romulans on this, Commander Mhaven will insist they have only just completed repairs, and that they can't expect to understand the intricacies of advanced Romulan technology with their simple Federation scanners. However, now they no longer have the excuse of engine damage the Romulans will have to advance the timeline. Commander Mheven will give the *Nightingale* crew an hour to get themselves in order before they take them to Romulus. This is essentially a way to tell their agent they have an hour to get what they came for before the Romulans leave!

SCENE 5: REPAIRING THE COMPUTER CORE

As detailed above, another system that is in need of repair is the computer core. While it is not damaged the Romulan Protocol has encrypted all the data within it. To decrypt the system will take several hours of work. However, this is not actually that critical. Only the data has been encrypted, not the computers control systems. So while some systems lack a certain amount of automation, the computer isn't required to get the *Nightingale* out of the Neutral Zone.

However, the computer does contain all manner of information that will be helpful to the Player Characters' investigation. It contains details on who has recently accessed which systems as well as many recordings of who was where on the ship and what they were doing. It also contains the personnel files on all of the *Nightingale* crew.

The problem is that while the information in the computer will potentially help the investigation, the Romulan agent aboard the *Nightingale* also needs the computer working. This agent has been in deep cover as a Vulcan geologist called Tellek for over eight years in Starfleet. He worked his way into a posting on the *Nightingale* and has been here for two years, thoroughly entrenched among the crew. The Romulans are very interested in knowing what Federation forces are lined up along the Neutral Zone. While a military vessel might prove more useful, it would also be more secure. By conducting many sensor sweeps along the border, the *Nightingale* has been privy to a large amount of highly useful data.

Tellek is a skilled geologist and secretly quite a good computer technician. But his greatest secret is that he is actually a Romulan agent. He was inserted into Starfleet over eight years ago after undergoing surgery to make him appear Vulcan. His cover story includes a note that he has Romulan ancestry in his past, making him about an eighth Romulan. This is to explain any Romulan DNA that turns up in routine beam ups or medical scans. However, a proper medical scan will turn up the truth of his biology. For this reason he has avoided several routine medical examinations, which Doctors put down to typical Vulcan insistence that he will only report to sickbay if he believes himself unwell.

While Tellek is a dedicated Romulan spy, he is not a fool and knows when to play his hand and when to fold. He won't be too pushy to get what he wants, following orders as required and then steering things back to his objective carefully. While he wishes to complete his mission, it is more important that he leaves no clear evidence of Romulan espionage. His body could be such evidence, and so if things go very wrong he will want to ensure no trace of him remains.

Tellek is improvising a new plan furiously, and it all depends on how much information he can get from the computer. His plans for escape are detailed later on in Act 3.

TRAITS: Romulan, Disguised as Vulcan, Dedicated Spy

VALUES:
- The Mission is Everything
- Everything I Do, I Do for Romulus

ATTRIBUTES

CONTROL	12	FITNESS	09	PRESENCE	09
DARING	08	INSIGHT	10	REASON	11

DISCIPLINES

COMMAND	02	SECURITY	03	SCIENCE	04
CONN	02	ENGINEERING	03	MEDICINE	02

FOCUSES: Deception, Espionage, Interrogation

STRESS: 12   **RESISTANCE:** 0

ATTACKS:
- Unarmed Strike (Melee, 4▲ Knockdown, Size 1H, Non-lethal)
- Dagger (Melee, 4▲ Vicious 1, Size 1H)
- Disruptor Pistol (Ranged, 6▲ Vicious 1, Size 1H)

SPECIAL RULES:
- **Guile and Cunning:** When attempting to remain hidden or unnoticed, a Romulan may spend one Threat to increase the Difficulty of enemy Tasks to detect them by one.
- **Ruthless and Determined:** Tellek may spend 2 Threat to gain the effects of a point of Determination, rather than the normal 3.
- **Wary:** Whenever a Romulan attempts a Task to notice or detect an enemy or hazard, they may re-roll one d20.

As downloading the data wouldn't take long, and Romulans like to play safe, the agent didn't collect this data as he went. If it was discovered in his possession his cover would be blown. Unfortunately, the Captain managed to activate the Romulan Protocol before he could download what he needed. Now the agent is desperately trying to get the computer back online so he can get what he needs and make an escape. If he can get the help of the Player Characters, it is all the better.

Commander Lewis is not convinced the computer needs fixing at this point. So 'Tellek' has played the concerned scientist card. He has insisted that several of his (and others) experimental data is in the computer. As scientists they should try to save it in case the Romulans allow them to leave without the ship. Commander Lewis didn't want to argue, and as Tellek wasn't great use anywhere else she told him he could see what he could do. Currently, Lewis has no reason not to trust a Starfleet officer she has served with for two years.

"JUST BLOW UP THE SHIP"

It is important the Romulans don't get hold of the *Nightingale* as a prize. Their technicians would love to go over all that lovely Federation technology, especially as the *Nova* class is such a new design. So the Player Characters might want to rig some way to destroy the *Nightingale* rather than let the Romulans have it (as long as it has been evacuated first!) as their ship is out of weapons range.

The best way to destroy the *Nightingale* is to activate its self-destruct sequence. Unfortunately it is currently offline. To repair it is another Extended Task (**Insight + Engineering** (Focus Warp Systems) Magnitude 2, Work 10, Difficulty 2). Once this repair is complete the sequence can be activated by at least three Star Fleet officers of rank Lt Commander or above. It must be done from the bridge or engineering, and the system will give one minute to evacuate before destroying the ship.

BORDER DISPUTE
ACT 3: ENDGAME

There is a lot going on in this mission, and many ways it can end, depending on the actions of the Player Characters. The endgame might come together in a number of different ways, from a tense phaser battle with a Romulan agent, to a gentle return to Federation space wondering what was really going on. We've summarised several endings and how they might play out. But ultimately it will be up to the Gamemaster to resolve the various plots depending on what the Player Characters have investigated.

One of the most important things the Player Characters need to discover is that there is a saboteur on board the *Nightingale*. There are several clues, which are worth collating here for convenience:

- An autopsy on Captain Blake's body will prove she was murdered

- An investigation of the navigation array will reveal it was sabotaged just before the *Nightingale* crossed the Neutral Zone

- If pressured, Tellek may prove a little too insistent that the computer needs to be fixed.

- Commander Mheven seems to be playing for time, which is odd, given she has the upper hand.

- A full medical tricorder scan of Tellek will reveal he is actually a Romulan. But he will do whatever it takes (including murder) to cover up this information. Introducing random scans of the crew will make him speed up his plan out of necessity.

- Tellek has a pulse device to signal that his extraction is required. This device is not specifically Romulan technology and he will insist it is used to send a pulse at a rock to gauge thickness and structure. A close examination will determine it couldn't do that. Should someone activate it, the Romulans will think it is time to commit to extraction! (See below)

RUNNING THE ENDGAME

There are several ways the end of this mission might play out, depending on what the Player Characters discover. However, it is likely that the end will fall into one of three options. Within these options the Gamemaster should feel free to adjust them depending on what the Player Characters have already discovered or planned.

OPTION 1: THE ROMULAN PLAN

If things go to plan and Tellek gets the data he wants before the Nightingale tries to escape, he will make his escape. If the Player Characters haven't figured him out already, it is probably too late. But if they happen to cross paths with him as he tries to escape they might be able to foil the plan. If all is going well, Tellek will do the following:

- First he sends a short pulse to the Romulan warbird. He has a small device for this that just emits a pulse on a specific wavelength that the Romulans are looking for. It just tells them to put the extraction plan into operation. Anyone doing a general scan from the bridge at this time may detect it with an **Insight + Conn Task** with a Difficulty of 3. If detected they will discover where it originated.

- Then the Romulan warbird will target the *Nightingale* where the pulse was transmitted with a tractor beam. They will insist they have seen some structural failure in the hull and are using the beam to maintain cohesion in that area (out of the goodness of their hearts). In fact the tractor beam will cause enough 'noise' to cloak their use of a transporter beam.

- With the tractor beam on the *Nightingale*, Tellek will set a decent sized relay to explode in the section he is in and remove his combadge. This explosion, a few seconds later, has possibly enough force to blow a hole in the hull.

- But before the relay explodes, the Romulan warbird will get a transporter lock on Tellek (using the pulse device — or whoever is holding it!) and beam him aboard. For this reason Tellek will need to ensure the *Nightingale* has not (or cannot) raised its shields.

The whole plan should make it look as if the Romulans detected a dangerously stressed area of the *Nightingale*, but sadly failed to act in time. Luckily only one crewman (Tellek) was in the area, but he was disintegrated in the blast.

It will be possible for Starfleet crew members to detect some of what is going on, but only if they are actively scanning at the time. Otherwise the pulse device is too small and low-powered to be automatically detected and the tractor beam will mask the Romulan transporter beam. But if someone is in the right place at the right time they might make a **Reason + Conn Task** assisted by the ship's **Sensors + Conn** to detect either or both pieces of subterfuge.

If the Romulans have what they want: their agent, the computer files and no evidence of their plan, they will be magnanimous. Commander Mheven will hail the *Nightingale* and say that she has been considering the situation. As long as Commander Lewis formally apologises for the actions of the Federation, the warbird will allow them to leave. Lewis will make the apology, and the Warbird will turn and cloak as it flies away. The *Nightingale* will be free to leave the Neutral Zone as soon as impulse power is restored. Having admitted fault in the incident, the Federation will find the Romulans

using this to their advantage in negotiations. But that's a lot better than losing any more people or submitting the *Nightingale* crew to Romulan justice.

But it is quite possible that everything won't go so well for the Romulans. So there are a few other ways the mission might turn out:

OPTION 2: IF THE NIGHTINGALE MAKES A RUN FOR IT

If the *Nightingale* has engine power but the computer is still offline, the agent has a problem. Time is basically up and the Romulan warbird will have to take the *Nightingale* back to Romulus or call it a day. The time has come to call their bluff.

Tellek's plan will depend on the state of the computer systems. If it is partially repaired, Tellek may cut his losses and make an escape with as many of the encrypted files as he can. It will take Romulan intelligence a long time to crack them, but the data is at least in there. Better to get encrypted files and leave undetected then get found out trying to

acquire an unencrypted version. If the Federation knows the files are stolen, they will reassign their forces on the border, making the files useless.

However, if Tellek is not quick enough to escape as planned, he will have to make a new plan. So he will attempt to sabotage something in engineering and get to a shuttlecraft as detailed in option 3.

For the Player Characters, attempting escape will be a tense ship-to-ship battle as they race to the border of the Neutral Zone. How far the *Nightingale* gets will depend on how well it has been repaired. If weapons and shields are not also available it will be a really short trip. The warbird will try to disable the *Nightingale* rather than destroy it, but that might be unavoidable given the damage it has already sustained. The fact they have an agent aboard is not really a concern to the Romulans at this point, and the agent knows the score.

If the Player Characters bring their own ship across the Neutral Zone, it will take them 2 Turns to be in weapons range. The warbird will focus on the *Nightingale* but if the *Nightingale* is not a threat they may be forced to deal with the Player Characters. Unfortunately, as the Player Character's ship has willingly entered the Neutral Zone (even to help their own) the Romulans will be looking to destroy and not disable them. Having said that, if they can take two Federation ships back to Romulus, then that will be quite a prize.

If the mission goes this way, it will end with a great ship combat climax, but the fallout will be bad for the Federation and the Player Characters. The Federation will be glad to see the crews escape (as long as there were no further deaths) but the diplomatic situation will be a nightmare.

If the *Nightingale* makes a run for it after the Romulans have their agent, they will let them go. But the Romulan diplomats will still kick up a fuss and milk 'how the Federation refused to face justice' for all it is worth.

OPTION 3: IF THE AGENT IS DISCOVERED

The only real danger for the Romulans is for their agent to be discovered. However, it is not just enough for the Player Characters to find out what is going on, they need proof. Even so, if they can just manage to stop the agent making off with the data they will have put an end to years of Romulan espionage.

The best outcome for the Player Characters is for them to discover Tellek is behind everything and manage to arrest him before he knows they are on to him. As a Tal Shiar agent, Tellek is not used to being outmanoeuvred. However, the Player Characters will have to be cunning. People being called away for private conversations, strange orders or a

build-up of security personnel will warn Tellek something is amiss. In such a case he may decide to bolt, whether he has the data or not. The Gamemaster should remember his orders are to get the data, but his priority is remaining undiscovered. The Romulans are pragmatic and would rather bide their time than risk failure.

It is important to remember that Tellek's body is evidence he doesn't want in the hands of the Federation. While he appears Vulcan, and has a backstory that gives him a little Romulan ancestry, a close medical scan will reveal him as pure Romulan. So, even his dead body is evidence of Romulan treachery. As a loyal Romulan, if all else fails, Tellek will do his best to see his body is disintegrated as thoroughly as he can manage.

If Tellek has to make an escape, he will try to do the following:

- Firstly he'll have to break away from any security. He is clever enough to see an arrest coming and should make a run for it beforehand, but otherwise he will have to escape any security officers making the arrest.

- If there is an opportunity, he will go to engineering and set up a relay panel to explode (possibly an overloading phaser at a push). This explosion will cause enough damage to take the impulse and warp drive offline so the *Nightingale* can't go too far before Tellek can escape. The explosion will also get the Player Character's attention and increase the tension.

- Tellek will then make for a shuttlebay. Transporters can be overridden from the bridge and take longer to set accurate coordinates. His journey to the shuttlebay will be beset with difficulties as there will be plenty of opportunities for Player Characters to give chase with a pitched running phaser battle (as Tellek will undoubtedly be armed at this point).

- If they Players have made steps to lock Tellek out of the shuttlebay, he will need to override the security measures. Tellek is very good at overriding security systems though. He and the Player Character trying to override each other's control will have to make an opposed **Reason + Security** challenge. The first one to win three such challenges locks their opponent out of the system. But each challenge takes 1 round, which may give the others a chance to catch up with Tellek.

- Once in control of the shuttlebay, Tellek will take a shuttle and leave. Commander Mheven will immediately hail the *Nightingale* and demand to know what is going on. She will announce that the shuttlecraft will not be given any asylum and will be considered an attempt to escape. Then the warbird will open fire on the shuttle and destroy it utterly!

- The warbird will then simply turn and leave without a word, cloaking as it slips back to the other side of the Neutral Zone. Whatever the result, Mheven will leave it to the diplomats to do what they can with the situation. The *Nightingale* would do well to leave as quickly as possible!

- While this might seem that the Romulans have decided to just clear up the mess, things are not so straightforward.

Anyone scanning the area when the warbird opens fire can attempt a **Insight + Conn Task** with a Difficulty 3. On a success they notice another beam, possibly a transporter, possibly a transmission appears to have been operating just before the warbird's disintegrator beam. Did they receive a transmission, or beam up their agent before the blast hit the shuttle? Perhaps the Federation will never know.

BORDER DISPUTE
CONCLUSION

This is a hard mission for the Player Characters to win outright, but they can still foil the Romulans' plans.

It is possible they will discover nothing about the plot and apart from some odd occurrences it will appear to be a win for the Federation. The Romulans did a bit of sabre rattling but eventually relented and allowed the *Nightingale* to leave. Starfleet will be disappointed the Romulans have a diplomatic stick to beat them with given they have broken the treaty, but at the end of the day, no more lives were lost.

What is more likely is that the Player Characters will discover some circumstantial evidence but not enough to prove the Romulans had a spy. If they play the game quietly and intimate to the Romulans they know what is going on, the Romulans will get the message and not push their luck. However, if the Player Characters make accusations they can't back up with hard evidence, the Romulans will have a field day. They will claim the Federation made all manner of baseless accusations after they had been the ones to break the treaty. Diplomats will have to offer several concessions to satisfy the Romulans

and the Player Characters will be reprimanded. However, most admirals understand how frustrating the Romulans can be, so as long as the Player Characters didn't start a war they will just get a slap on the wrist.

CONTINUING VOYAGES...

If the Player Characters uncovered the agent and stopped him passing on the data, they will be commended. If the Player Characters handed him over to the Romulans in the end the Admiral will be glad they didn't risk another war. Far better to stop the plot than gain leverage against the Romulans at the cost of Federation lives.

If they are beaten, the Romulans will accept it with grace. They don't have the same ego as Klingons and will grudgingly respect anyone who can outmanoeuvre them. They won't admit that of course, but they will remember the Player Characters and look forward to their next encounter...

LCARS 208-32

65-3920

66-2849

70-4742

72-4299

75-3800

DEUTERIUM CONTROL CONDUIT

OUTER THERMAL BLANKET

POWER TRANSFER CONDUIT

SECONDARY VALVE BLOCK

MATTER REACTANT INJECTOR

UPPER MCS CAP

MAGNETIC CONSTRICTION SEGMENT

VERTICAL TENSION MEMBER

PHASE ADJUSTMENT COIL

REACTION CHAMBER

DILITHIUM HOUSING

PRESSURE VESSEL TOROID

LOWER MCS CAP

ANTIMATTER REACTANT INJECTOR

MRI1	122
MRI2	103

5930-26 2890
22 2595-11 3805
293-44 1185
98-38 4020
490

MCS1	256
MCS2	152

380-50 7180
27-29 2793

VTM1	28
VTM2	25

20-52 2807
2810

PAC1	244
PAC2	145

1368-89 0065
20 3593-00 0000
820

RAC1	606
RAC2	598

3 2493-97 3892
48 2840-19 4300
284-27 2995
12 8848
379

PVT1	76
PVT2	100

38 2693-39 2920
67 7290-28-9339
229-80-1148

ARI1	108
ARI2	104

10 2790-54 3782
4 2739-11 1930
27 3890-31 4990
389-22 2014
295

88-5020

89-4458

2612-4840	42020	104730	69-213849	2402	248450	1506313	1739	55-38503005	330 3002482	338-44593-496
3002-5068	219059	384922	40-381984	52040	314029	4890320	4920	18-28108997	174 1840937	173-37482-700
5012-3692	2957	74027	128-359437	2849	329390	1394620	2849	14-27492820	294 3630035	329-47829-274
5836-9671	130119	243002	36-274920	24947	182470	1937292	1370	18-92759900	420 1038330	226-29461-294
1049-3460	19204	184920	144-269209	18460	149204	3236501	1957	45-37815822	148 1844949	118-37492-558
2348-5119	249202	45927	145-850228	138493	250201	1548289	593	12-38590211	249 6734575	290-25082-199

ENGINEERING

CHAPTER 04.00

ENTROPY'S DEMISE

BY ANTHONY JENNINGS

80684268
1129821303201

Situated near the Federation's border with the Romulan Empire, Carina VII is an idyllic world with lush forests, a pleasant climate, and abundant resources. Until recently, Morgan's Hope, the colony's capital, had thrived, but in the last year, strange events have been occurring: people residing on the planet have aged rapidly, structures that should have lasted for decades, crumble in days. Crops that were planted in the morning mature overnight and are rotten before the next afternoon. Even more disturbing, the colonists are spreading rumors that Romulans have been sighted in the system. The Player Characters' ship has been dispatched to Carina VII in the hopes that they can discover the cause of the rapid aging of people, structures, and plants.

After transporting down to the planet, the Player Characters interview the residents of Morgan's Hope and discover that these occurrences are not new but have only recently

increased in both severity and quantity. The Player Characters search eventually leads them to a cloaked Romulan science outpost. After dispatching the crew of the outpost, the Player Characters discover that the Romulans have also been studying the phenomena on Carina VII.

After studying the colony and the new information gleamed from the Romulans, the Player Characters are able to deduce that the problems on Carina VII have been caused by massive tachyon emissions emanating from the tenth planet in the system. Hidden in the rings of the gas giant, the Player Characters discover a *Constitution*-class ship, the *U.S.S. Hamilton*. Research into the history of the *Hamilton* uncovers a weapons test for a powerful tachyon device; however, the crew lost control of the device leading to the perceived destruction of the *Hamilton*. Unknown to the Federation, the *Hamilton* was thrown forward in time, leading to problems on Carina VII.

OTHER ERAS OF PLAY

For those Storytellers from the *Enterprise* and the Original Series eras, there are a wide variety of options you can use to make your games compatible with the *The Next Generation* era game. The important thing to remember is to have fun with it and use whatever options you think will work. Here are a couple of suggestions you can use for your Players:

• **For *Enterprise* era Players**, replace the Takarans with the Antarans. Antarans are a militant race that has been "at war" with the Denobulans on numerous occasions and may attempt to gain Starfleet's favor. As such, the Klingon House of Duras can be replaced by the Orions, who may be attempting to profit from the stealing of military secrets. They have been hired by an anti-Antaran faction of Denobulans who want the weapon, a new and improved version of Starfleet's photonic torpedo. Now, the Players must retrieve the device from the Orions, who no doubt wish to double-cross the Denobulans for their own power-hungry, nefarious reasons, as well as avert another war between two long-time adversaries, whose populations still feel a deep-seeded hatred for each other. This, of course, provides

any Denobulan characters with moral choices of their own throughout the scenario, as well as advancing the duplicitous nature of the Orion Syndicate for further play in games of that era.

• **For Original Series era Players**, the obvious choice to play the antagonists are the Klingons. However, it might be just as fun, if not more so, to use other races. One such suggestion may be to have the Tellarites play as the Takarans and using their age-old adversaries (and fellow Federation allies), the Andorians, in place of the Romulans (used in *The Next Generation* era setting of this game). The Tellarites raid an outlying Andorian research base and steal plans for an upgraded photon torpedo. Why would they do that? Perhaps an insecure faction with the Tellarite government, or a rogue scientist with a particular grudge against the Andorians. Our blue-skinned friends would have no problem taking back what they believe is theirs and, suddenly, the Players must fight to keep a civil war from igniting between two of its founding members.

Because of the intensity of the tachyon emissions around the *Hamilton*, the Player Characters must take a shuttlecraft to the ship, but they are not the first to arrive. A Romulan shuttlecraft has already landed in the shuttlebay with a cadre of Romulans hoping to capture the plans for the weapon. As the tachyon bursts worsen and the *U.S.S. Hamilton* disintegrates around them, the Player Characters must not only defuse the tachyon weapon but stop the Romulans from capturing the plans to the weapon.

DIRECTIVES

In addition to the Prime Directive, the Directives for this mission are:

- The Temporal Prime Directive (although you may only wish to bring up the Temporal Prime Directive to Players if it becomes relevant)

Gamemasters begin this mission with 2 points of Threat for each Player Character in the group.

CHAPTER
04.20

ENTROPY'S DEMISE
ACT 1: TROUBLE ON CARINA VII

SCENE 1: GROWING UP FAST

When the Players are ready, read the following:

An urgent transmission from Starfleet Command is patched through to your ship. On the main viewscreen you see a female Vulcan Starfleet officer that you recognize as Admiral T'Lara, a member of Starfleet Operations. Although her expression remains passive, you get a sense that something grave must be occurring if an admiral is contacting you directly.

"Captain," she begins, "Starfleet Command needs you to re-direct your ship to the colony on Carina VII. The colony's governor, Syreeta Sebastian, is reporting a series of strange phenomena that threaten the colony's safety. She states that children born on Carina VII are aging rapidly, the native flora and fauna are growing rapidly and just as rapidly withering, and structures that should have lasted decades are falling apart.

"Your ship is the closet to the colony, and it is imperative that you discover a solution to the colony's problems."

The Player Characters may attempt **Reason + Science Task** with a Difficulty of 1, if they are successful they recall some information about the colony on Carina VII. If they fail the check, Admiral T'Lara will share information with the crew.

On a successful Task, the Player Characters learn that Carina VII is a small agricultural world that specializes in viticulture or wine-making. Although synthehol can reproduce the taste to some degree, connoisseurs of wine claim that wine created by replicators is an inferior product. Carina VII's climate is perfect for producing an enormous variety of wines and the viticulturists there have been able to reproduce wines that can approximate unique early 20th century strains from the North American continent such as those that once flourished in Napa Valley, California, or the central regions of Virginia. These wines are a popular trade item with species such as the Ferengi.

Admiral T'Lara is willing to answer questions about the colony that the crew might have. She knows the following information:

- The colonists' survival is of paramount importance to the Federation. Whatever effects that are causing the aging and structural decay may represent an unknown threat to the Federation.

- The colony was settled approximately two decades ago by a group of winemakers hoping that the climate would be conducive to growing a wide variety of grapes.

- The colony lies near the Romulan Neutral Zone and represents one of the furthest outposts that the Federation has in that region.

CARINA VII

The Carina system has a G-type main sequence star with a yellowish hue that will remind humans of Sol. The system has six small planets that orbit too close to the star to be habitable. Only Carina VII falls within the habitable zone, and beyond Carina VII are 3 gas giants and finally a series of small, icy planetoids. From space Carina VII is a blue marble with large green continents and white polar ice caps. This Class-M planet is as close to ideal for humans as any planet in the sector.

As soon as the Player Character's ship arrives in orbit of Carina VII, they may use the ship's sensors to scan the planet with a **Reason + Science Task** with a Difficulty of 2. If successful, the Player Character making the check will notice low level interference affecting their scanners in the system but will be unable to locate a source for the interference. If unsuccessful, the Player Character notices only that Carina VII is as described. The tachyon emissions are causing this interference, and a successful **Reason + Science Task** with a Difficulty of 3 will inform the Players of this fact.

▪ The colony's success is integral to several ongoing Federation trade deals with the Ferengi who trade for the wine. The gold-pressed latinum is used as currency with other groups.

SCENE 2: INVESTIGATING MORGAN'S HOPE

MORGAN'S HOPE

Morgan's Hope is a small, idyllic settlement that is the capital of Carina VII. The rest of the settlers are spread out across the planet on large, self-sufficient farms. The colonists have, for the most part, stuck to a central subtropical region of the planet noteworthy for its rolling hills, tall deciduous trees, and pleasant climate. All of these factors make this area a perfect region for growing grapes and making wine. Beyond the settlement, the citizens of Morgan's Hope have planted enormous vineyards that stretch to the horizon in long parallel rows of grape vines.

Morgan's Hope has all the comforts of a 24th century town including a small hospital, schools, replicators, etc. The buildings are mostly single story, and there are large

warehouses for the storage of wine as well as facilities for creating wine bottles. The colony also grows cork trees they use to make the corks for the wine.

When the Player Characters beam down to Morgan's Hope, read aloud the following:

You arrive in a small grove of cork oak trees with a stone path leading towards a large home. A middle-aged woman of Indian descent who speaks with a slight accent reminiscent of Earth's England approaches with a worried look on her face that fades to relief, "You arrived quicker than I imagined. I am Syreeta Sebastian, the governor of this colony. Please excuse my rudeness, but we don't have time for a tour. The situation here is only getting worse."

Syreeta is available to answer any questions about Morgan's Hope. She will also act as a guide to the various places where the worst phenomena have occurred. She recommends that Player Characters visit the Mackley household where their child, Efren, is aging rapidly. She notes that other colonists have also noticed signs of abnormal aging, but the effect on Efren Mackley is the most pronounced. She also suggests that the Player Characters visit the vineyards to see the effects the phenomena are having on the grapes, and the site of a recent building collapse.

If questioned about their winemaking, Syreeta explains that some things cannot be synthesized in a replicator and that some things are best when done traditionally.

SYREETA SEBASTIAN [NOTABLE NPC]

The governor of Morgan's Hope the largest settlement on Carina VII, Syreeta Sebastian has served her people for nearly 5 years, but the last year has been especially difficult. The increasing number of problems at the colony has forced Syreeta to swallow some of her pride and call the Federation for help. She is anxious to see these issues resolved and will be as helpful as possible.

TRAITS: Human

VALUE: I Will Protect the Colony to the Best of My Ability

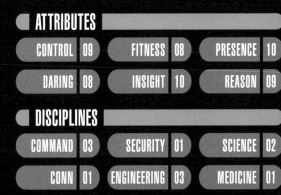

ATTRIBUTES		
CONTROL 09	FITNESS 08	PRESENCE 10
DARING 08	INSIGHT 10	REASON 09

DISCIPLINES		
COMMAND 03	SECURITY 01	SCIENCE 02
CONN 01	ENGINEERING 03	MEDICINE 01

FOCUSES: Negotiation, Organizer

STRESS: 9   **RESISTANCE:** 0

ATTACKS:
- Unarmed Strike (Melee, 2▲, Knockdown, Size 1H, Non-lethal)
- Phaser Type-1 (Ranged, 3▲, Vicious 1, Size 1H)

SPECIAL RULES:
- Syreeta Sebastian reduces the Difficulty of all Tasks involving viticulture by 1.
- Syreeta Sebastian reduces the Difficulty of all Tasks that involve negotiating with her fellow colonists by 1.

CARINA VII COLONIST [MINOR NPC]

Colonists on Carina VII pride themselves on two things: their wines and their self-sufficiency. They are experts at making wine, and many can talk for hours about the grapes they grow, the bottles they make, or cork that stoppers the bottles. Overall, they are a gregarious and happy people who take to their work with delight and are proud of the quality of their wines. Use the following statistics to represent any of the colonists other than Syreeta Sebastian.

TRAITS: Any Federation

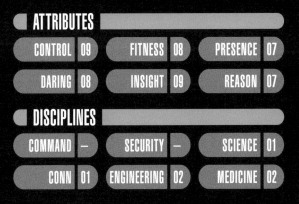

ATTRIBUTES		
CONTROL 09	FITNESS 08	PRESENCE 07
DARING 08	INSIGHT 09	REASON 07

DISCIPLINES		
COMMAND —	SECURITY —	SCIENCE 01
CONN 01	ENGINEERING 02	MEDICINE 02

FOCUSES: Viticulture

STRESS: 8   **RESISTANCE:** 0

ATTACKS:
- Unarmed Strike (Melee, 1▲, Knockdown, Size 1H, Non-lethal)
- Knife (Melee, 1▲, Vicious 1, Size 1H)

THE MACKLEY HOUSEHOLD

Read aloud the following:

A tall, broad shouldered human greets you as enter the home. "I'm Wes," he introduces himself, "and this is my wife Aurelia and our son Efren. We're so relieved that you came. We weren't sure how long it would take for Starfleet to send a ship." Wes's relief is obvious and his wife is holding their child in her arms. The child appears to be about six years old but is babbling like an infant.

Wes has been a farmer all of his life. He has the serious demeanour of a man who understands the ups and downs of farming, especially raising grapes. His wife is also a vintner and worked among the grapevines alongside her husband until she got pregnant. Both of them grew up on Carina VII, met, and fell in love.

Wes Mackley and his wife Aurelia explain that Aurelia gave birth to Efren six months ago, but for some unexplainable reasons, their child grew rapidly, and now Efren has the physical body of a six-year-old, but retains the mental state of a six-month-old. The Mackleys have taken Efren to the colony's hospital, and at first the colony doctors believed that Efren had progeria, a genetic disorder that causes rapid aging, but when tested Efren lacked the genetic markers.

The doctors on Carina VII have assured the Mackleys that Efren isn't developmentally stunted, but they believe something environmental might be the cause of his rapid growth. The doctors assure the Mackleys that Efren is exactly where he should be developmentally for a six-month-old, even though his body is that of a six-year-old.

WHAT IS PROGERIA?

Progeria is a rare genetic disorder that was incurable in the 21st century. Its primary symptom is the appearance of rapid and premature aging. Persons with progeria have a short life span and rarely live past thirteen. This disorder was never found outside of the human race. By the 24th century, doctors were able to diagnose and treat progeria prior to the birth of the child. A rare few cases still occur in the 24th century, usually on distant Federation colonies that do not have the most modern medical equipment.

The Mackley family is happy to let the Player Characters examine Efren. They explain that Efren has the mental capacity of a six-month-old and continues to socialize as a normal infant would. Aurelia will explain that Efren has not started speaking yet, and he is unable to walk but does crawl.

A successful **Reason + Medical Task** with a Difficulty 1 reveals that Efren is a perfectly healthy six-year-old. Further investigation reveals what the colony's medical staff has already deduced: Efren is developmentally six months old, and the child has no underlying genetic disorders that would explain any of this.

A successful **Reason + Medical Task** with a Difficulty 2 reveals that Efren's condition will likely persist at its current rate: for every month that passes Efren's body will age a year. That means that Efren will die of old age in less than 100 months.

Before the Player Characters leave the Mackley's home, Wes begs the Player Characters to help their child and for reassurances that the Player Characters will be able to fix whatever is wrong. The Player Characters may decide to transport the Mackley family to their ship's sickbay where the medical staff can monitor Efren closely.

The Player Characters can also detect signs of advanced aging in the other colonists. A similar **Reason + Medical Task** with a Difficulty 1 also shows that anyone who has resided on Carina VII for more than a few days has experienced some form of advanced aging (including the Romulans who the Player Characters will encounter later in the mission). The Player Characters should not suffer any of the effects of rapid aging, but if they take their time exploring Carina VII, they should all add 1d6-1 to their ages.

THE VINEYARDS

When the Player Character enter the vineyards, read aloud the following:

Long rows of grape vines stretch out in front of you, running parallel to each other until they disappear beyond the horizon. The leaves on the vines are withered as if it were already fall and the vines are heavy with shriveled grapes as if the colonists had forgotten to pick the grapes on these vines. Tending to the grapes is a slim female humanoid with blonde hair. She shakes her head and mumbles something under her breath. When she sees you approaching, she stands and introduces herself, "I'm Se'irrah."

This is Se'irrah's vineyard. She is the daughter of one of the earliest families to settle on Carina VII. Once she hears that the Player Characters are on Carina VII to discover the cause of the strange phenomena, she is more than willing to answer their questions. Se'irrah explains that her crop has undergone rapid growth and then rotting several times. The grapes will appear to be mature on the previous day, but after a single night the grapes are shriveled and useless. Syreeta can substantiate her claim and explains that most of the other vintners have had similar experiences.

A successful **Reason + Science Task** with a Difficulty of 1 reveals this is usually the right time of year for grapes to be harvested; yet they are hanging shriveled on the vines.

VITICULTURE IN THE 24TH CENTURY

Winemaking and the cultivation of grapes is a 7,000-year-old art and science. Grapes used in winemaking require a specific climate, soil type, and other conditions to mature properly. The grapes are grown on the slopes of hills within the temperate latitudes of a planet capable of sustaining agriculture. Not every planet is capable of producing a worthy crop of grapes for making wine. Carina VII was fortunate enough to reside in the habitable zone of a star system and with the correct climate and geography for the cultivation of grapes. Grapes are typically harvested from late summer through early autumn. The harvest time is dependent upon the type of grape grown.

After the atomic horror of World War III, entire countries were irradiated from the nuclear fallout. Regions that had previously been famous for their vineyards — such as the French countryside; Napa Valley, California; and Central Virginia — were unfit for cultivating any agriculture. Viticulture was lost for much of the mid to late 21st century as the remaining farmland was necessary for the cultivation of foodstuffs rather than luxury items such as wine. While some vintners continued to make small batches of wine, it was only after the formation of the United Earth government in 2150 and the alleviation of famine that viticulture returned in earnest.

A successful **Reason + Science Task** with a Difficulty of 2 reveals nothing inherently wrong with the grapes or the vines. The Player Characters' tricorders don't detect any sign of herbicide, parasite, or disease that would explain what has happened to the grapes.

As a good host, she invites the Player Characters to her home where she offers them some of her family's wine; but when the Player Characters taste the wine it is sour. Se'irrah is shocked when the Player Characters tell her this. Even the bottles of wine stored in her cellar have spoiled and turned.

A successful **Reason + Science Task** with a Difficulty of 0 reveals nothing unusual in the wine. It has merely been exposed to oxygen and due to the chemical reactions, the wine naturally turned sour. This effect could be caused by either improperly corking the bottles or the wine has been sitting for far too long.

COLLAPSED STRUCTURES

Read aloud the following:

Syreeta leads you to one of the collapsed structures: a warehouse that was built within the last year. The outer shell of the warehouse has a faux wood veneer but underneath is a prefabricated metal structure. A simple examination of the warehouse reveals that several of the support columns broke apart and the entire structure collapsed shortly afterwards.

To anyone with a Focus in Engineering, this is problematic. The Federation constructs buildings like this warehouse out of tritanium alloys, the same material they use for their starship hulls. If something is happening to the metal in these buildings it could be disastrous for the Federation's fleet.

A successful **Reason + Engineering Task** with a Difficulty of 1 with a tricorder reveals that the metal collapsed due to fatigue caused by aging. This sort of metal fatigue would be expected in a structure that had been standing for over a hundred years not a building that was erected within the last year.

The warehouse stored empty wine barrels. Studying the wine barrels, the Player Characters discover significant rust on the steel bands and some of the barrels have wood that is rotten and so fragile from age that it falls apart when touched. Syreeta claims that the colonists had built those barrels just a few years previous and that wine barrels can last for decades.

SCENE 3: THE ROMULAN RUMORS

Once the Player Characters have investigated the situation around the rest of Morgan's Hope, an angry colonist approaches them and demands that they investigate the Romulans near his vineyard. The man angrily shouts at Syreeta and the Player Characters until they acquiesce to his demands. He tells them his name is Zane Knoll and that everything happening here is the Romulans' fault!

If asked Syreeta will explain that that Zane Knoll has claimed for weeks to have seen a Romulan skulking around his vineyard cutting down several of his vines and digging in the soil on multiple occasions. Syreeta doesn't believe Zane, and she thinks that he is likely seeing things due to the stress of these recent events. She tells the Player Characters that Zane is stubborn, but the rest of the colonists agree that he is earnest and not known for embellishments. He, however, is proud of his wine, and some of the other citizens of Morgan's Hope may be jealous of the quality of his white wines.

Zane Knoll is a young male human vintner with a small vineyard nestled in a hilly and rocky region not far from Morgan's Hope. This region is especially well suited for growing white grapes as the rocky soil is ideal for the variety of grape he uses to make wine. Zane is as stubborn as the soil his grapes prefer. He is initially standoffish when the Player Characters come to his vineyard as many of the other colonists believe that Zane is hallucinating Romulans. If the Player Characters listen to Zane and are at least willing to believe his story about the Romulans then he opens up and offers as much help as he can.

The Romulan, he claims, was cutting off grapes and digging in the soil. An **Insight + Command Task** with a Difficulty of 0 reveals that Zane believes what he is saying is true. Zane describes the Romulan carefully and makes specific mention of the Romulan's uniform and V-shaped forehead. If asked if he thinks it might have been a Vulcan colonist, Zane says that he can't be completely sure, but why would a Vulcan skulk around in his vineyard?

Zane is happy to take the Player Characters to the spot where he most recently saw the Romulans. There, the Player Characters discover that several grape vines have been cut, one has been up rooted completely, and the ground nearby

has a small hole in it. The hole is perhaps the strangest. It is approximately 1 meter deep and .25 meters in diameter. A successful **Reason + Engineering Task** Difficulty 2 will reveal that the hole could be from a device designed to take soil samples.

If the Player Characters attempt to look for tracks or other signs that a Romulan was here. They may make a **Reason + Security Task** with a Difficulty of 1 to notice strange scuff marks nearby. If asked, Zane says that he attempted to follow the trail, but that he lost the tracks at the bottom of the nearby hills. If they follow these scuffmarks, the Player Characters discover a path with several small, trampled bushes and small scrub trees that have broken limbs. The path leads further into the hills.

The Player Characters may also wish to have the crew of their starship scan the planet for likely places that a Romulan might hide. If the Player Characters choose to have their starship scan for energy sources, the starship finds nothing as the Romulan outpost is cloaked and well-hidden in the rocky hills near Zane's farm.

ENTROPY'S DEMISE

ACT 2: ROMULAN OUTPOST

Once the Player Characters discover the Romulan Outpost, they will be one step closer to understanding what is happening in the Carina System. The Romulans established this outpost two years ago to monitor Federation activity in the region. When the Romulans discovered the tachyon emissions several weeks ago, they immediately called for a science team to investigate the tachyons. Unfortunately, the Romulans became aware of the Player Characters as soon as their ship entered the system, and the Romulans are in the process of evacuating their outpost. They are taking anything useful and anything that can be replaced has been destroyed. So far, most of the command staff of the base has left, but a few Romulans remain to finish the evacuation. Subcommander D'Tok, the primary researcher, is in charge of the evacuation while the Romulan Commander is enroute to the source of the tachyon emissions.

SCENE 1: ROMULAN OUTPOST EXTERIOR

The Romulan Outpost is hidden in a series of caves in the hills a short hike from Zane Knoll's Vineyard. The caves have been enlarged and the Romulans have reinforced the caves with prefabricated buildings that house a large scientific laboratory, a barracks, and administrative offices along with a large power supply and a cloaking field generator.

THE MAIN ENTRANCE
Read aloud the following:

Hidden by the cloaking field, the main entrance appears as nothing more a sheer cliff. However, close inspection of the ground reveals lots of tracks going to and from the base of the cliff. The tracks are recent, and it appears someone is in a hurry.

Finding the entrance to the outpost is easy because the Romulans are swiftly evacuating the base. They are no longer making any attempt to hide their tracks.

SCIENTIFIC LABORATORY

Read aloud the following:

As the doors open, you peer into a dimly lit room. Overhead lights flicker and the smell of burning plastic and ozone permeate the room. From just a single glance you realize this was an observation post the Romulans hastily converted to a large laboratory. Given the destruction, it's unlikely that anything will be salvageable. The computer banks and consoles have disruptor burns, and smoke pours forth from the holes, and the floor is littered with smashed PADDs and other equipment. The Romulans must have evacuated this facility in a hurry because they have destroyed some sophisticated equipment that would be difficult to replace.

INTERROGATING D'TOK

If the Player Characters interrogate D'Tok, they learn that he and his team of scientists recently arrived at the Romulan Outpost after the discovery of the tachyon emissions. He brought with him a special tachyon detection device that was capable of locating the source of the tachyon emissions in the system.

He lies and claims that he is the only one left at the outpost and the rest of his team has already beamed aboard their ship. D'Tok tells the Player Characters that as soon as they arrived in the system, the Romulan outpost's sensors detected their ship and the Romulans began to evacuate. Their investigations have led them to believe that the source of the tachyon emissions is on or near the tenth planet in the Carina system, a gas giant known as Carina X. He also claims that his team was unable to determine the exact cause of the tachyon pulses but they suspect that it was artificial.

A successful Opposed **Insight + Science Task** against D'Tok's **Control + Science** with a Difficulty of 1 will reveal that D'Tok is lying. Unless the Player Characters further interrogate D'Tok or threaten him, he will not reveal any more than that. D'Tok will fold under any threat of physical

D'Tok is the lead the scientist at this outpost. His specialty is in tachyon emissions and time dilation due to gravitational effects. He was assigned here when the Romulans at the outpost detected strange tachyon emissions from this system. They originally thought the emissions were a natural occurrence, but since arriving D'Tok and his team have determined that the emissions are actually artificial. They have been studying the effects of the tachyon emissions on the planet's flora and fauna as well as the planet's colonists.

SPECIES AND TRAITS: Romulan, Suspicious, Curious

VALUE: Through Science I Will Help the Romulans Ascend to Greatness

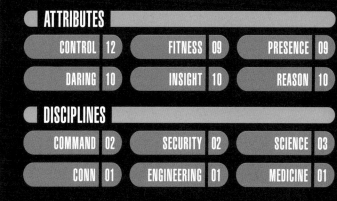

ATTRIBUTES

CONTROL 12	FITNESS 09	PRESENCE 09
DARING 10	INSIGHT 10	REASON 10

DISCIPLINES

COMMAND 02	SECURITY 02	SCIENCE 03
CONN 01	ENGINEERING 01	MEDICINE 01

FOCUSES: Subatomic Particles, Physics

STRESS: 11   **RESISTANCE:** 0

ATTACKS:
- Unarmed Strike (Melee, 3🅐, Knockdown, Size 1H, Non-lethal)
- Disruptor Pistol (Ranged, 5🅐, Vicious 1, Size 1H)

SPECIAL RULES:
- Due to his expertise and training, D'Tok's difficulty to complete Tasks related to the study of tachyon particles is reduced by 1.
- D'Tok's experience as a lead scientist allows him to reduce the Resistance of any Extended Task by 1 so long as he is working with a team.

TACHYON PARTICLES

Tachyon particles are either naturally occurring or artificially generated. Some regions of space naturally generate excess tachyon particles. Cloaked ships also generate tachyon particles. Tachyon particles are also present after nearly every instance of time travel or time-associated phenomena. Nearly every spacefaring species studies these faster-than-light subatomic particles, but none have solved all their mysteries.

The use and effects of tachyon particles are far reaching. The Federation has used tachyon detection grids to detect cloaked Romulan warbirds entering the neutral zone, and the Borg have used tachyons pulses to open transwarp conduits. As research into tachyon particles continues, further uses for these strange particles will be developed.

punishment and tell the Player Characters as much as he knows about the Romulans in the rest of the base.

With a successful **Insight + Science Task** with a Difficulty of 3, the Player Characters find a PADD with some scant bit of information on it regarding Morgan's Hope. The information includes not only data on the population but also notes about the phenomena that have occurred with specific mentions of the Mackley family and their child. Given the timeline of events on the PADD, the Romulans have been studying the colony for at least two years.

With a successful **Reason + Engineering Task** with a Difficulty of 2, the Player Characters can repair one of the Romulan terminals well enough that it will function; however,

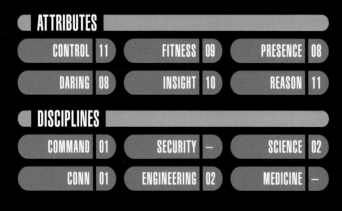

ROMULAN SCIENCE OFFICER [MINOR NPC]

Romulan science officers are ruthless in their search for ways to exploit science and technology to gain advantage over their foes. The rivalries amongst Romulan scientists push them to often take dangerous risks that other scientists might avoid. The payoff can be astounding, but they court disaster with each new experiment.

SPECIES AND TRAITS: Romulan, Curious

ATTRIBUTES

CONTROL	11	FITNESS	09	PRESENCE	08
DARING	08	INSIGHT	10	REASON	11

DISCIPLINES

COMMAND	01	SECURITY	—	SCIENCE	02
CONN	01	ENGINEERING	02	MEDICINE	—

STRESS: 9   **RESISTANCE: 0**

ATTACKS:
- Unarmed Strike (Melee, 1▲, Knockdown, Size 1H, Non-lethal)
- Disruptor Pistol (Ranged, 3▲, Vicious 1, Size 1H)

SPECIAL RULES:
- Romulan science officers may re-roll one d20 on any task involving Science.

TACTICS:
Romulan science officers will fire a couple of blasts with their disruptor pistols and then attempt to contact their ship and beam away. They have no plans of being caught by the Federation. If they are caught, they will give relatively the same information that D'Tok has but with less detail.

all the data has been erased or is corrupted. The disruptors simply did too much damage and the Romulans have been too thorough in their destruction for any information to be gleamed from these terminals.

SCENE 2: BARRACKS

Through the eastern door, you enter a long hallway with six doors along the opposite wall and a seventh door at the far end of the hall. Each of the doors is labeled with a number in the Romulan language starting with one and ending with six. The seventh door has a name on it written in Romulan.

Characters who can read Romulan understand the writing on the door: Subcommander Taleria. A successful **Reason + Command Task** with a Difficulty of 4 reveals that Subcommander Taleria is a Romulan science officer who was recently promoted to be the second-in-command of the Romulan warbird *Belorex*.

The six rooms along the eastern wall are the barracks for the science officers and and *uhlans* who work at this outpost. They are all of a similar design. They each have four bunks and underneath the mattress pad of each bunk is a storage compartment with personal effects such as family photos and spare uniforms. Everything is still neatly packed into these storage spaces. Each room has a single replicator and a pair of small desks with chairs. The replicators are non-functional due to a lack of power.

A successful **Insight + Command Task** with a Difficulty of 0 reveals that the Romulans must have evacuated as quickly as possible if they left behind their personal belongings.

In the fourth room, two Romulan science officers are hiding. They stayed behind to finish destroying the last of the outpost's research. Unless the Player Characters are being cautious and trying to sneak through the base, the Romulan science officers should make a **Reason + Security Task** with a Difficulty of 1. On a success, the Romulans are aware of the Player Characters and will lie in ambush for the Player Characters.

SUBCOMMANDER TALERIA'S SUITE
Read aloud the following:

Entering this room, you are nearly overwhelmed by the smell of burning plastic as an acrid smoke fills the air. Every PADD, every computer terminal, even the subcommander's storage space under her bunk has been destroyed with a disruptor. Just from a cursory glance you don't expect to find anything in here of use. Subcommander Taleria has been thorough in her destruction.

SCENE 3: ADMINISTRATIVE OFFICES

Read aloud the following:

Once these doors slide open, you see a dark corridor with flickering overhead lights. Red lights glow from beneath the metal grates on the floor, an obvious warning of danger. Directly ahead of you is an open door with smoke billowing out. To your left is another door. This one is closed. The corridor turns to the right where you see two more doors. Each door is closed and has Romulan writing on it.

ROOM 1 (SUBCOMMANDER TALERIA'S OFFICE)

Read aloud the following:

Thick plumes of smoke billow off the smouldering remains of a large desk. The room appears as though a bomb was set off in it. The furnishings have burn marks and the terminals are smoking as they continue to meltdown. The scent of burning plastic and melted metals burn your noses. A quick study of the room suggests that it served as the outpost commander's quarters.

A successful **Reason + Security Task** with a Difficulty of 1 reveals the likely cause of this damage was a disruptor set to overload.

A search of this room reveals nothing except smoking wreckage. Whatever the Romulans had in this room they had no intention of letting anyone else discover what it was.

ROOM 2 (SUBCOMMANDER D'TOK'S OFFICE)

On the exterior of the door is a word written in Romulan. Characters who understand the Romulan language or who scan the text with a tricorder realize it says, "Subcommander D'Tok, Department Chief Particle Physics."

The door to this room is locked. A successful **Reason + Engineering Task** with a Difficulty of 2 is required to open this door.

Once the Players are inside, read aloud the following:

This is the office of the lead scientist for this outpost, Subcommander D'Tok. It appears that he has done a thorough job of destroying all of his research. Both of the computer terminals in his office have burning holes in them from disruptor fire. It also appears that he has blasted all the PADDs in his office with a disruptor as well.

A search of this room and a successful **Reason + Security Task** Difficulty 1 will allow a Player Character to discover a still-functioning PADD that has a copy of D'Tok's work on it. If the Player Character's captured and questioned D'Tok this PADD further confirms what they already know. If not, it has the same information on it that D'Tok would have given them.

ROOMS 3 & 4

Romulan staff and logistics personnel primarily used these rooms. The small terminals are smoking wrecks from disruptor fire and the desks have been overturned. Any search through the wreckage reveals nothing except damaged PADDs and smashed equipment.

SCENE 4: POWER SUPPLY ROOM

Read aloud the following:

Even before you open the door you can hear the humming of a power generator coming from this room. When you open the door, you see both the power supply and cloaking device for the Romulans' outpost. Large conduits run overhead carrying power to the rest of the outpost. On the far side of the room, two Romulans are attaching a device to the fusion generators main regulator. They are so intent on their work that neither of them looks up at you.

As soon as the Romulan *uhlans* notice the Player Characters, one Romulan turns to attack with his disruptor while the other continues attaching a bomb to the main generator. A successful **Reason + Engineering Task** with a Difficulty of 0 allows the Player Characters to identify what the Romulan security *uhlan* is doing.

The Romulans fight until the Romulan *uhlan* successfully completes a **Reason + Security Task** with a Difficulty of 2 to set the explosive. Once that is done, both Romulans will beam out of the base on their next actions.

If the Romulans successfully set the explosives, the Player Characters will have four rounds to disarm the explosive. Disarming the explosive requires a successful **Reason + Engineering** or **Reason + Security Task** with a Difficulty of 2.

The Player Characters will have four Rounds to attempt to disarm the bomb, if this time elapses and the Player Characters have failed to disarm it, the explosion will completely destroy the outpost, collapsing the cave, and killing anyone inside. However, the Player Characters can still escape the explosion by calling to be transported out. Allow each Player Character to make a **Control + Command Task** with a Difficulty of 1. If the Player Character is successful, they are able to contact their ship and have the transporter chief evacuate them. Otherwise, the Player Characters suffer an Injury. Avoiding this Injury will cause a personal Complication related to symptoms of the blast.

SCENE 5: CLEAN ROOM

Read aloud the following text:

You enter this room through two sets of heavy doors much like an airlock. The inner doors are thicker and heavier than the outer doors. As you pass through the vestibule, you see several sensors along the wall that are non-functional. Unlike the rest of the Romulan outpost, this room has not been touched. Nothing is damaged, and you see no disruptor burns. This room's floor, walls, and ceiling are made from a different material than the rest of base. The room also has its own power supply sitting in the far corner next to a large console. The fusion reactor is still on, but the console is off. You also see a sturdy square table about the length and width of an average human. Several conduits hang from the table and lead back to the computer console and fusion reactor. They were likely attached to a device of some kind.

If a Player Character carefully studies the room with a tricorder and succeeds on a **Reason + Science Task** with a Difficulty of 2, they will discover that the Romulans designed the materials that make up the walls of this room to filter out most subatomic particles with the exception of the tachyons.

With a successful **Reason + Engineering Task** with a Difficulty of 0, the Player Characters may restart the computer console in this room.

Although the Romulans have wiped most of the data from the computer's memory, the Player Characters may attempt a **Reason + Science Task** with a Difficulty of 3 to reveal that this computer was dedicated to a single device used to detect, measure, and track tachyon emissions. Given the sophisticated nature of this equipment, the Romulan device is more advanced than anything the Federation has. It might be able to detect tachyon emissions from as far as way as several dozen light years. This would explain how Romulans detected the Tachyon emissions in the Carina system.

SCENE 6: RETURN TO THE SHIP

After searching the Romulan science outpost, the Player Characters will likely want to return to their ship and recover while they put together the clues they've uncovered so far. If the Player Characters have captured D'Tok they may want to further question him regarding the tachyon emissions and what it means for the planet. D'Tok has no additional information but will suggest that any damage done by the tachyon particles is irreversible.

The Player Characters may also decide to return to Morgan's Hope to recuperate. If they do, the citizens of the colony are happy to provide whatever assistance to the Player Characters that they can; however, their supplies are limited in comparison to what's available aboard the Player Character's starship. If the Player Characters confirm the Romulan presence to the colonists (either by telling the colonists or marching in a group of Romulan prisoners), the colonists will be outraged and blame the Romulans for their colony's problems.

ENTROPY'S DEMISE

ACT 3: FATE OF THE USS HAMILTON

SCENE 1: INVESTIGATING THE HAMILTON

After the Player Characters have transported back to their ship, they should have enough information to focus their search for the tachyon emissions on Carina X, the largest planet in the Carina system. A series of colourful rings encircle Carina X, and the composition of those rings plus the disruptions caused by the tachyon bursts make any attempts to scan the planet more difficult. However, with the information from the Romulan outpost, the Player Characters have the information necessary to focus their search.

Scanning for the source of the tachyon emissions is a **Reason + Science Task** with a Difficulty of 1. A successful scan reveals that the tachyon emissions are coming from a *Constitution*-class starship. The registry of the ship is the *U.S.S. Hamilton* NCC-1145.

A successful **Reason + Command Task** with a Difficulty of 0 reveals that the Federation decommissioned the *Hamilton* nearly 40 years ago, stripped the ship of all its core components, and recycled the metals per the Federation's standard procedure in decommissioning their starships. Yet, the *Hamilton* is right there on their main viewscreen and is obviously the source of the tachyon emissions. Further attempts to investigate the *Hamilton* will be met with dead ends as all data on the *Hamilton* has been classified by Starfleet.

Depending on the personalities of the Player Characters, they may attempt one of two options: Player Characters who are more independent-minded or distrusting may attempt to access Starfleet's computer system without permission and gain knowledge of the *Hamilton*. Player Characters who trust the Federation may contact Admiral T'Lara and request information from her. In either case, the Player Characters will gain the same information.

HACKING STARFLEET'S RECORDS

If the Player Characters wish to override the Starfleet's computer system's security protocols to discover the secret behind the *U.S.S. Hamilton's* appearance in the Carina system, the Player Characters must succeed on a **Reason + Engineering Task** with a Difficulty of 2. Success indicates that the Player Characters have been able to defeat

Starfleet's computer security and gain access to the data about the *Hamilton's* final mission.

TALKING TO ADMIRAL T'LARA

As a member of Starfleet Operations, Admiral T'Lara is aghast that the Federation is directly responsible for the problems on Carina VII (although her Vulcan demeanor does not allow her to express this emotion). She accesses Starfleet's classified files on the *Hamilton*, and she explains that the Federation was testing a new weapon at the time and gives the Player Characters access to the Captain's Log entries below. She informs the Player Characters that the *Hamilton* was believed lost after the tachyon weapon test.

THE WEAPON'S TEST

Regardless of whether the Player Characters broke into Starfleet's computers, spoke directly to Admiral T'Lara, or found another way to discover information about the *U.S.S. Hamilton*, they uncover the following captain's logs detailing the *Hamilton's* last hours.

Read aloud the following sections giving breaks for the Player Characters to take notes when necessary:

After skimming through the log entries of the U.S.S. Hamilton, *you discover three that are pertinent to the tachyon emissions. Captain Tal'lek Shran, an Andorian, is terse in each entry, and as the logs progress she becomes more worried.*

The Captain's logs can be ound on the following page.

A **Reason + Science Task** with a Difficulty of 2 allows the Player Characters to establish that the explosion of tachyon particles likely caused the *Hamilton* to be moved forward in time.

The Player Characters uncover additional files attached to the Captain's Logs. The files include the location of the tachyon weapon (in engineering) and the location of the weapon's plans (on the bridge). The Player Characters should understand if the Romulans capture either the weapon's plans or the weapon itself the Federation's most dangerous enemy will have access to a new and dangerous weapon. The Player Characters should understand by now the dangerous effects of a tachyon's harnessed as a weapon.

CAPTAIN TAL'LEK SHRAN'S LOGS

CAPTAIN'S LOG. STARDATE 1425.7

Having arrived in the Carina system we are ready to begin testing of the tachyon weapon. Mr. Spruell, the weapon designer and our chief engineer, Lt. Matis, have assured me that all indications point to a positive and successful test. Mr. Spruell claims that the weapon will harness directed tachyon bursts to degrade any structure, artificially aging it, and thus disabling any potential threat.

CAPTAIN'S LOG. STARDATE 1426.6

Despite the best efforts of Chief Engineer Matis, the tachyon weapon is drawing ever increasing power from our engines. The process appears irreversible. All efforts to stop or contain the weapon have failed. My first officer has suggested that we attempt to destroy the device, but Mr. Spruell is convinced that

damage to device could cause a simultaneous core breach and explosion of tachyons so powerful that the entire Carina system could be destroyed.

CAPTAIN'S LOG. STARDATE 1426.8

The device has drained so much energy from the ship that we no longer have impulse power and life support is beginning to fail. Reports are coming in from all ship's departments of structural failures in the ship's bulkheads and superstructure. All attempts to regain control of the device have failed. Antimatter containment is beginning to fail, and I have ordered a general evacuation.

CAPTAIN'S LOG. STARDATE 1426.8, SUPPLEMENTAL

Captain Shan's log has no commentary. Instead you see images of the *Hamilton* disappearing in a brilliant flash of light.

CAPTAIN'S LOGS

FEDERATION WEAPON EXPERIMENTS

The *U.S.S. Hamilton*'s accident occurred on Stardate 1426 putting the accident firmly in the time period covered in *Star Trek: The Original Series* in the year 2265 CE or approximately 100 years prior to the current stardate. This period of Federation history is controversial, especially with the Federation's involvement in the development and testing of the Genesis Device as well as the creation and destruction of the Genesis Planet. With the Klingons already involved, knowledge of the existence of the Genesis Device and the planet it created spread through the Alpha and Beta Quadrants.

Although the Federation did not intend the Genesis Device to be a weapon, its potential as a weapon was unheralded. Both the Romulan and Klingon governments argued that the development of weapons of that magnitude represented a major threat to peace between the three governments and demanded the Federation stop all development of future weapons of mass destruction. Starfleet decided it was best to classify all previous failed weapons experiments including the tachyon weapon aboard the *U.S.S. Hamilton*.

Along with the information gathered from the captain's log, the Player Characters discover the plans to the tachyon weapon that Mr. Spruell had built and tested onboard the *Hamilton*.

With a successful **Reason + Engineering Task** with a Difficulty of 3, a Player Character is able to recall that Daymond Spruell was a weapon's researcher for Starfleet during the early 23rd century. He is responsible for the development of several experimental torpedo designs. His later research focused on detecting and eventually generating tachyon particles. Much of his later work went into the development of contemporary deflector dishes.

SCENE 2: APPROACHING THE HAMILTON

At this point the Player Characters should have an accurate idea of what is happening to the colony: a series of tachyon bursts have been causing the premature and rapid aging of organic and inorganic matter on the planet. With information from the Romulan Outpost, the Player Characters also have discovered the cause of the tachyon bursts, a *Constitution*-class starship orbiting Carina X.

Once in orbit of Carina X, the game master should have the Player Characters make a **Reason + Science Task** with a Difficulty of 0. On a success, the Player Characters discover that due to the interference from the tachyon particles any attempts to transport onto or off the *Hamilton* will end fatally for the away team.

Piloting a shuttlecraft to the *Hamilton* is the only option, but it is not without dangers. The rings encircling Carina X are made of rocks and dust. Some of the rocks are large enough to do damage to a shuttlecraft. The Player Characters must succeed on a **Daring + Conn Task** with a difficulty of 1 to pilot their shuttle craft through the rings without sustaining damage. Failure indicates that the shuttle craft was damaged and all further Tasks involving piloting the shuttle increase their Difficulty by 1.

Once the Player Character's shuttle reaches the *Hamilton*, read aloud the following:

As your shuttlecraft approaches the Constitution-class starship you see that it is in much worse condition than you expected, given the amount of damage that the ship has taken, you wonder if the hull is still intact and if the ship still maintains a breathable atmosphere. The tachyon bursts from the weapon are causing the ship to deteriorate at a much faster rate than you expected. The starboard warp nacelle is badly damaged from meteor impacts, and as your shuttlecraft circles the Hamilton, *you can see that the ship's shuttlebay doors are open and a Romulan shuttlecraft has landed. The Romulans have beaten you to the* Hamilton!

Prior to landing on the *Hamilton* the Player Characters may use the shuttlecraft's instruments to scan the ship; however, due to the massive amount of tachyon particles in the vicinity very little information may be gleamed.

A **Reason + Security Task** with a Difficulty of 1 to determine that that a Romulan shuttlecraft has space for two helmsmen and up to 10 passengers.

Landing on the *Hamilton* will require the Player Characters to succeed on a **Daring + Conn Task** with a Difficulty 1.

Once their shuttle has landed, the Player Characters will be able to scan the *Hamilton*. A **Reason + Science Task** with a Difficulty of 0 determines that parts of the ship are no longer air tight and it would be wise if the Player Characters wore EV suits.

SCENE 3: SHUTTLEBAY

Please read the following out loud:

You step off the shuttlecraft and into the deserted shuttlebay. The sickly green of the Romulan shuttlecraft draws your attention first. You notice that it is sealed up tightly. Otherwise, the shuttlebay is littered with trash and the remains of a quick evacuation. Several large containers sit against the wall with their lids opened. From the state of things, you can assume that the U.S.S. Hamilton was evacuated very quickly.

PCs may attempt to a **Reason + Engineering Task** with a Difficulty of 3 to unlock the Romulan shuttle.

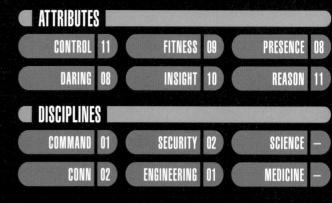

ROMULAN HELMSMAN [MINOR NPC]

Trained at the finest academies in the Romulan Empire, Romulan Helmsmen and pilots are some of the most ruthless in the Galaxy. Although they may serve as helmsmen today, all are eyeing the Commander's chair and believe that it's only a matter of time and cunning before they prove themselves and rise in rank.

TRAITS: Romulan

ATTRIBUTES

| CONTROL 11 | FITNESS 09 | PRESENCE 08 |
| DARING 08 | INSIGHT 10 | REASON 11 |

DISCIPLINES

| COMMAND 01 | SECURITY 02 | SCIENCE — |
| CONN 02 | ENGINEERING 01 | MEDICINE — |

STRESS: 11   **RESISTANCE:** 0

ATTACKS:
- Unarmed Strike (Melee, 3⏶ Knockdown, Size 1H, Non-lethal)
- Dagger (Melee, 3⏶ Vicious 1, Size 1H, Deadly, Hidden 1)
- Disruptor Pistol (Ranged, 5⏶ Vicious 1, Size 1H)

A single Romulan Helmsman remains in the Romulan shuttlecraft. He will not attack, but immediately alerts the other Romulans that a Federation ship has landed. If the Player Characters investigate the Romulan shuttle they discover him and can take him prisoner, but he will resist. His orders are to protect the shuttlecraft as it is the Romulans' only means of escape. If they do not investigate the ship, the Romulan will attempt to disable the Player Characters' shuttlecraft.

If questioned, the Romulan helmsman, Jaron, will admit that the captain of the Romulan warbird, Commander Merrok, has no interest in the existing tachyon device. He wants the plans so that the Romulan Empire can reverse engineer the tachyon weapon and build something that's actually effective — unlike the incompetent Federation.

SCENE 4: HALLWAY

This room has a thin atmosphere. Without EV suits, the Player Characters cannot breathe.

Read aloud the following:

As you exit the shuttlebay, you enter the main corridor that runs the length of the ship. At the far end of the corridor is the turbolift that leads to the bridge. Along this corridor, you will also be able to access engineering. The corridor is crowded with debris from the original crew's evacuation. The deck has started to disintegrate due to the effects of the tachyon emissions making crossing the corridor fraught with danger.

Warned by their colleague on the shuttlecraft, the Romulans have set up an ambush here. Two Romulan security *uhlans* are hidden in partially opened doorways waiting for the Player Characters to enter the hallway. The Player Characters will notice the Romulan ambush with an **Insight + Security Task** with a Difficulty 1 opposed by the Romulans' **Control + Security**.

The GM should use threat to introduce environmental hazards as the ship deteriorates: falling beams, holes opening in the floor, etc.

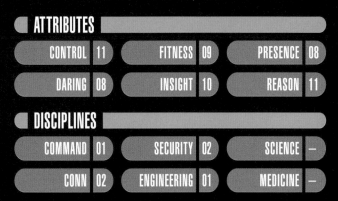

ROMULAN UHLAN [MINOR NPC]

The Romulan *uhlan* is the lowest ranking officer in the Romulan Guard and makes up a substantial number of their personnel.

SPECIES AND TRAITS: Romulan, Suspicious

ATTRIBUTES

CONTROL	11	FITNESS	09	PRESENCE	08
DARING	08	INSIGHT	10	REASON	11

DISCIPLINES

COMMAND	01	SECURITY	02	SCIENCE	—
CONN	02	ENGINEERING	01	MEDICINE	—

STRESS: 11   **RESISTANCE:** 0

ATTACKS:
- Unarmed Strike (Melee, 3▲ Knockdown, Size 1H, Non-lethal)
- Dagger (Melee, 3▲ Vicious 1, Size 1H, Deadly, Hidden 1)
- Disruptor Pistol (Ranged, 5▲ Vicious 1, Size 1H)
- **Escalation** Disruptor Rifle (Ranged, 6▲ Vicious 1, Size 2H, Accurate)

SCENE 5: ENGINEERING

When the Player Characters reach engineering, read aloud the following:

Approaching engineering you hear the unmistakable hum of an active warp core still powering the ship. Continued signs of the ship's deterioration give you pause. Panels hang loosely from the walls with only thin, worn wiring to hold them up. Most of the consoles here are malfunctioning or not working at all. The consoles that appear to be functioning, however, risk shorting out at any moment.

A cylindrical device is attached directly to the antimatter intermix valve. The device is approximately 2 meters in height and 1 meter in diameter, very similar in appearance to a photon torpedo, if it were stood on one end.

Using one of the still functioning consoles, Player Characters can make a **Reason + Engineering Task** with a Difficulty of 1 to determine that the warp core is no longer stable.. The Player Characters should surmise that the tachyon device's continual drain from the core and the tachyon bursts are causing disruptions to the antimatter containment fields. The *Hamilton* only has hours before a core breach destroys the ship.

DEFUSING THE TACHYON DEVICE

Disabling the tachyon device is an Extended Task with a Difficulty of 3. The Work track for this Extended Task is 18, with a Magnitude of 3. Successfully defusing the tachyon device requires a **Reason + Engineering Task** (PCs may use Focuses such as Physics, Computers, or similar.) The Player Characters have 9 Intervals to defuse the device. Due to the limited amount of space around the device, only two Player Characters may attempt to disarm it.

CONSEQUENCES

FAILURE

If the Player Characters fail, the device causes the *U.S.S. Hamilton* warp core to completely destabilize, and the Player Characters will have only minutes to escape. The resulting explosion will saturate the star system with tachyon particles further exacerbating the problems on Carina VII and making it uninhabitable. A full evacuation of Carina VII will be necessary to save the colonists, but the environment of Carina VII will never recover.

SUCCESS

Successfully disarming the device means that the *Hamilton's* warp core will stabilize and the device will stop emitting the dangerous tachyon bursts that threaten the colony.

When the Player Character's make their first Breakthrough, they are attacked by Subcommander Taleria and three Romulan *uhlans* who enter the engineering bay with plans to capture the weapon so their scientists can reverse engineer

Subcommander Taleria first distinguished herself with her knowledge of subatomic particles while at the Romulan Fleet Academy. With her knowledge of physics and her command ability, Taleria has risen quickly through the ranks. Taleria has served with distinction aboard the *I.R.W. Belorex* since assigned to the ship as its executive officer. Her first thought is always for the crew of her ship and she is well liked by her subordinates. Commander Merrok has already petitioned the Romulan Fleet for Taleria's promotion.

Taleria lacks the innate hatred and distrust of the Federation common to most Romulans. She is willing to talk and consider alternate outcomes. Her goal after her service in the Romulan Fleet is to become an ambassador. Despite her preference to avoid violence, Taleria will not undermine the Romulan's position, and her cunning almost ensures that when she negotiates a bargain the Romulans will always have the better side of it.

SPECIES AND TRAITS: Romulan, Negotiator, Cunning

VALUE: The Romulan Empire Will Prevail, but Violence Isn't the Only Solution.

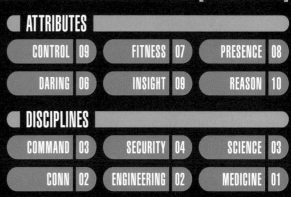

ATTRIBUTES

CONTROL	09	FITNESS	07	PRESENCE	08
DARING	06	INSIGHT	09	REASON	10

DISCIPLINES

COMMAND	03	SECURITY	04	SCIENCE	03
CONN	02	ENGINEERING	02	MEDICINE	01

FOCUSES: Subatomic Particles, Leadership, Quick Wits

STRESS: 13   **RESISTANCE:** 2

ATTACKS:
- Fists (Melee, 5▲, Knockdown, Size 1H)
- Knife (Melee, 5▲, Hidden 1, Deadly, Vicious 1, Size 1H)
- Disruptor Pistol (Ranged, 7▲, Vicious 1, Size 1H)

SPECIAL RULES:
- Subcommander Taleria grants all Romulan NPCs under her command an additional Task each turn.
- Subcommander Taleria may attempt to Negotiate or Intimidate as an additional Task on her turn.

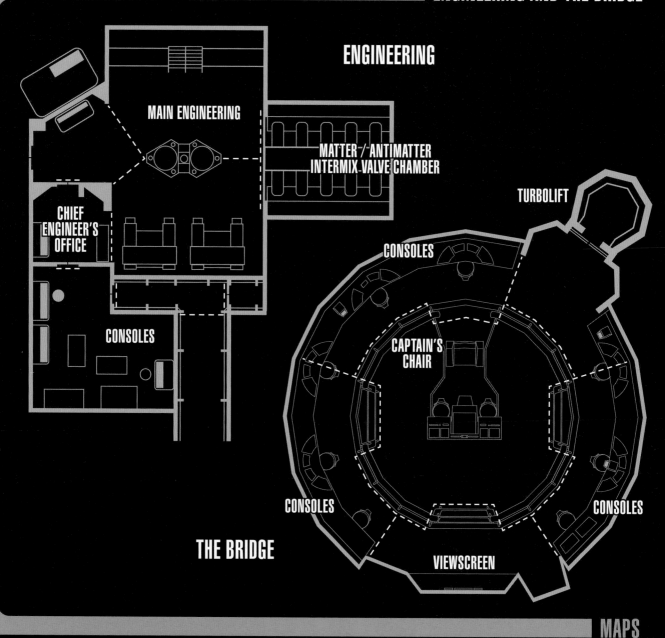

ENGINEERING

MAIN ENGINEERING

MATTER / ANTIMATTER
INTERMIX VALVE CHAMBER

TURBOLIFT

CHIEF
ENGINEER'S
OFFICE

CONSOLES

CONSOLES

CAPTAIN'S
CHAIR

CONSOLES

CONSOLES

THE BRIDGE

VIEWSCREEN

it. Unknown to the Romulans the tachyon device could cause the destruction of the *Hamilton* at any moment. The Romulan's main goal is to capture the device and capture or kill any Federation officer in engineering.

Subcommander Taleria may listen to reason if the Player Characters make an effort to talk and explain the situation.

SCENE 6: THE TURBOLIFT SHAFT

This room has a thin atmosphere. Without EV suits, the Player Characters cannot breathe.

Read aloud the following:

The doors to the turbolift have been pried open. On the opposite wall is the emergency ladder that offers your only path to the bridge. The rungs look sturdy, but you can see where a few have started to corrode and hang loosely from their mountings.

The climb to the top is a **Daring + Security Task**. The Difficulty is 0, but the GM should spend Threat to make sure that the Player Characters struggle to make it to the top by increasing the Difficulty of their climbing by 1. This Extended Task has a Work track of 10 and a Magnitude of 2.

As soon as the Player Characters begin their ascent, a pair of Romulan security *uhlans* begins firing at them.

When Player Characters are halfway to the top (achieved their first Breakthrough), two Romulans begin firing disruptors at them. The Romulans have cover from their perch at the top. As soon as one of the Romulans is wounded, they both retreat.

If the Player Characters have persuaded Subcommander Taleria to assist them in stopping Merrok, then the Player Character's will have the Difficulty of negotiating with the Romulan *uhlans* reduced to 1.

SCENE 7: THE BRIDGE

Read aloud the following:

As you pull yourselves up the final rungs of the turbolift shaft, you peek through the opened doors and see a tall Romulan with the rank insignia of a commander leaning over the science officer's station accessing the ship's computer. Beside him is a pair of watchful uhlans.

"Hurry up," the Romulan commands, "We've got to get out of here before those Federation fools arrive."

The bridge is in worse shape than the rest of the ship. The captain's chair has been overturned, a part of the bridge's ceiling has collapsed, and several of the computer consoles are spitting sparks. The ship is starting to decay faster and faster.

As soon as the Player Characters make themselves known, the Romulan commander orders his *uhlans* to attack. The *uhlans* take cover and fire at the Player Characters while the commander continues to download the plans to the tachyon weapon.

The Romulan captain will gain the plans so long as he succeeds at an Extended Task with a Work track of 8, Magnitude of 2 and Difficulty of 3. After which he will have his two *uhlans* cover his escape. The only escape is through the turbolift shaft behind the Player Characters.

Unable to transport away, Commander Merrok and his security team will fight to the last man. If they are able to bypass the Player Characters, they will rush down the turbolift shaft and towards their shuttle hoping to escape back to their ship.

The Player Characters may attempt to negotiate with Commander Merrok, but Merrok is loath to talk to any member of the Federation. The only chance they Player Characters have of ending this confrontation without violence is if they have befriended Subcommander Taleria. Nevertheless, all negotiations with Merrok have an increased Difficulty of 1.

Commander of the Romulan warbird, the *D'deridex*-class *Belorex*, Commander Merrok rose rapidly through ranks of the Romulan military thanks to his cunning and calculated risk taking. He allows no dissent among his crew and expects each of them to excel at the tasks assigned to them. More than a few officers on the *Belorex* have been reassigned to outposts on distant and frigid worlds.

Merrok has no love for the Federation and sees them as a growing threat to the Romulan Empire. The tachyon emissions that his ship discovered in the Carina system are more evidence of the Federation's constant hypocrisy. While the Federation claims to be a peaceful organization, their military arm, Starfleet, continues to build dangerous new weapons.

SPECIES AND TRAITS: Romulan, Ruthless

VALUE: I Will Do Whatever It Takes to Stop the Federation

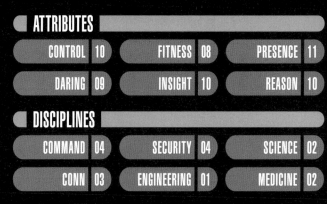

ATTRIBUTES

CONTROL 10	FITNESS 08	PRESENCE 11
DARING 09	INSIGHT 10	REASON 10

DISCIPLINES

COMMAND 04	SECURITY 04	SCIENCE 02
CONN 03	ENGINEERING 01	MEDICINE 02

FOCUSES: Command, Deception, Disruptors

STRESS: 12 **RESISTANCE:** 2

ATTACKS:
- Unarmed Strike (Melee, 5🗡, Knockdown, Size 1H)
- Knife (Melee, 5🗡, Hidden 1, Vicious 1, Size 1H)
- Disruptor Pistol (Ranged, 37🗡, Vicious 1, Size 1H)

SPECIAL RULES:
- **Threatening 2:** When the Player Characters encounter Merrok, add two threat to the threat pool.
- Unless a Player Character has a higher Daring than Commander Merrok, Merrok always acts before the first Player Character.
- Merrok grants all Romulan NPCs under his command an additional task each turn.

ENTROPY'S DEMISE
CONCLUSION

Having defused the tachyon weapon and defeated Commander Merrok, the Player Characters make their way back to their shuttlecraft and return to their ship.

If the Player Characters have befriended Subcommander Taleria, she will request that the Player Characters allow her to take the remaining Romulans and return to their ship as well. If the Player Characters attempt to take her hostage, she will fight back. Otherwise, the Player Characters and Romulans part as foes who have earned each other's respect.

If the Player Characters have captured any Romulans, the Romulan warbird, the *Belorex* will decloak once the Player Characters return to their ship and the new commander of the ship, Subcommander T'Plag, will attempt to negotiate for their release. If the Player Characters argue against the release of the Romulans, Subcommander T'Plag will suggest that the Galaxy will not look to kindly on the Federation once word of the tachyon weapon spreads. In exchange for the return of the prisoners, T'Plag will agree not to spread rumors of the Federation's weapon research.

CONTINUING VOYAGES...

On Carina VII, the effects of tachyon emissions subside; however, the damage that the tachyons have done is irreversible. The vineyards will survive; although, most of the wine has turned sour. It will take several years before the colony recovers completely. The buildings on Carina VII will no longer suffer from structural failures. Unfortunately, the rapid aging of young Efren Mackley is irreversible, but although he will struggle for the next few years, eventually his mind will catch up with his body.

The greater question is: How will the Player Characters explain to the colonists that this entire episode was caused by a Federation experiment gone awry? And what sort of mission with their explanation create in the future?

TACHYON EMISSION SUBHARMONIC ANALYSIS

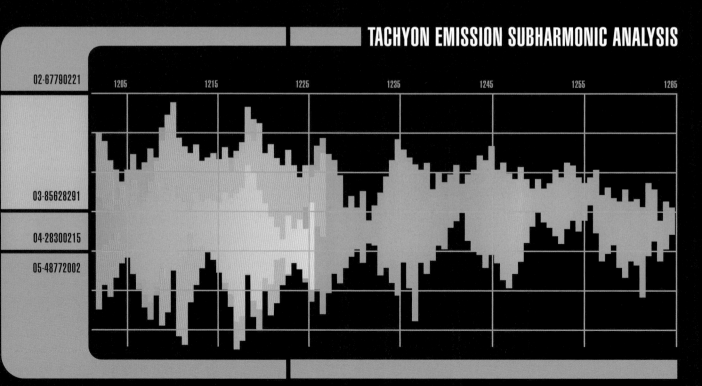

02-67790221
03-85628291
04-28300215
05-48772002

1205   1215   1225   1235   1245   1255   1265

CHAPTER 05.00

FORESTS OF THE NIGHT

BY DARREN WATTS

22122983987283
1035918587

SYNOPSIS

The Players' starship has been assigned to explore a new sector, which is filled with unusual numbers of ion storms. After weeks of cataloguing of supernovae, quasars and uninhabited systems, they pick up a strange metallic object on their sensors, and realize it must be an alien ship! It's spinning slowly, moving slower than light, and emitting a strange radiation that is similar to the types of ion storms that plague this sector. However, it does seem to contain indistinct life signs, and since the ship's transporters are untrustworthy in this energy field, the Players will likely have to send over a shuttlecraft to find out what's inside.

Once there, the crew discovers the ship contains a massive forest, inhabited by strange alien plants as well as a few animals. They'll have to deal with ghostly lights, dangerous plants, and something moving in the shadows stalking them through the terrifying terrain, in order to solve the mystery of the Forests of The Night!

DIRECTIVES

In addition to the Prime Directive, the Directives for this mission are:

- Explore and Map this New Sector
- Make Peaceful Contact with New Civilizations

The crew should quickly discover that whoever built the ship has basic interstellar capacity, so the Prime Directive will frame their response.

Gamemasters begin this mission with 2 points of Threat for each Player Character in the group.

BACKGROUND

The Player Characters have been assigned to explore a new sector of space just beyond the current borders of the Federation. This sector is home to an alien race called the Vahari, who now live on a planet they call New Vahar after the destruction of their original homeworld. The Vahari are

humanoid beings, distinguishable from humans only by their bluish skin and their greater range of vision into the ultraviolet range thanks to the differences in spectrum emissions from their original home star. Their society has advanced politically to the point where they would be welcome in the Federation, having united their various nations and outlawed war. Though they have not yet discovered warp drive, they were in the early stages of exploring space in their original system, having colonized several other worlds and moons in their own system and sent unmanned sublight probes to nearby stars. They have not yet encountered another sentient species, and whether they are alone in the universe is a question that concerns them deeply.

Approximately sixty years ago, the Vahari discovered abnormalities developing in the core of their sun, which was our spectral class B4 and approximately eight times as massive as Sol. The core was slowly collapsing for unknown reasons, and the sun's conversion into a supernova was unavoidable. Fortunately, the Vahari discovered this while decades remained in the star's life, and immediately dedicated their entire society to building a massive fleet of slower-than-light colony ships to carry their population (and as complete a representation of their world's animal and plant life as possible) to a recently-discovered habitable planet in a star system only about sixteen light-years away. It took them twenty years to assemble this fleet and launch it into space, placing the future of their entire people into the hands of fate.

By the time the fleet was ready to leave Vahar, its sun's instability had caused it to generate localized interplanetary and even interstellar-level ion storms, which raged throughout the local sector. The Vahari ship's navigators were hard-pressed to avoid these hazards, which form unpredictably and inflict enormous damage despite their shields (Ion storms can overload the plasma circuits, cause massive computer shutdowns, and otherwise disrupt ship's systems like communications). Though most of the convoy's ships successfully made the trip to New Vahar, a small number of them were destroyed or driven off-course by the terrifying storms.

One of those lost was the *Grif Balata*, part of the section of the convoy dedicated to transporting native plant species of Vahar. In this case, the collected plants were from a heavily forested continent that had been maintained partially in a naturally wild state by the Vahari government. Though none of the plant species were truly sentient, they were more advanced than any Earth plant species; some were mobile, capable of tracking and following animal prey, while others could communicate in a crude language of pheromones that carry powerful emotional cues. Many were quite dangerous if mishandled, and the *Grif Balata* carried a small crew of well-trained botanists and biologists who served months-long shifts caring for them before rotating off to other ships.

The *Grif Balata* was caught in one of these unpredictable ion storms approximately four years into their journey to the new home, and was separated from the convoy. The intense radiation penetrated the shielding of the ship, and the crew was killed along with most of the higher animal forms by the high-temperature burst. This also killed a lot of the active plants but left root colonies and seedlings capable of growing back. The engines were partly damaged, causing the ship to continue on a new heading away from the convoy at approximately 1/10th the speed of light. That course and speed has placed it currently 3.6 lightyears from the site of the storm striking it, five light years from the neutron star that used to be Vahar's sun, and about eighteen light years from the system where the colony of New Vahar was successfully established by the rest of the convoy about ten years ago.

OTHER ERAS OF PLAY

Storytellers from the Original Series era of *Star Trek* should be able to use this scenario as written. For *Enterprise* era Players, the crew will have been assigned to explore this particular sector by Starfleet in coordination with the Vulcan High Command, presumably as one of the follow-up missions behind the *NX*-class *Enterprise*. The effects of ion storms are probably much less well-known to the crew, and the prospect of being caught in one with insufficient shielding is likely much more frightening. The absence of advanced universal translator technology should provide additional Complications in linguistics when dealing with the ship's computer terminals. If the Gamemaster decides to add another ship seeking to salvage or claim the *Grif Balata,* then obviously it should not be Ferengi prior to their first contact with the Federation in 2364. Orions might be appropriate in either period.

In addition, the artificial intelligence that ran the computers, life-support, and general maintenance of the ship and its "forest" was disrupted by the radiation burst, causing it to lose large portions of its library database and some of its higher problem solving faculties, leaving it functionally "insane." Despite these infirmities, the *Grif Balata's* systems have continued to maintain and care for the regrowing forest it carries within. It's at this point that the Player Characters encounter the sub-light ship.

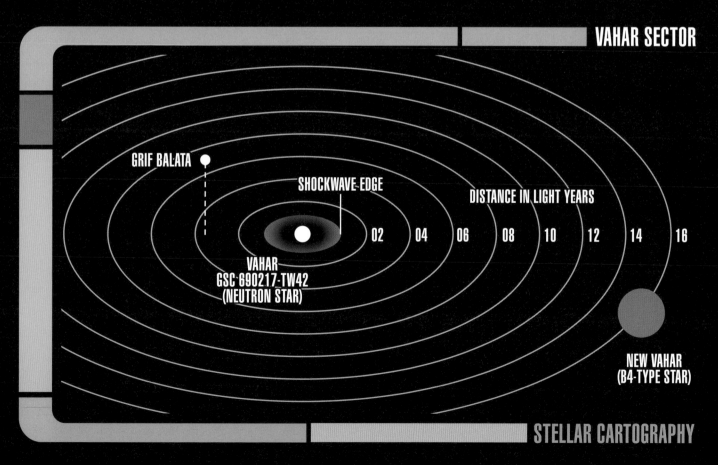

GRIF BALATA

SHOCKWAVE-EDGE

DISTANCE IN LIGHT YEARS

02   04   06   08   10   12   14   16

VAHAR
GSC-690217-TW42
(NEUTRON STAR)

NEW VAHAR
(B4-TYPE STAR)

FORESTS OF THE NIGHT
ACT 1: A NEUTRON STAR

CAPTAIN'S LOG

STARDATE 47439.5

We've been searching this sector of space for a while now and three days ago astrometrics reported a new supernova, only about twenty years old, on long range sensors. I've ordered us into a distant orbit around the neutron star it created and fired off several probes to measure the size and extent of the supernova's impact on surrounding space. It seems the shockwave has been traveling at about thirteen kilometers per second since the supernova, which means that the shock wave itself has traveled slightly less than a light-year at this point. The crew are busy analysing the data, and I should have an update soon.

SCENE 1: A NEUTRON STAR TEMPORARILY RELIEVES ROUTINE

The Player Characters' starship has been on assignment in this space sector for a couple of months, exploring and mapping a section of space on the leading frontier border of the Federation. Star systems are not particularly dense in this area, and while the assignment has been a bit slow for officers accustomed to more adventurous postings, the scientists aboard are thrilled with the constant stream of new data. Most of the crew has had plenty of time recently to work on their own projects and hobbies. If this scenario is part of a long-term campaign, the Gamemaster might choose to include personal scenes advancing any subplots at this point.

This is a good point for the Players to attempt some introductory Tasks, analysing the neutron star. **Reason + Science Tasks** and **Control + Engineering or Science Tasks** can be called for to use the probes' telemetry and data capturing to work on the information being collected. These should be fairly routine Tasks at a Difficulty of 1 or 2, perhaps with the *Launch Probe* action decreasing the Difficulty, allowing the Players to gather some interesting information about the star.

The expanding shock wave of gases is still detectable from considerable distance; it's been traveling at about thirteen kilometers per second since the supernova, which means that the shock wave itself has traveled slightly less than a light-year at this point.

This star, of course, was once the home star of the Vahari, GSC 690217-TW42. Successful Tasks can gain this basic information:

- The star that was here has collapsed into a neutron star, only about ten kilometers in diameter.

- This star contains twice the mass of Earth's own sun.

- The *Obtain Information* Momentum spend can inform the Player Characters further, per point:

- Had the initial star been larger than it was (about 8 solar masses), it might have collapsed instead into a black hole.

- Even as it is, neutron stars are hazards to navigation and need to be carefully cataloged, as their immense gravitational fields mean their escape velocity is about 1/3 light speed (approximately full impulse for a starship) and their time dilation effects on the immediately-surrounding space are significant. Entering its gravitational field will mean a "Gravity" Complication for any **Engines Task** attempted with the starship's Systems, with its Complication range increased by 1 for those Tasks.

Once the Players have gathered as much information as they can, the ship leaves. The science departments begin analyzing their probe reports, while the rest of the crew returns to the routine of the mission. As yet, whether this star had any planets at the time of it turning nova remains a mystery, though obviously the hope is that if so, none were inhabited. That's when ship's sensors report an unidentified metal object entering sensor range.

SCENE 2: A SHIP ADRIFT!

The object sensors detect is a metallic object, shaped like a child's spinning top toy. A **Reason + Science Task** assisted by the ship's **Sensors + Science** with a Difficulty of 1 will give the following information:

- It consists of a rotating disk 2500m in diameter, with vertical protrusions emerging from the center of both sides of the disk that taper upwards for about 1000m, starting at about 200m in diameter and coming to a sharp point at the top. The disk is extremely thin, only about 40m in height.

- The object seems to be giving off unusual radiation readings (which have increased any Difficulties relating to any Sensor Tasks attempted on the object).

Any *Obtain Information* Momentum spends will grant the following, point for point:

- There are no signs of an active propulsion system- if it's a ship, its engines are apparently off and it is moving by inertia alone.

- There are obvious docking doors on the rim of the main disk. On the top and bottom surfaces of the disk near the doors are engraved and painted symbols, words in an alien language that presumably represent the ship's name or other identification. They match nothing in the ship's libraries.

- The vessel is giving off definite, but indistinct life readings — these are difficult to nail down mostly because of the radiation.

With further analysis it is clear that the ship is currently traveling at approximately thirty thousand kilometers per second, or about 1/10th the speed of light. It's slowly being pulled in by the gravitational field of a nearby red star. A success using Astrometrics or a similar Focus reveals that the unknown vessel will eventually enter orbit a few months from now unless it changes course. However, that orbit will probably not be stable and the ship or station will almost certainly burn up at that point. Further analysis suggests that wasn't the intended course, but that instead the ship has been pulled off its original course by the star's gravity and nobody on board has compensated (which would be a simple Task and usually automated).

The ship is generating a "strange radiation field" Trait that is very similar to that of ion storms, which increases Difficulty to Sensors and Communications Tasks. Once the Players' ship is within about twenty thousand kilometers, increase the intensity of the Trait to "strange radiation field 2", the ship's screens become fogged with static and the sensors begin returning nonsensical readings.

Medical or science officers are uncertain whether the radiation would in fact be harmful to human life, but one success on a **Medicine Task** lets them realize short-term exposure (for example, a few days' worth) is probably harmless and the threat can be reduced even farther with hyronalin anti-radiation injections.

Once identified as a ship, it will be clear that the engines are fusion-based and not warp-capable; indeed, the top speed of such a ship is probably around half light speed, which is somewhat faster than starship impulse power. This may spark a Prime Directive discussion, as one of the primary standards for approving first contact with an alien species is warp capability; however, it's clear that the ship is interstellar in capacity and therefore contact is allowable anyways based on the judgment of the officers involved.

Presumably the Players will be ready to head over and explore the strange vessel at this point. If they require any

prompting, the Gamemaster should remind them of the indeterminate life signs and the likely fate of the ship when it gets drawn into the nearby sun. The Strange Radiation Field Trait prevents the creation of a stable transporter lock, so a trip by shuttlecraft will be much safer. Players who wish to attempt transporting anyway can do so by getting four successes, and will need to repeat this every time they attempt to use the transporter while within a thousand kilometers of the ship. Failure should usually only result in a failed transport and the characters remaining in place, but with any Complications generated, they may instead wind up somewhere other than where they were aiming.

The away team should include at least one engineer and one science officer with some Focuses in Life Sciences, as well as someone to pilot the shuttle and probably at least one security officer. Depending on the makeup of the Player group, Supporting Characters might be required to fill out the away team.

FORESTS OF THE NIGHT
ACT 2: INTO THE FOREST

SCENE 1: GETTING INSIDE

The shuttle trip over is largely uneventful and only takes a couple of minutes. Up close, anyone attempting new sensor readings at a much closer range can confirm large amounts of biosignatures as well as a breathable nitrogen-oxygen atmosphere with a **Reason + Science Task** assisted by the small craft's **Sensors + Science** with a Difficulty of 1. This is supported by additional readings showing that some sort of atmospheric life-support systems are still functional, as are internal gravity control and inertial damper systems not terribly different from Starfleet standards. Though the ship is rotating, it is at far too slow a speed to provide artificial gravity itself. The ship clearly has no deflector shields active, and no sign of the ability to generate them; instead, it seems to rely entirely on the thick hull plating, which can easily withstand small meteor strikes or similar space hazards but would not last long under attack by starship weaponry. A quick orbit around the outside of the ship shows scattered

bits of scarring; a single success from either a **Reason + Engineering** or **Security Task** suggests the damage resulted from ionic flares during an ion storm rather than coming from another ship's weapons. At one point on the periphery of the disk a clear docking point with external doors is seen, but no attempts to establish communication have any effect.

The shuttle can "dock" anywhere on the perimeter of the disk, but it's considerably easier to do so at the main doors, which are thinner and lighter than the rest of the hull. The hull material is quite thick and durable, but there is an outer manual control mechanism behind a panel that can be penetrated with even a hand phaser after a sufficient amount of time and offers little resistance to a phaser drill or rifle. The doors currently are receiving no power from the engines, and so won't respond to efforts to pick them electronically unless the Player Characters connect some kind of power supply (or perhaps spending Power from the shuttle itself combined with some kind of **Engineering Task**. Although, that should be considered a security risk, though it will in fact have no negative effect.

Behind the doors is recognizably an airlock of some kind, which is functional though not currently active. An **Engineering Task** with a Difficulty of 3, and a Power requirement of 1, turns the equipment on inside and allows the lock to cycle properly, protecting the interior from vacuum exposure.

Passing through the airlock leads the away team into a corridor that runs around the outer circumference of the disk. The corridor is dark, though light fixtures along the walls can be easily identified; examination reveals they are functional, but receiving no power. There are also computer terminal screen stations every 100 meters or so, which are similarly depowered. If the Players brought along a portable generator, an **Engineering Task** with a Difficulty of 2 will allow them to hook it up to the alien systems, which will allow them to provide light in the corridor and activate the terminals. Unfortunately, the terminals are connected to the damaged ship's computer and therefore will only display static interspersed with random feeds of Vahari entertainment, mostly drama or comedy with the sound turned off. However, if the Players think to do so, they can connect their tricorders to these broadcasts and start the universal translator programs required to understand Vahari, which may save them time when they finally encounter the ship's main computer terminal inside the forest (see below.)

The corridor has high ceilings, about six meters up, which is of course considerably less than the height of the disk and should suggest (incorrectly) that there are several floors. The corridors are eerily silent, and there are mild odors of flowers and fruit with no obvious source. Once the Players are inside the ship, they receive much less interference on their tricorders and can determine that there are in fact enormous biosignatures on the other side of the corridor wall. However, the interference with attempts to hail or signal the Player's ship are increased by a similar amount, increasing the Difficulty of related Tasks by 2.

Approximately 500 meters down the corridor (in either direction) there is a large door leading further into the center of the disk. The door is locked shut by an internal electronic mechanism, which can be defeated either by another **Engineering Task** or cutting open a panel with a phaser (the internal walls are much less dense and resistant than the outer ones) and manipulating the controls manually.

No matter where else Players may attempt to dock at the edges of the disk, they will enter the same corridor at some point past the entry airlock, as it spans the entire circumference of the ship. If they try to enter from either surface of the disk, remind them that there are no signs of any force field generators on this ship, and therefore they'd be opening the interior of the ship to vacuum. If they insist on doing so, particularly tolerant Gamemasters may offer them a second chance to notice the damage they're

doing while the hole is still small and can be patched; otherwise, they expose the forest below to space, losing atmosphere and presumably killing pretty much everything inside by freezing.

If they instead decide to start with the engines, they are located at the ends of the two pillars above and below the disk. The "engine rooms" revealed by opening the ship here are small, designed for only one or two human-sized occupants, and have Jefferies tube-style entry points into parts of the engines themselves in case repairs are needed. There are consoles, alien in design but easily understandable by anyone with an **Engineering Task** with a Difficulty of 1. The consoles reveal the fact that the engines are active but not providing any propulsion; instead, they are maintaining life-support and a number of other systems in the disk that can't be identified from here. The engines *can* be turned on from here, and the ship can be steered from here as well (should anyone want to pull the ship out of the grip of the red giant star). There is also a single long shaft running the thousand-meter length of the pillars, including a maintenance ladder; the shaft is dark and the internal gravity is oriented towards the center disk on both sides. The shaft turns at a ninety-degree angle at the surface of the disk and then runs along the "roof" for another thousand meters, and then exits into the circumferential corridor. Those doors are also not working currently.

SCENE 2: I'D TURN BACK IF I WERE YOU

The door leading further into the ship is locked, but again can be opened by either phaser or some electrical engineering done on the mechanisms behind the nearby wall panel. When it opens, the Players are at first assaulted by a wave of odors released from behind the environmental seals; fruits and other plants, animal scents, and powerful pheromone-laced emissions, strong enough to overwhelm anyone accustomed to the antiseptic smells of a starship. A **Control + Command Task** with a Difficulty of 2 is required, otherwise the character is affected by a "Overwhelmed senses" Trait, increasing the Difficulty of all Tasks. The room is dark, though characters who haven't been overwhelmed will quickly adjust to the gloom and realize they are looking into an enormous jungle forest maintained within the ship itself, clearly large enough to fill the disc's vast interior. There are sounds as well, the buzz of insects and trills of small bird analogues (and perhaps additional creatures), but less than one might expect from a wilderness like this appears to be.

The plants and trees of the forest are bewildering in variety. There are trees that stretch up twenty meters or more, with vines and epiphytes like Spanish moss that connect the higher branches in a messy canopy overhead and block the view of the ceiling in most places. From the doorway, entering the forest involves stepping down onto a steep slope covering several meters in height at a sharp angle, so characters should take care or risk tripping in the near-darkness.

The lighting inside the ship is always dim. No matter when the crew enters, it's approaching "sundown" in the lighting schedule. Vahar was more distant from its sun than many planets, and its sun's light tended farther into the ultraviolet portion of the visual spectrum. By human standards, therefore, the planet was dark even during the daylight hours. Since the plants' chlorophyll analogue is also somewhat different than those familiar to the crew, their typical colors run more to blues and purples than green, though there are flowers and other features in an array of other hues. The entire forest has the Location Trait of Near-Darkness. This Trait increases the Difficulty of Tasks like seeing farther than Close Range by 1 per zone, though it lowers the Difficulty of Tasks like sneaking up on someone by the same amount. (Remember, in Opposed Tasks the Difficulty only applies once.)

Any Player succeeding at a **Sensor Task** with a Difficulty of 0 will confirm the jungle is full of biosignatures, with any *Obtain Information* Momentum spends making them aware of the lower levels of the same ionic radiation encountered outside the craft. Also, there are large energy signatures ahead, suggesting the presence of electrical devices drawing large amounts of power (presumably from the ship's engines). There is no particular cleared path through the jungle, though there are certainly areas that are easier to walk through than others. Eventually it will be clear that there's no alternative to exploring this mysterious forest.

THE JUNGLE

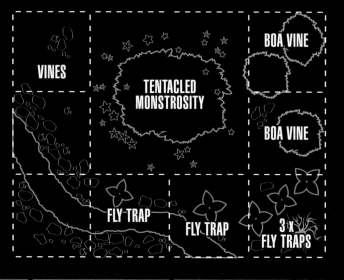

MAP

SCENE 3: INTO THE DARK

GM Guidance: Exploring the forest is the central part of the mission, and the Gamemaster should be prepared to let the Players set the pace. They probably will want to proceed with caution, looking for traps and staying on their guard, and the Gamemaster should be willing to reward them for that caution without slowing down the game too much. Be sure to play up the spookiness of the setting. Give plenty of description of their surroundings, and concentrate on their own senses and perceptions. Describe the sounds of soft breezes in the trees, the hum of insects and occasional hoots and chatters of small animals. Don't forget the overwhelming smells of the flowers, and the occasional scent of sickly-sweet fruits and something resembling decaying meat. Every so often point out the sensation of a character's boot sinking into wet mud, or an unseen spider-web brushing against someone's neck.

Player Characters will probably still be concerned about levels of radiation in here. Though their tricorders remain balky and occasionally return bursts of static instead of readings, they will generally find that this portion of the ship actually has the *lowest* readings of ionic radiation they've encountered so far. This is because the plants in the forest include radiotrophic fungi that have absorbed much of the internal radiation — too late to save the crew, alas, but it has made the interior much safer over the last few years.

Anyone taking the time to do a complete biological scan with **Reason + Science Task**, even with their balky equipment, will be able to determine that this entire forest likely suffered a nearly catastrophic event only a couple of decades ago, where many of the plants suffered some amount of structural damage and many died — perhaps some sort of forest fire? The plants have mostly recovered over the years, but it's unlikely they would have been this successful without some sort of outside, intelligent assistance and curation. On the other hand, though the forest has sufficient room to move through (mostly), it does not seem to have been either planned growth, nor are there any signs that this was ever a park or a garden.

Once the party has spent a few minutes in the forest, they will begin to be subtly affected by the pheromones given off by the brainflowers (see p.80). This is a group Hazard and should cost the Gamemaster a total of 2 Threat to create the Trait "Overwhelmed senses", though the effects will probably not be noticed at first. The Gamemaster should ask each Player for a **Control + Command Task** with a Difficulty of 2. Players who get fewer than two successes will find the pheromones affecting their judgment and will give them the Trait, or enhance it by 1. Gaining the "Overwhelmed senses 2" Trait will increase the Complication range of any Task by 1, with any Player who gets a Complication suffering from hallucinations and eventually becoming overwhelmed with fear at some point during the

VINES [MINOR NPC]

These plants extend long burrowing vines underneath the soil, extending for tens or even hundreds of meters away from their central stalks (which are stubby, pinkish shrubs covered with bristle cones on the surface). They will grab unsuspecting targets by the ankles when they pass over a portion of the soil that is particularly loose and sandy, yanking them down with extraordinary force and then pulling them backwards through the tunnels they have dug to the main stalk. Generally, humans are a bit large for them to manage, but a quick yelp of surprise and they've been knocked down!

TRAITS: Vahari Plant, Root network

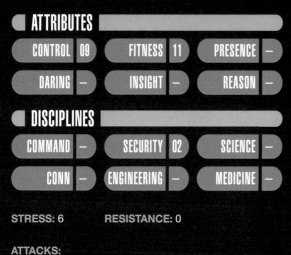

ATTRIBUTES

CONTROL 09	FITNESS 11	PRESENCE –
DARING –	INSIGHT –	REASON –

DISCIPLINES

COMMAND –	SECURITY 02	SCIENCE –
CONN –	ENGINEERING –	MEDICINE –

STRESS: 6   **RESISTANCE:** 0

ATTACKS:
- Vine (Melee, 3▲, Non-lethal, Knockdown)

SPECIAL RULES:
- **Root Network:** Individual vines are part of the "Root network" so rarely act alone. Each root has an individual 6 Stress, but while a vine is still present in the encounter, the Gamemaster may bring in 1 more vine by spending one point of Threat at the start of its turn.

BOA VINE [MINOR NPC]

These vines grow on and in the trees like the moss-like epiphytes, which the boas use for camouflage. Should someone linger beneath a tree for too long, the vine will lower a thick tendril slowly toward them, and then spring at it in an attempt to wrap multiple coils around the torso (and particularly the throat if it can reach). The coils will then tighten with remarkable strength in an effort to either crush or strangle its prey. Other characters can attempt to assist with overpowering the vine, but it is generally more effective to target the bladderlike body of the boa vine, which will have attached itself to a high branch in the tree with gluey secretions.

TRAITS: Vahari Plant

ATTRIBUTES

CONTROL 10	FITNESS 09	PRESENCE –
DARING –	INSIGHT –	REASON –

DISCIPLINES

COMMAND –	SECURITY 02	SCIENCE –
CONN –	ENGINEERING –	MEDICINE –

STRESS: 11   **RESISTANCE:** 0

ATTACKS:
- Wrap (Melee, 4▲, Non-lethal)
- Crush (Melee, 5▲, Lethal)

SPECIAL RULES:
- **Camouflage:** When the vine is in foliage, any search for the vine requires an **Insight + Security** or **Reason + Security** Task, with a Difficulty of 2, to locate it.

---

scenario. If the Gamemaster desires, they may expand the possible effects of the alien pheromones to include emotions other than fear; perhaps the characters become sleepy, or suggestible, or argumentative, spending one point of Threat for each strange thing that happens to them. These changes might be linked to the species of the character, providing clues to the nature of the effect.

*GM Guidance: At first, Gamemasters should only play up the eeriness of the situation for the entire party. Once they've had one or two of the following encounters, however, any Player who failed their **Control + Command** Task should begin to be penalized on any Tasks that involve concentration or seem to place them in any sort of potential danger.*

The following encounters do not have to be presented in any particular order, though in general they should escalate in tension and danger as the scenario continues, and the brainflowers should be one of the final encounters before finding the main terminal.

ENCOUNTER: DANGEROUS FLORA

The forest contains many hazardous carnivorous plants that the characaters might encounter. The Gamemaster should mix in as many of these as seem interesting with the various robot encounters.

DART THROWER [MINOR NPC]

A Dart Thrower is a sessile plant that can fire small poisonous darts or thorns at targets). The stem and flower of a Dart Thrower can rotate to effectively target someone who comes too close, and the darts make a loud "puff!" sound when fired.

TRAITS: Vahari Plant, Poisonous

ATTRIBUTES

| CONTROL 12 | FITNESS 06 | PRESENCE — |
| DARING — | INSIGHT — | REASON — |

DISCIPLINES

| COMMAND — | SECURITY 02 | SCIENCE — |
| CONN — | ENGINEERING — | MEDICINE — |

STRESS: 8   **RESISTANCE:** 0

ATTACKS:
- Dart (Close range, 5▲, Lethal, Debilitating)

SPECIAL RULES:
- **Night Vision:** The plant can detect its prey even in pitch darkness
- **Poison:** The darts are coated with an organic poison similar to saponin, making its way to the target's heart. If a character suffers an Injury from a dart and recovers from either *Avoiding an Injury* or receiving first aid, in the next round or at the end of the encounter a second Injury is immediately dealt to the target character.

TENTACLED MONSTROSITY [MAJOR NPC]

The Monstrosity is not obviously a single plant; rather, it looks like a number of small plants ringing a small pond, which is filled with a slightly sweet-smelling liquid. The blossoms and buds of this plant are masses of thick, overlapping blue leaves. They cover several long tendrils that are folded under them, which the Monstrosity will slowly and carefully unfurl when it detects the presence of nearby prey. It will then lash out with its tendrils acting like tentacles, allowing it to make grabs at characters at Medium Range. The tendrils are extremely strong, and they will attempt to pull any targets they capture into the central pool, where the watery liquid inside acts as a paralyzing drug. Anyone making contact with it loses the ability to move their limbs; once they are subdued in this fashion the Monstrosity will drown them and slowly digest them.

SPECIES AND TRAITS: Vahari Plant

ATTRIBUTES

| CONTROL 08 | FITNESS 12 | PRESENCE 02 |
| DARING 10 | INSIGHT 07 | REASON 01 |

DISCIPLINES

| COMMAND — | SECURITY 04 | SCIENCE — |
| CONN — | ENGINEERING 01 | MEDICINE 01 |

FOCUSES: Poison

STRESS: 16   **RESISTANCE:** 2

ATTACKS:
- Tentacles (Ranged, 4▲, Non-lethal, knockdown)
- Paralyzing Fluid (Melee, 8▲, Lethal, Vicious, Intense)

SPECIAL RULES:
- **Immune to Fear**
- **Grappling Vines:** Whenever a Knockdown effect is dealt to a target, the Gamemaster may spend 2 Threat to immediately move the target one zone closer to the Tentacle Monstrosity

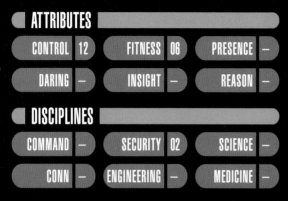

TOXICOLOGY

ORG	441	
		2011-32 0120
	149	3567 1920-22 2167
		12 1920-23 1066
		987-12 0020
		128-21 3844	3844
END	21	22 1877-15 2002
		98-00 1881	67720
EXO	10		380002
			20913
RAD	33		12

A flytrap in this jungle conceals its constituent "trapping leaves" in a collection of brush and moss. The Gamemaster should call for the Players to make an **Insight + Security** or **Science Task** with a Difficulty of 2 when they enter this area; the Player who misses by the most has drawn the plant's attention by stepping on or brushing against the flytrap's sensory cilia. If one of the *other* Players spends Momentum to *Obtain Information* they see the "trap" preparing to snap shut, and can yell (allowing the targeted character to attempt a **Daring + Security Task** with a Difficulty of 2, to leap out of the way) or substitute that with their own Task to dive at their teammate and try to knock them out of the way. If *this* Task fails, both characters will be caught in the massive plant's trapping leaves.

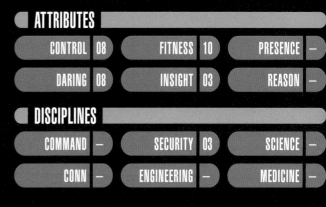

TRAITS: Vahari Plant, Carnivorous

ATTRIBUTES

CONTROL 08	FITNESS 10	PRESENCE —
DARING 08	INSIGHT 03	REASON —

DISCIPLINES

COMMAND —	SECURITY 03	SCIENCE —
CONN —	ENGINEERING —	MEDICINE —

STRESS: 13   **RESISTANCE:** 1

ATTACKS:
- Shells (Melee 5▲ Non-lethal, Vicious 1)

SPECIAL RULES:
- **Enzymes:** The round after it closes, the flytrap will begin to secrete digestive enzymes, which make an additional **Fitness + Security** (Melee, 2▲, Lethal, Debilitating) attack every round that the Player remains within it.

CHAPTER 05.40

FORESTS OF THE NIGHT
ACT 3: THE MAINFRAME

SCENE 1: THE TRIBBLE STOCK

In a patch of grassy stalks the Players find a small pack of three baby tribble-analogues, munching away and trilling contentedly. Like tribbles, these mammalian creatures are small, furry, adorable and not very intelligent. They are born in a birthing matrix in an underground chamber in this part of the forest and released periodically by the AI as part of the reproductive cycle of some of the seeding plants — the tribbles eat the flowers and later pass the seeds through

their digestive tracts elsewhere in the forest. They also serve as prey for the carnivorous species. Unlike actual tribbles, these creatures are completely sterile. They will generally ignore the Players.

If the Players are lost or seem frustrated with their progress, the Gamemaster can have them be present when a new batch is released into the wild, and see the opening into the chamber below. While the chamber itself is too small for a human to climb into, a **Medicine** or **Science Task** can identify its purpose; and an **Engineering Task** will allow a

Player to determine how the chamber receives power and directions for growing and releasing new tribbles by thin fiber-optic cabling running underneath the soil level, and therefore the direction and an estimated distance to the AI's main terminal.

Should somebody feel the need to actually attack a tribble, they have Stress 3 and no Soak and no attacks, though they may try to escape!

BRAINFLOWERS

The most advanced plants are the brainflowers. They resemble oversized sunflowers, with large flat purple flower heads made up of a central disk surrounded by florets, which sit at the top of thick stalks that average three meters tall. At the bases of the stalks are thick roots, which surround a bulbous organ protected by a wood-like "case" that sits directly on the ground beneath the flower. This organ is a primitive brain analogue, which gives the brainflowers approximately the same level of intelligence as, say, an Earth fish or amphibian.

They communicate with each other (and to a much more limited extent the other plants in the forest) with emotion-linked pheromones, which most of the crew are likely to be susceptible to. (The Vahari have evolved alongside these creatures and know how to manage their physical responses to these pheromones. Indeed, they use them culturally for recreation and religious purposes by choice.) The brainflowers in the forest have been under a lot of stress, and therefore much of their communication with each other has been tinged with fear for many years. Once they detect the presence of the away team in their forest, the amount of fear-related pheromones they release ramps up to the point where most every breathing creature is affected.

There are a dozen or so brainflowers, growing on either side of a small artificial stream that emerges from some rocks fifteen meters from their copse and runs down to another pond between some particularly tall trees. As the Players approach them, the scent of the pheromones becomes actively detectable even by inferior human senses, and anyone who has been suffering the effects of the failed resistance Task earlier will become even more paranoid and jumpy. Anyone who earned a Complication at that point will be overcome with fear at this point, and depending on their own Talents and Traits will either attempt to run away, huddle in place, or attack the brainflowers themselves in a panicked rage.

Even if nobody failed the resistance Task, the entire party will feel apprehensive about the flowers themselves, and will note that the sensation becomes stronger the closer they approach. If anyone gets close enough to one of the brainflowers to touch it (or run a scanner over it), the terrified plant will release a concentrated burst of pheromones as a defense mechanism, directly into the face of the character. (The spray will be so thick that it actually will be visible as a fine mist to anyone else close enough to see it.) Make an Opposed Task, using the plant's **Presence + Medicine** versus the Player Character's **Control** or **Fitness** and applicable Discipline, with a Difficulty of 1. If the plant succeeds, the unfortunate victim will then suffer their own panic attack, with the same effects as those for the Complication listed above. If the Player succeeds, allow them to resist the spray and perhaps *Obtain Information* on the plant.

The only physical consequence for anyone who does suffer a panic attack (barring hurting themselves or their fellow crewmembers trying to restrain them in their temporary mania) is the possibility of attracting security robots, as the brainflowers have no means of defending themselves physically (though of course some in the crew might have determined the partial sentience of the creatures and wish to protect them). Once the pheromones have been detected, a **Medicine Task** with two successes can allow for the creation of an antidote to the pheromones themselves.

MAINTENANCE ROBOT [MINOR NPC]

TRAITS: Vahari Robot, Hive Mind

FOCUSES: Botany

STRESS: 11 **RESISTANCE:** 2

ATTRIBUTES

CONTROL 08	FITNESS 07	PRESENCE 04
DARING 04	INSIGHT 04	REASON 10

DISCIPLINES

COMMAND –	SECURITY 04	SCIENCE 01
CONN 02	ENGINEERING 02	MEDICINE 01

ATTACKS:
- Tool (Melee, 3▲, Non-lethal)

SPECIAL RULES:
- Immune to Fear
- Immune to Pain
- Machine 2
- Night Vision

ENCOUNTER: STRANGE LIGHTS AND SOUNDS

At any point during the Players' journey through the forest they may encounter strange lights moving though the brush, behind trees and in and out of bushes. They also may hear low whistles, insect-like hums and buzzes, or the crackle of dried twigs and leaves being moved or stepped on. They should constantly feel as though they are being watched. Have this happen once or twice before you allow them to actually see what's causing the sounds and lights, in order to play up the suspense, perhaps mixing in a dangerous plant encounter below first so that they suspect the noises to be coming from actual lifeforms.

These sounds and lights are actually coming from maintenance robots tending the jungle itself on behalf of the *Grif Balata*'s controlling artificial intelligence system. Small and boxy, they are designed to be as unobtrusive as possible, explaining why they are relatively difficult to catch in action. They fly on small antigrav thrusters, and have several "limbs" ending in various tools and sensors useful for gardening, including small trowels and clippers. They are variously sized, with some units being approximately the size of a human fist, while others are roughly half a meter tall and weigh ten kilograms.

The small robots are in no way designed for combat, though they move quickly and are difficult to either hit or grab. Some of their tools can make nasty small cuts if handled incorrectly. Once one has been captured, their purpose can be determined, and dismantling one can reveal to anyone attempting an **Engineering Task** that they periodically return to the main computer terminal to recharge, download information about the health of the plants they are monitoring, and receive their next set of maintenance instructions. This will provide Players with directions to the terminal, so reserve this sort of encounter until you are ready (or nearly ready) to have them escape the forest.

ENCOUNTER: SECURITY ROBOTS

The *Grif Balata* is also equipped with a small number of larger maintenance robots designed specifically for corralling larger lifeforms. This model is used by the artificial intelligence to keep the plants under control normally, but is also used on other ships to manage animals, and if the AI detects the Players damaging either the plant life or the general ecosystem of the forest (for example, by trying to dig up the soil to get to the wiring and gear underneath), it will deploy several robots to stop them.

FORESTS OF THE NIGHT
CONCLUSION

Once the Players have either defeated or successfully reprogrammed the *Grif Balata*'s AI, they can easily access its original programming, including the history of the Vahari as described above and the location of the proposed New Vahar settlement. It's in a star system eighteen light years from here. The ship can be taken under tow by a starship of sufficient tractor beam capacity, or the Players may decide to put that off and simply go notify the Vahari of its whereabouts as part of a first contact protocol.

Depending on the interests of the Gamemaster and Players, that first contact can be reduced down to a single satisfying ending scene of the Captain shaking hands with the Vahari president with smiles and cheers all around, or can be expanded out into a full first contact mission where the crew follows the McCoullough Protocols, selecting scientists and politicians to contact privately after careful covert observation and sending down disguised observation teams to blend in with and observe their culture, as in *The Next Generation* episode "First Contact."

CONTINUING VOYAGES...

If this scenario is running as part of an extended campaign (or as the introduction to one), then the Vahari might benefit from some additional attention to their society than is given here. They are the only sentient species in their sector which includes only a small handful of star systems with habitable planets. While the Vahari have not yet invented warp drive, their society is quite advanced in other fields, and may have considerable knowledge or technology that would be valuable to the Federation in trade (perhaps in pharmaceuticals and other biologically-derived sciences thanks to the fascinating array of plant life on their homeworld!) Their society has undergone a great deal of stress in the last few decades, from the discovery of their sun's imminent destruction and the decision to leave their homeworld to their extended journey through space and then the hardships of colonizing their new world. Their population might welcome the discovery they are not alone, or the shock of that news might be the proverbial last straw that leads to chaos.

PHEROMONIC ANALYSIS

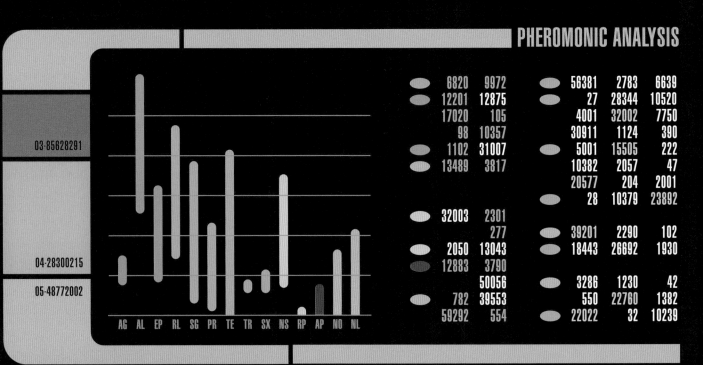

CHAPTER 06.00

BIOLOGICAL CLOCK

BY FRED LOVE

4981652931867 2
3021239494

BIOLOGICAL CLOCK
SYNOPSIS

CAPTAIN'S LOG

KAVIAN STELLAR CIRCUIT 831.11

My first collection run to Optera IV as commanding officer of the *Ko'Falgrin* is now underway, and I confess that I'm as conflicted as ever. The lifeforms will emerge soon, and we'll be there to herd them into the pens and take them back to Kavia Prime. Our best scientists assure me they're nothing more than giant, mindless bugs that happen to produce the tetryons that power our civilization, yet I can't help but pity them. They'll spend their remaining decades restrained in crates, linked to a power grid that drains them of their very essence. Poor devils. Still, at this point in Kavian history, we've grown so dependent upon them that I doubt it's even possible for us to disentangle ourselves from these creatures. My duty to my people is clear. The collection on Optera IV must proceed.

– From the log of Captain Sharama Kaladok,
  commanding officer of the Kavian collection barge
  K.E.S. Ko'Falgrin

INTERCEPTED LOGS

"Biological Clock" is a scenario that presents the crew of a Starfleet vessel with an ethical dilemma weighing the future of an intelligent species against the Prime Directive, Starfleet's most important regulation that outlaws interference in the development of alien societies. The mission also gives Player Characters the opportunity to solve a mystery on a remote planet and initiate first contact with a strange race of aliens who originate from a place beyond the confines of normal space and time.

The mission opens when the crew's vessel picks up unusual tetryon emissions from an unexplored planet known as Optera IV. Investigating the tetryons will lead the crew to encounter giant insectoid creatures that spend the first 74 years of their lifecycle in subterranean caverns before they emerge all at once on the planet's surface to lay eggs and take flight into space. The crew may dismiss the insectoids as unintelligent at first, but they'll quickly discover the tetryon emissions are actually a form of communication employed

by the insectoids. Once the Starfleet personnel open communications with these creatures, the insectoids ask for help in returning to their home in subspace.

As the first contact situation unfolds, an unidentified spacecraft enters orbit, and its captain, identifying herself as a member of a species called the Kavians, demands the Starfleet vessel leave the system. Teams of Kavians pilot shuttles to the planet's surface and begin rounding up the insectoids into pens for transport back to Kavia Prime. The Kavian captain explains that her people claimed Optera IV centuries ago and return every 74 years to "harvest" the insectoid creatures in order to use the tetryons they produce as a powerful energy source.

The Starfleet crew will have to decide whether to clash with the Kavians, leave the insectoids to their fate as slaves or broker some kind of compromise between the two species. Each option comes with its own difficulties, testing the courage and intelligence of all involved.

A permanent solution to the impasse will require the Player Characters to venture into a dangerous facility built centuries ago by the Kavians near the core of the planet, where the crew can shut down the technology preventing the Opterans from making their voyage home.

DIRECTIVES

In addition to the Prime Directive, the Directives for this mission are:

- Directive 010: Before Engaging Alien Species in Battle, Any and All Attempts to Make First Contact and Achieve Nonmilitary Resolution Must Be Made.

Gamemasters begin this mission with 2 points of Threat for each Player Character in the group.

OTHER ERAS OF PLAY

This mission works well for games set during the *Enterprise* and Original Series eras. The scenario features original races and locations, so Gamemasters don't need to worry about running afoul of established *Star Trek* history. However, Gamemasters running early-era games may wish to scale back the statistics of the *Ko'Falgrin* to make it an appropriate challenge for less advanced Starfleet vessels. Additionally, because the universal translator was still at an experimental stage during *Enterprise*, crews from that era may run into increased Difficulty when attempting to decipher the tetryon-based language of the Opterans.

CHAPTER 06.20

BIOLOGICAL CLOCK
ACT 1: STRANGE NEW READINGS

SCENE 1: ANOMALOUS SENSOR READINGS

Gamemasters may read or paraphrase the following to begin the mission:

The bridge hums with activity as officers at computer consoles go about their duties, and stars streak by at warp speed on the viewscreen. Suddenly, an alert rings out from the long-range sensors. The readings show strengthening tetryon bursts emanating from the planet Optera IV. Tetryons occur naturally only in subspace, making these readings particularly strange and worth investigating.

The Player Characters may have questions about the nature of the tetryons, and conn or science officers should be allowed to conduct a more in-depth sensor scan if they like. Tetryons have a random momentum, making it impossible for sensors to track them with any precision under normal circumstances. Player Characters may overcome this problem by creating an Advantage, such as recalibrating the sensors or applying subspace theory in some innovative way. Creating an Advantage requires spending 2 Momentum or 1 Determination. The crew can generate Momentum by performing Difficulty 0 Tasks such as adjusting course for Optera IV or other routine shipboard duties. With an Advantage in place, Player Characters may make a precise sensor sweep of the tetryons with **a Reason + Science**

CAPTAIN'S LOG

STARDATE 48214.73

The ship is proceeding through a little-explored sector of space, according to our orders. This region was mapped and surveyed 40 years ago at long range, but that mission gathered only the most general data on the nearby systems and planets. And, in any case, a lot can change in four decades.

Task, assisted by the ship's **Sensors + Science Task** with a Difficulty of 2.

A successful Task yields the following information:

- The tetryons originate from a multitude of sources scattered across and within Optera IV. The vast majority of tetryons appear to originate from under the planet's surface.

- The tetryons occur in repeated patterns, which are then answered by nearly identical patterns at a local level. These call-and-response bursts are increasing in frequency.

The call-and-response nature of the tetryon patterns suggests an intelligence at work on the planet, and it may even occur to the sensor operator that the emissions represent conversation among lifeforms. If the crew attempt to apply the universal translator to the tetryon bursts its calculations reinforce that these sensor readings likely point to language, but there's not enough information for the computer to decipher it. To learn more, the crew will have to visit Optera IV.

The crew may also consult the ship's library computer to see what Starfleet knows about Optera IV. Doing so does not require a Task. The ship's database reports that a Federation survey mission charted the Optera system and its six planets roughly 40 years ago but found no evidence of advanced civilizations. Accordingly, the system was not heavily explored. Optera IV is a class-M world with three moons and a diverse climate. The planet likely supports an abundance of animal and plant life. The database offers no further information about the Optera system.

GM Guidance: This introductory scene is meant to function as the prelude for the episode, a way of teasing the mystery to come. It's recommended that Gamemasters keep this scene short and move quickly to scene 2, which introduces more opportunities for exploration and action.

SCENE 2: OPTERA IV

Dropping out of warp near the Optera system will allow the Player Characters to run more accurate sensor sweeps of the planet. Making a sensor sweep requires a **Reason + Science Task**, assisted by the ship's **Sensors + Science Task**, with a Difficulty of 2. This becomes a Difficulty 1 Task if the crew created an Advantage earlier. A successful scan confirms what the ship's library computer had on file regarding Optera IV. The Class-M world is home to a wide range of organisms and climate types, with several oceans of liquid water. Its nitrogen-oxygen atmosphere appears breathable to most humanoid species. Sensors detect no cities, road networks or industrial activity. However, the sensor sweep does reveal some interesting readings. The planet's core has achieved an entirely liquid state that creates regular subspace inversions, allowing for the stable formation of solanogen throughout the planet's crust. Solanogen, like tetryons, usually occurs in subspace. In addition, the sensor scan reveals the following:

- A **mysterious power signature** operating on the surface of a landmass indicates the presence of some kind of technology in the middle of an otherwise uninhabited desert.

An enormous concentration of tetryon bursts is located in a vast **subterranean cavern**, which is connected to a tangled network of tunnels running throughout the planet's substrata.

- Smaller, more localized readings indicate some tetryon activity near a major **mountain peak**.

- **Anomalous readings** near the planet's core show a blind spot that reflects sensor scans back to their point of origin, possibly indicating shielding technology.

The power signature in the desert and the localized tetryon readings in the mountain range are easily accessible by transporter and do not require a Task to send an away team. The highly concentrated tetryons in the subterranean cavern, however, cause significant interference, requiring a **Control + Engineering Task** with a Difficulty of 3 for a successful transport. This Task is assisted by the ship's **Sensors + Engineering Task**. Failing the task causes the away team to rematerialize on the ship's transporter pad. The crew may create a new Advantage to reduce the difficulty of transporting through the tetryon interference by one.

The fourth location near the planet's core is a Kavian facility that prevents the Opterans from returning to subspace. An energy shield surrounds the facility, and any sensor scans or transporter beams intended to penetrate the shield are reflected back. Gaining access will require the crew to pinpoint the exact frequency of the shields protecting the installation. The crew may attempt to figure out the shield frequency through trial and error, but that process will take days. An in-depth description of the installation can be found in act 3 under the section titled "The Shielded Core Facility."

GM Guidance: Gamemasters should let the crew investigate any of the sensor readings listed above that interest them in whatever order they choose. Exploring Optera IV will introduce them to the insectoid creatures and force the crew to attempt communicating with them. This first contact situation forms the heart of this act of the mission, and establishing communication with the Opterans will lead directly to the final scene of this act, outlined in the "Lost in the Dark" section that appears later. If the Player Characters show a reluctance to beam down to the planet, or if the game stagnates for other reasons, they may still come into contact with the insectoid aliens in the optional "Space Swarm" encounter also described later in this act. Each encounter is detailed in its own section.

Many of the encounters in this act put the Player Characters into contact with tetryon radiation, though often at low levels. If Player Characters suffer prolonged or intense exposure, or if the Gamemaster wishes to increase the danger of a particular scene, the Gamemaster may spend 2 Threat to

Create a Complication related to rising radiation levels. This Complication increases the Difficulty of all Tasks attempted by affected characters until they leave the irradiated environment and receive medical attention. Player Characters may negate this Complication by creating an appropriate Advantage or if a medical officer completes a **Reason + Medicine Task** with a Difficulty of 4 to create an inoculation against tetryon radiation.

SCENE 3: THE MYSTERIOUS POWER SIGNATURE

If the crew investigates the location of the unidentified power signature on the planet's surface, the away team materializes in a barren desert.

The whine of the transporter fades and is replaced by the roar of a harsh, burning wind. Cracked and sun-bleached rocks litter the otherwise flat surface of the desert, which extends to the horizon in all directions. Optera IV's three pale moons hover overhead in a cloudless sky. Roughly 50 meters away, you can see a tall tower bristling with electronic instruments.

The tower is the power source sensors detected from orbit. If the away team approaches the tower, they spot something else of interest:

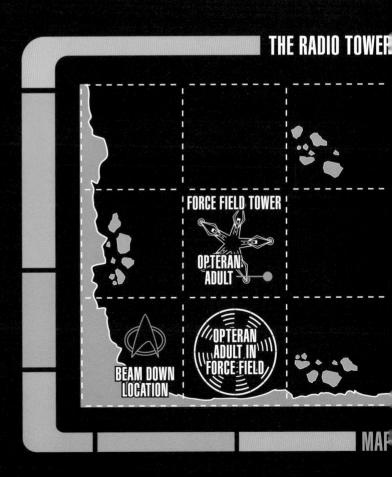

THE RADIO TOWER

FORCE FIELD TOWER

OPTERAN ADULT

OPTERAN ADULT IN FORCE FIELD

BEAM DOWN LOCATION

MAP

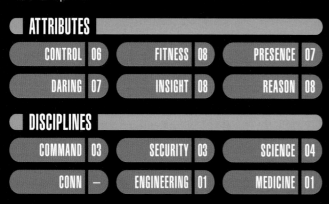

TRAITS: Opteran

ATTRIBUTES

CONTROL 06	FITNESS 08	PRESENCE 07
DARING 07	INSIGHT 08	REASON 08

DISCIPLINES

COMMAND 03	SECURITY 03	SCIENCE 04
CONN —	ENGINEERING 01	MEDICINE 01

STRESS: 11   **RESISTANCE: 1**

ATTACKS:

- Pincers (Melee, 4 ▲, Knockdown)

SPECIAL RULES:

- **Flight:** Adult Opterans that have shed their skin can fly and may travel to any location within long range as a minor action.

Emerging from the ground like an orange bubble is a dome of crackling energy, a force field! Trapped inside the force field is a large insectoid creature with six spindly appendages and glowing red eyes set atop a strange mouth-like orifice surrounded by short tentacles. Another seemingly identical creature circles the tower a short distance away and thrashes its pincers against it in a useless attempt to free its companion.

This section of the desert, along with many other sites on the planet's surface, was booby trapped by the Kavians to imprison Opterans for delivery back to Kavia Prime. The two Opterans, as the insectoids are called in this text, are a mated pair and the beginning of a wave of insectoids that will soon migrate from their subterranean communities to the planet's surface.

The free Opteran understands that the tower controls the force field that has entrapped its mate, a sign of its intelligence. But it can't manage to operate the tower's controls. Examining the tower reveals a removable metal panel that grants access to a computer console. It requires a **Reason + Engineering Task** with a Difficulty of 3 to decipher the alien technology well enough to disable the force fields.

The force field dome surrounding the trapped Opteran is roughly 10 meters in diameter and extends underground in a spherical shape to prevent Opterans from burrowing out

and escaping. Individual force fields can be overloaded with phaser fire. Each force field has 8 Stress, with a Resistance of 3. Exhausting a force field's Stress overloads it and shuts it down permanently.

The Opterans will take a hostile attitude toward the Starfleet officers and assume they're responsible for the force field. The free Opteran will move protectively between the away team and its mate. Combat may break out, but the Opterans will not make the first move. If the Player Characters move cautiously and non-threateningly, they may be able to avoid violence. Players may spend Determination on Tasks attempting to avoid combat, in accordance with the nonviolence Directive that applies to this mission.

As the scene plays out, Gamemasters may spend 1 point of Threat to trigger additional force fields that imprison Player Characters or 2 Threat to summon more Opterans that burrow up to the surface from underground and join the standoff. In the event that a fight becomes unavoidable, the Opterans will not kill an adversary and will surrender if they feel they are outmatched. The Opterans value peace and do not wish to harm other living creatures unless forced.

If a Player attempts to disable the force fields in the middle of combat, they may use the Daring or Control attributes for the task. If the Player Characters manage to free the trapped Opteran or otherwise shut down the force fields, the Opterans will assume a peaceful posture.

RESOLUTION

Once the encounter has been resolved, either through combat or through the Starfleet crew rescuing the trapped Opteran, the creatures will begin to emit a series of brilliant colored lights from the mouth-like orifices on their faces. These lights take the form of roughly circular bands of pulsing radiation. A tricorder scan shows that the energy signature created by the radiation is identical to the tetryons detected by the ship's sensors. Moreover, if two or more Opterans are present, they respond to one another in the same call-and-response patterns the crew may have observed from space. The crew should figure out from this turn of events that the Opterans are intelligent and use tetryon radiation to communicate.

This tetryon-based language will make it difficult to establish a dialog. If the Player Characters attempt first contact with the Opterans, they'll have to do so without help from the universal translator, at least initially. However, it is possible for the crew to establish a rudimentary exchange with the Opterans without the aid of technology. If the Player Characters act peacefully, the Opterans will remain in the area, curiously observing the away team. The Opterans may attempt to mimic the actions of the away team as a means of making a connection, though their alien physiology likely would hinder such an effort. This may even present the opportunity to introduce some humor into the scene.

The crew may try to apply the universal translator to the Opteran language. Doing so is possible, but requires the completion of a Gated Challenge, which is outlined in a later section of this act. The Player Characters may wish to begin this challenge immediately after their first contact with the Opterans or they may wish to explore the planet further. Or they may split up and pursue both options simultaneously. Gamemasters should let the Players choose how to proceed.

The posture of the Opterans eventually will begin to droop, and their movements will slow from exhaustion. Any member of the crew who attempts a tricorder scan of the creatures at this juncture can sense they are beginning to undergo a major change in their biology.

Eventually, the Opterans will stop communicating and curl up on the ground. Cracks in their exoskeleton will appear, and they will begin pulling free of their old skin as they metamorphose. Characters who successfully complete a **Reason + Science Task** with a Difficulty of 1 can deduce that this is a natural development in the Opteran lifecycle.

Once free of their former exoskeletons, the Opterans look much the same, though their new exoskeletons glisten in the sunlight. They also grow a pair of translucent wings on their backs that initially appear shriveled and weak. The Opterans will remain motionless for a time as they gather strength. They will eventually fly away together to a secluded location to mate and lay eggs. Crewmembers who successfully made the previous **Reason + Science Task** can also guess at this eventuality.

THE OPTERANS

The intelligent insectoid creatures referred to in this scenario as Opterans actually originate from a tertiary subspace manifold outside of normal space and time. Their molecular structure is based on solanogen, a material that normally exists only in subspace. The Opterans possess an innate ability to produce tetryons. They communicate with one another by emitting tetryon radiation, manipulating the frequency and wavelength of the radiation to create a syntax and vocabulary. They can also propel themselves through space by discharging tetryon-based energy in a way similar to an old-style space rocket.

Centuries ago, their native subspace manifold experienced a prolonged period of turbulence, causing many members of the species to seek refuge by passing through a spatial tear that connected subspace with the substrata of Optera IV due to the unique properties of the planet's molten core. For generations, the Opterans passed freely through the spatial tear to escape periodic outbreaks of subspacial turbulence, treating Optera IV like a safe port in a raging storm. Over time, they built a vast network of tunnels beneath the planet's surface.

Everything changed when the Kavians discovered the Opterans and the potential energy supply their naturally occurring tetryon emissions could provide. The Kavians built a dampening facility near the planet's core that permanently closed the spatial tear by flooding the area with polarons. Now trapped on Optera IV, the Opterans developed an unusual lifecycle as an adaptation to foil the Kavians seeking to capture them. The speed with which the Opterans implemented this adaptation suggests intelligence, as does their complex form of tetryon-based communication.

The Opterans spend decades in a period of immaturity in their underground communities, constantly emitting bursts of tetryons that illuminate the dark caverns with brilliant flashes of light amplified by Optera IV's naturally occurring solanogen deposits. These immature nymphs resemble large insects with six spindly appendages, large red eyes and stubby bodies covered in thick brown exoskeletal plating.

The Opterans return to the planet's surface in one massive migration every 74 years. This migration relies on strength in numbers to prevent the Kavian collection ships from abducting more than a small fraction of the population, ensuring that most of the Opterans will mate successfully and give rise to a new generation. Once above ground, each Opteran sheds its skin and becomes a mature adult specimen, complete with a set of wings. The mature Opterans mate and lay eggs, then take flight into the cold reaches of space in search of a spatial tear capable of sending them back to their home in subspace. The eggs they leave behind hatch, and the new generation of nymphs burrows underground, beginning the cycle anew.

The only Federation survey mission to scan the region passed through during a point in the Opteran lifecycle when the creatures were underground, leaving the surveyors with the mistaken impression that the planet was uninhabited by intelligent life.

Opteran lifespans stretch on almost indefinitely as long as they are allowed to recharge periodically near some sort of energy source. The Opterans that leave the planet rarely linger near such an energy source for long, however, due to their nearly irresistible biological compulsion to search for a new spatial tear. Nearly all of the Opterans die after weeks or months drifting through space at sub-warp speeds.

SCENE 4: THE SUBTERRANEAN CAVERN

If an away team manages safe transport to the massive tetryon readings deep within the planet's crust, the Player Characters materialize in an enormous cavern mostly composed of solanogen crystals.

You stand along the edge of a vast cavern. Brilliant flashes of kaleidoscopic light assault your vision the instant you materialize. The lights seem to emanate from dozens of outcroppings made of crystal. In the instant the lights flash brightest, you can see the motionless shapes of large insect-like creatures clustered around the outcroppings. There appear to be hundreds of these creatures in the cavern. Contrasting sharply with the psychedelic light show, the chamber is eerily quiet.

These Opterans are preparing for their mass migration to the surface. The crystals to which they cling amplify the tetryon bursts from the creatures into a wondrous chorus of multi-colored light, like a silent fireworks display. This has a disorienting effect on the away team and imposes a Complication that adds 1 to the Difficulty of any Tasks they attempt for as long as the Opterans continue the light show.

The crew may scan the crystals that make up much of the chamber's walls with a successful **Reason + Science Task** to determine that the crystals are solanogen-based, just as the Opterans are. These solanogen deposits seem to provide ideal habitat for the insectoids.

The Opterans are too focused on their impending trip to the surface to pay much attention to the new arrivals unless the away team acts in a provocative manner. In

that case, several Opterans may surround the crew and attack. However, if the Player Characters have managed to assemble a means of communication, the Opterans may relate much of the information contained in the Opteran sidebar above. They may also explain that they originate in a place "outside space and time" and wish only to return to their homes, a clue that these beings are native to a tertiary subspace manifold.

Once the away team has had a sufficient chance to explore the subterranean chamber, the tetryon light show suddenly ends, cloaking the entire cavern in darkness. A loud clattering sound fills the darkened chamber as the Opterans begin to scale the walls and enter the tunnel network leading upward to the planet's surface.

Any Player Characters in the chamber risk getting caught in a stampede as the Opterans migrate upward. Gamemasters should allow the Players to take whatever actions they feel might help them survive the stampede, such as climbing the crystalline outcroppings, hiding behind rocks or even simply beaming back to the ship. However, Gamemasters could spend Threat to cause the ship's transporter operator to lose his or her sensor lock on the away team, or increase the difficulty for successful transport,, due to interference from the solanogen crystals.

Any action requiring a Task is governed by each character's Daring attribute. The unfolding chaos imposes a dire distraction on the Starfleet crew, making any defensive actions Difficulty 4 tasks. On a failed task, characters suffer 3 ▲ damage from being trampled by fleeing Opterans. Gamemasters may spend 2 Threat to trigger a rockslide as the Opterans skitter across the cavern's ceiling and charge into the network of tunnels overhead. If this happens, Gamemasters should allow each character to attempt another defensive action of Difficulty 4 to protect themselves from falling debris. Any failures result in the character taking another 3 ▲ damage.

RESOLUTION

The crew may find themselves alone in the empty chamber. A Difficulty 2 **Reason + Science Task** will allow the away team to track the movement of the Opterans through Tricorder scans to where they will emerge on the planet's surface. This Task may also be completed by the ship's sensors from orbit as well.

If the Player Characters locate the Opterans, they find the creatures sprawled by the thousands across a massive prairie filled with exotic plants. The Opterans begin to shed their skin over the span of several hours, then take flight in a chaotic swarm of mature creatures. The swarm generates a nearly deafening buzz. Over time, the Opterans begin to pair off to mate before the females lay eggs.

Sensors indicate similar scenes playing out across the surface of the planet. The mass migration of the Opterans has begun.

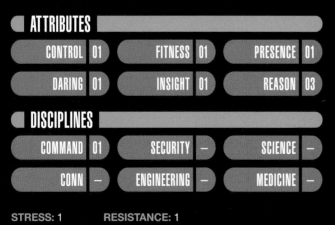

OPTERAN NYMPH

TRAITS: Recently Hatched and Immature Specimens of the Opteran Species

ATTRIBUTES

CONTROL	01	FITNESS	01	PRESENCE	01
DARING	01	INSIGHT	01	REASON	03

DISCIPLINES

COMMAND	01	SECURITY	—	SCIENCE	—
CONN	—	ENGINEERING	—	MEDICINE	—

STRESS: 1   **RESISTANCE: 1**

SCENE 5: MOUNTAIN PEAK

If the crew investigates the localized tetryon bursts originating from a major mountain chain, the away team will have to transport to a rocky and frigid peak at high altitude.

A bone-chilling cold sets in as soon as the transport is complete, freezing your breath and making it visible as you exhale. You stand on a rocky ledge overlooking a magnificent mountain chain that stretches beyond the horizon. Ahead of you on the ledge, you see a pile of cracked and empty eggshells, each about the size of a melon. A sticky, mucus-like substance, still surprisingly warm, holds the eggshells together in a nest. Several trails of this ooze lead from the nest into a nearby cave. The ledge near the outer edge of the nest appears to have given way in a landslide, and some of the eggs may have fallen below.

This was a nest where two mature Opterans laid their eggs and migrated into space. The eggs recently hatched, and the immature nymphs crawled into the mountain's cave network and will find their way eventually to one of the major underground communities. If the Player Characters investigate the nest, they can see that one of the eggs rolled off the ledge in the landslide and fell into a chasm about 30 meters below. Luckily, the chasm is filled with snow at the bottom, softening the egg's landing.

Peering into the chasm reveals one Opteran nymph curled up into a ball, struggling to stay alive in the cold.

The nymph emits a weak flash of tetryons every few minutes to indicate its distress. Its injured legs won't allow it to climb out without help, and the layer of snow and ice prevents it from burrowing underground.

The crew may attempt to rescue the Opteran nymph. This may be done in several ways, the most obvious of which is transporting the nymph to safety. This requires a **Control + Engineering Task** with a Difficulty of 2. Or Player Characters may attempt to climb down into the chasm, which requires a **Daring + Security Task** with a Difficulty of 3. On a failed attempt, the character triggers a rockslide that does 3⚔ damage to the character, the nymph and any other characters attempting to climb into or out of the chasm. Player Characters must attempt another Task if they wish to climb back out of the chasm.

RESOLUTION

If the Player Characters rescue the nymph, they may take the opportunity to study its biology or establish communication. Studying the nymph with the instruments on board the ship will grant the crew new insight into the Opteran lifecycle. The nymphs are born with an instinctual awareness of how to use their tetryon bursts to communicate basic feelings and impressions, but, if the Player Characters try to use the universal translator, the nymph will manage only rudimentary messages. The crew may also set the nymph free on the ledge where it was supposed to hatch. In this situation, the nymph crawls into the mountainside cave to rejoin its siblings.

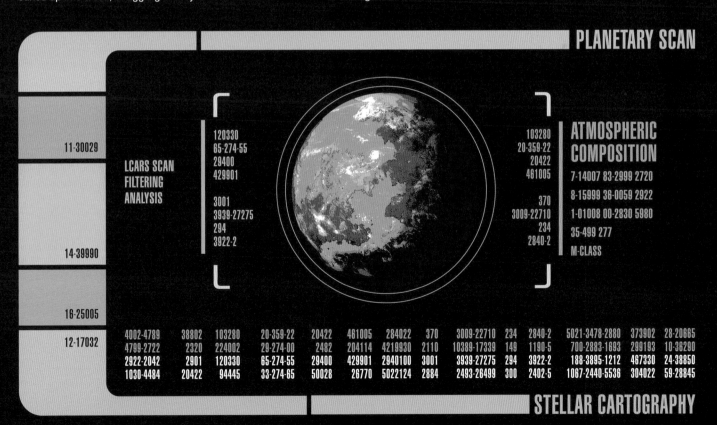

PLANETARY SCAN

					ATMOSPHERIC COMPOSITION
11-30029		120330 65-274-55 29400 429901		103280 20-359-22 20422 461005	7-14007 83-2999 2720
	LCARS SCAN FILTERING ANALYSIS				8-15999 36-0059 2922
		3001 3939-27275 294 3922-2		370 3009-22710 234 2840-2	1-01008 00-2830 5980
14-39990					35-499 277
					M-CLASS
16-25005					

12-17032	4002-4789	38802	103280	20-359-22	20422	461005	284022	370	3009-22710	234	2840-2	5021-3478-2880	373902	28-20665
	4799-2722	2320	224002	29-274-00	2482	204114	4219930	2110	10389-17339	149	1190-5	700-2883-1693	299193	10-36290
	2922-2042	2901	120330	65-274-55	29400	429901	2940100	3001	3939-27275	294	3922-2	188-3895-1212	467330	24-38850
	1030-4484	20422	94445	33-274-65	50028	26770	5022124	2884	2493-26499	300	2402-5	1067-2440-5536	304022	59-28845

STELLAR CARTOGRAPHY

BIOLOGICAL CLOCK
ACT 2: THE LANGUAGE BARRIER

CAPTAIN'S LOG

SUPPLEMENTAL

We've stumbled onto a mystery. Tetryon emissions on Optera IV, an unexplored world, have led us to investigate a sentient but intelligent native species of insectoid. Due to the unusual and unstable nature of tetryons, particularly in normal space, I felt warrented in sending away teams to discover and decode the source. It appears the Tetryon emissions may be some form of communication for the instectoids and so we have decided to attempt to translate these emissions. Any damage done by beaming down, in relation to the Prime Directive, will have inadvertently already been done and so an attempt at first contact, no matter if it proves futile, should at least be made.

SCENE 1: PROGRAMMING THE UNIVERSAL TRANSLATOR

Making the universal translator useful in communicating with the Opterans will require the completion of a Gated Challenge composed of two Extended Tasks. The Extended Tasks likely will necessitate a return to the ship for the use of its specialized equipment, but the Player Characters are free to begin the process any time they choose. It could be immediately after their first encounter with the Opterans or after an extended period of exploring the planet.

The first Extended Task, which must be completed before moving to the second, is employing the universal translator to construct a syntax matrix that deciphers the tetryon-based communication and encodes it as audible language. This will allow the crew to understand the Opterans. Doing so is a moderate challenge, since this is what the universal translator was designed to do. Accordingly, the Extended Task has a Work track of 13, a Magnitude of 3 and a Base Difficulty of 3. The basic Task is **Reason + Science**.

The next Extended Task poses more of a challenge because it will force the engineering officers to find innovative new

uses for existing technology. In order to allow the Starfleet personnel to speak to the Opterans in the tetryon-based language, they will need a means of manipulating tetryon radiation as the Opterans do. Linking the universal translator to an engineering tool such as a portable phase coil resonator will do the trick, but this Extended Task has a Work track of 18, a Magnitude of 4 and a Base Difficulty of 4. The Basic Task is **Reason + Engineering**. This Extended Task may only be attempted 5 times because the limited timetable won't allow for thorough field testing of the translator before it's put to use.

Failing to complete either of the Extended Tasks does not prevent the construction of a tetryon communication translator. Rather, failure allows the Players to succeed at a cost, creating a Complication in the form of a miscommunication between the crew and the Opterans due to an imperfection in the technology. A miscommunication may lead to a garbled message at a critical moment or a mistranslation that could cause inadvertent insult on either side.

Gamemasters may consider alternative solutions to establishing direct communications with the Opterans, should the crew wish to try something different. Any proposal, however, should meet a minimum level of challenge due to the truly alien nature of the Opterans' mode of communication.

Figuring out how to apply the universal translator to the tetryon-based language transforms the crew's discourse with the Opterans from a basic exchange of gestures and body language to a relationship in which either side is capable of communicating complex and specific thoughts. Once the crew has completed the Challenge, either successfully or unsuccessfully, the Players gain access to a means of direct communication with the Opterans. This new device, which can be attached to a tricorder, records the wavelength and frequency of tetryon bursts from the Opterans and translates them into audible speech. Conversely, the device also translates speech into tetryon bursts that can be understood by the Opterans.

RESOLUTION

With this new tool in play, the first Opterans the Player Characters encounter, whether on board the Starfleet vessel or on Optera IV, will make a request that leads directly to the encounter in the next section, "Lost in the Dark." It is highly

THE KAVIANS

The Kavians are a spacefaring race of humanoids who annexed Optera IV roughly 400 years ago, attracted by the tetryon bursts used by the Opterans to communicate. Quickly realizing the value of their discovery, the Kavians began herding Opterans into large collection ships and linking the Opterans to their power grid, harnessing the natural tetryon emissions as an energy source. The long Opteran lifespan made them an ideal source of sustainable energy, and the Kavians now depend almost exclusively on tetryons to power their society and economy.

The Kavian Expeditionary Force observed the Opterans moving between subspace and their underground network of communities on Optera IV via a spatial tear and set about devising a means of trapping the Opterans in normal spacetime. Kavian engineers, eager to test the limits of their revolutionary new energy source, built a shielded facility near the core of Optera IV that draws on tetryon emissions harvested from captured Opterans to release continuous polaron bursts into the planet's

core. These polarons closed the spatial tear that allowed the Opterans to enter normal spacetime and prevent it from reforming. The facility, considered one of the greatest feats of Kavian ingenuity, is heavily automated and shielded to prevent anyone from tampering with it. The original four captive Opterans that power the facility remain there, kept alive by the installation's power grid in a vegetative state.

In response to their newfound captivity, the Opterans swiftly adopted a complex lifecycle in which they surface only once every 74 years. Accordingly, the Kavians leave the planet abandoned until the "harvest," during which they round up as many Opterans as possible for transport to Kavia Prime. Captain Sharama Kaladok of the *K.E.S. Ko'Falgrin* is leading the current harvest, the fourth such occurrence in the history of Optera IV.

Kavians are mammalian in appearance, with widely spaced eyes positioned near their temples. Tufts of soft hair, ranging in color from light tan to dark brown, start on top of their heads and extend down their necks and backs. Kavians descended from herd animals and often display a strong collective instinct.

The tetryon-based technology employed by the Kavians has allowed them to make impressive advances in the last few centuries, including powerful starships and deadly weapons. However, the unpredictable nature of tetryon energy made the Kavians hesitant to embrace transporter technology, especially in cases of transporting lifeforms. The Kavians rely on shuttles for most short-range transportation as a result.

recommended that the Players complete that encounter before proceeding to the final act of the mission.

Soon after the crew engages the Opterans with the universal translator, one of the creatures will ask for help identifying foreign technology discovered decades ago in their network of subterranean tunnels. The Opterans abandoned the tunnels near this mysterious machine in case it was dangerous. They believe the technology may have something to do with the "hunters" that all Opterans fear. The Opterans can provide coordinates that pinpoint the mystery object's location among a dense cluster of underground solanogen crystals. The crew may use the coordinates to beam directly to the location.

In addition to the request for assistance, any Opterans will gladly explain who they are, where they come from and their desperation to return to subspace. The Opterans will explain that they came to the planet through a spatial tear created by Optera IV's unique core, but something beyond their control is preventing them from reopening the tear and returning home. Most Opterans now believe that it was a horrible mistake to venture into normal spacetime. They also will display a willingness to work with anyone who might help them get home. If asked about the force fields or the shielded facility in

the planet's core, the Opterans will recount stories of "hunters" who scour the planet and abduct adult Opterans. However, the current generation of Opterans has had no direct experience with the Kavians, so their knowledge is limited.

SCENE 2: LOST IN THE DARK

This scene should take place once the Player Characters have established communication with the Opterans via the universal translator. The outcome of this scene will provide the shield frequency the crew will need to explore the installation in the planet's core, the final piece of the puzzle that will propel the story toward its climax and decide the fate of the Opterans.

You beam into a dark cavern at the intersection of several tunnels the Opterans once used as a crossroads but have since abandoned. Protruding from the ceiling of the cavern at an odd angle is the damaged hull of a small metallic craft. The canopy of the craft's cockpit hangs open, and its two seats appear to be empty. This must be the strange technology the Opterans asked you to investigate.

The Player Characters can determine using their Science or Engineering Disciplines that the craft was outfitted with a laser drill on its front end and was likely designed to traverse the planet's crust. Determining this requires a Task with a Difficulty of 0. Examining the cockpit shows that the craft still has minimal power available in its auxiliary reserves, but powering up the instruments reveals that the craft's propulsion, communications and laser-guidance systems were badly damaged by a violent impact. The computer's logs and mission briefings remain intact, however, and may be accessed easily. If the Player Characters call up the logs, Gamemasters should read or paraphrase the following section.

The logs contain audio entries from a pair of engineers named Raymar and Cyvala who worked for something called the Kavian Expeditionary Force. Their mission was to travel to a shielded installation near the planet's core to perform maintenance 74 years ago, but they struck a cluster of solanogen crystals and became stuck. The log entries grow increasingly panicked as the engineers report their communications systems inoperable. After several days of waiting for a rescue that never came, they opened the cockpit door and wandered into the underground tunnels. "Our supplies are exhausted, and we have no other option but to take our chances outside," the final log entry reports. "In our worst nightmares, we never dreamed we'd die hundreds of light years from Kavia Prime, buried alive on a distant world."

The crew may also access the craft's mission briefing, which contains information and schematics on the core facility. Using the mission briefing, the away team can determine the following information:

- The Kavian engineering team's mission was to strengthen the link between four captive Opterans and the power grid of a shielded facility built near the planet's core. The Kavians supply the massive amounts of energy the facility requires by channeling the tetryons produced by the captive Opterans.

- The Kavians constructed the core facility to trap the Opterans on the planet.

- The core facility contains a polaron generator that injects bursts of radiation directly into the planet's core, canceling the subspace properties of the solanogen crystals and preventing the formation of a spatial tear.

- The core facility's shield modulation frequency is 257.5.

GM Guidance: This is a valuable opportunity for the crew to learn about the Kavians, and Gamemasters should use the scene to foreshadow the Kavians' return to the planet in the next act. The Players may guess that shutting down the polaron generator is the only way to send the Opterans home. This knowledge may prompt them to transport to the core facility immediately. The Kavians should arrive just before they can do so, creating a hurdle that the crew will have to deal with first. If the Player Characters enter the core facility anyway, the Kavians will notice and send a team of six foot soldiers, led by Captain Kaladok, to remove them by force. If the Player Characters successfully convince Kaladok to work with them, she may help them in their efforts to shut down the generator rather than hinder them.

Once the crew ascertains the shield frequency for the core installation, the Gamemaster may begin act 3 of the mission.

RADIATION ANALYSIS

POLARON VARIANCE

	1105	1108	1111
56381	2783		
300	26903		
26999	291		
502	10038		
49	29200		
20001	6495		
780	33023		
	931		
77890	2992		
277			
1002	39553		
505	2000		
44211			

416

2-122-0566

3-272-0943

4-315-1178

SCENE 3: SPACE SWARM ENCOUNTER

This optional encounter should take place if the Player Characters show reluctance to make first contact with the Opterans on the planet's surface or if the Gamemaster feels the game could use a jolt. It may also come in handy later in the game if the crew considers abandoning the Opterans and allowing the Kavians to continue to treat them as property.

A swarm composed of dozens of mature insectoid creatures from the planet's surface has taken flight and is heading in the direction of the ship. The creatures are traveling at a high sub-warp velocity, and some of them appear to be on a collision course!

These mature Opterans are leaving the planet to try to find a way back to subspace, and some of them are naturally attracted to the energy output from the ship. Although most of the swarm will continue into interstellar space, several

creatures intend to attach themselves to the vessel's exhaust ports to feed on its plasma discharge.

The crew may raise shields or even open fire on the creatures. Firing weapons may destroy some of the swarm but won't take out all of the creatures. Raising shields will keep the Opterans from attaching to the ship's hull, but, in that case, the creatures simply attach to the shields and begin to drain them. Moving the ship away from the swarm takes too much time as the Opterans propel themselves through space at high impulse speeds by discharging jets of highly pressurized tetryon energy.

Once the Opterans have secured themselves to either the ship's hull or its shields, they begin emitting their tetryon-based language at each other to signify their curiosity about the orbiting vessel they've just discovered. These Opterans, probably no more than five, mean no harm to the vessel or its crew. They've simply found a source of nourishment.

Any crew member who attempts a sensor scan of these Opterans will deduce that the tetryon bursts are a complex form of language. This may lead them to begin the Challenge outlined in the "Programming the Universal Translator to Communicate with Tetryons" section of this act, in which case the ship's deflector dish may be used to emit the tetryon-based language.

RESOLUTION

If the Opterans attach themselves to the ship's exhaust ports, they absorb the vessel's plasma exhaust but cause no harmful effects. However, the creatures weaken the ship's shields by two points every hour if they attach to them.

The crew may remove the Opterans by any number of means. The most direct way would be to transport them aboard the ship or into space. The crew may also reverse the polarity of the ship's energy output, essentially "curdling the milk" and forcing the Opterans to detach themselves. Finally, the Opterans will not be able to maintain their grip on the vessel if it goes to warp. Gamemasters should consider any other creative means the crew may devise to extricate themselves from the swarm. This encounter is not intended to put the ship in mortal danger. Rather, it's a direct means of forcing the Starfleet personnel to make contact with the Opterans.

BIOLOGICAL CLOCK
ACT 3: ENTER THE KAVIANS

GM Guidance: *This final act includes the first appearance of Kavians in the Opteran system. The Kavian arrival will lead to the story's climax, in which the crew must decide whether the Prime Directive applies to the situation or if there's a way to send the Opterans back to subspace. This act features branching paths that could lead to open conflict with the Kavians, a high-stakes negotiation to strike a compromise that satisfies all parties or a less satisfactory ending in which the Starfleet personnel leave the Opterans to their fate as slaves exiled from their home.*

Much of the drama in this act hinges on the crew understanding both the gravity of defying the Prime Directive and the limitations of its application. Gamemasters should encourage Players to wrestle with this ethical dilemma and then make the difficult choice about how to proceed.

CAPTAIN'S LOG
SUPPLEMENTAL

We've made first contact with a race of intelligent insectoids on the planet. These creatures originate from subspace and use tetryons as a form of communication. We've also uncovered evidence that a second species visits the planet to capture the insectoids and tap their tetryon discharges as an energy source. These Kavians have constructed an automated facility near the planet's core that prevents the insectoids from going home.

SCENE 1: STANDOFF WITH THE KES KO'FALGRIN

This act begins when the *Ko'Falgrin*, a lumbering though durable spacecraft, enters orbit and its captain demands the crew's ship leave the area immediately.

A massive cargo ship of alien configuration enters orbit and opens hailing frequencies. A stern-looking woman with large, widely spaced eyes and military-grade body armor appears on the viewscreen. "I am Captain Sharama Kaladok, commanding officer of the collection vessel K.E.S. Ko'Falgrin of the Kavian Expeditionary Force," she says. "This planet belongs to Kavia. You will return any Kavian property on your vessel and withdraw from this system immediately. We will tolerate no interference with our harvest."

Soon after the *K.E.S. Ko'Falgrin* enters orbit, a dozen shuttles detach from the massive cargo vessel and make their way to the planet's surface. Kavians rarely use transporters to move personnel or sensitive equipment due to the sometimes unstable nature of their tetryon-powered technology. Sensors show each shuttle has a team of six Kavians aboard. These shuttles will touch down near the locations of the force field towers, where the Kavian crews

will load up any ensnared Opterans and take them back to the *Ko'Falgrin* for processing.

GM Guidance: *The Prime Directive should factor into how the crew decides to respond to Kaladok's demands. This directive, also known as Starfleet General Order 1, states that interference in the natural development of less technologically advanced species is prohibited. This Directive always applies and could inform whether the crew decides to intervene on behalf of the Opterans. If the Player Characters don't raise this concern on their own, perhaps a junior officer on the bridge, speaking nervously and out of turn, points out that the Prime Directive may tie the crew's hands when it comes to helping the Opterans.*

On the other hand, some of Starfleet's most celebrated figures set aside the Prime Directive under the right circumstances. Captain James T. Kirk, for instance, freed a primitive population of intelligent humanoids from the oppression of a tyrannical computer known as Vaal on the planet Gamma Trianguli VI (Original Series episode "The Apple"). Players may draw some compelling parallels between that situation and the current circumstances on Optera IV. The point here is to get the Players discussing the ethics of the Prime Directive, in the proud tradition of Star Trek storytelling, before making a principled decision about what to do.

If the Players decide the Prime Directive requires them to turn their backs on the Opterans, Gamemasters should make sure they understand the consequences of their decision. If there are any Opterans aboard the ship, they will have to be turned over to the Kavians. These Opterans will plead for Starfleet's help in the most desperate terms, perhaps even requesting asylum. If no Opterans are aboard the ship, a new swarm of mature Opterans will take flight into orbit, fleeing from the Kavian collection teams. The Kavian vessel will target some of these Opterans with tractor beams, but a few may attach themselves to the Starfleet vessel or its shields and beg for assistance. The remainder of this act, however, assumes the crew will decide to help the Opterans.

NEGOTIATING WITH CAPTAIN KALADOK

Dealing with Captain Kaladok presents an opportunity to use the Social Conflict system. Kaladok intends to capture and transport as many Opterans as possible because her people's economy and society depend on tetryons for energy production. If the Player Characters simply ask her not to carry out her mission, she may respond with force. A smart crew that engages in skillful negotiation, however, stands a much better chance of resolving the situation without phasers and photon torpedoes.

Asking Captain Kaladok to abandon her mission requires a Persuasion Task with a Difficulty of 6, making it impossible when the *K.E.S. Ko'Falgrin* arrives. This is because doing so would pose serious risk to Kaladok's career and massive effort on the part of the Kavians to produce enough energy without a fresh collection of Opterans. Using Social Tools, however, can change Kaladok's thinking.

Kaladok feels empathy for the captured insectoids and suspects they may be more intelligent than she has been led to believe. If the Starfleet personnel provide solid evidence that the Opterans are intelligent, they gain an Advantage that reduces the difficulty of their Persuasion Task to 5. Further, if they can negotiate an alternative means of providing

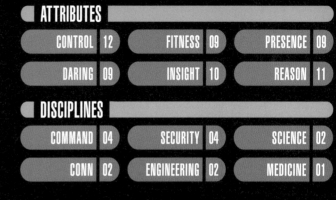

CAPTAIN SHARAMA KALADOK [MAJOR NPC]

TRAITS: Kavian

VALUES:
- Tough but Fair
- The Collection on Optera IV Must Proceed

ATTRIBUTES

CONTROL 12	FITNESS 09	PRESENCE 09
DARING 09	INSIGHT 10	REASON 11

DISCIPLINES

COMMAND 04	SECURITY 04	SCIENCE 02
CONN 02	ENGINEERING 02	MEDICINE 01

STRESS: 13   **RESISTANCE:** 1

ATTACKS:
- Unnarmed Strike (Melee, 5▲, Knockdown, Size 1H, Non-lethal)
- Tetryon Disruptor Pistol (Ranged, 7▲, Vicious 1, Size 1H)

SPECIAL RULES:
- **First into Battle:** When Kaladok makes a successful attack, she may spend 3 Momentum to assist anther Kavian's next attack with her **Daring + Command**.
- **Supreme Authority:** Whenever a Kavian currently under Kaladok's command attempts a Task to resist persuasion or intimidation, Kaladok may spend 1 Threat to allow that Kavian to re-roll, even if Kaladok is not present in that scene herself.
- **Wary:** Whenever a Kavian attempts a Task to notice or detect an enemy or hazard, they may re-roll one d20.

ROLE PLAYING CAPTAIN KALADOK

Sharama Kaladok is an experienced officer in the Kavian Expeditionary Force with a deep sense of duty to her people. Kaladok points out that the Kavian claim to Optera IV stretches back centuries. She believes she's on strong legal ground in a confrontation with Starfleet, and she will argue forcefully to that effect. She frequently refers to Optera IV and its inhabitants as Kavian "property."

However, as evidenced in her log entry at the beginning of this mission, she's not blind to the suffering of the Opterans that her people capture and press into servitude as living energy

sources. She's also less likely to turn a blind eye to signs that the Opterans may be intelligent creatures, if the Players make a persuasive argument to that effect. Gamemasters should play Captain Kaladok as tough but honest and open to the possibility of a compromise if a satisfactory agreement seems feasible.

Kaladok speaks in short, declarative sentences with the air of someone who is used to having her orders followed to the letter. She also carries a thin baton in one hand, a symbol of her rank, with which she gestures as she speaks.

the Kavians with tetryons, the difficulty of the Persuasion Task drops to 4. The crew may spend Determination to aid them in the negotiation, in accordance with the Directive of nonviolence that applies to this mission.

Where might the crew find an alternative source of tetryons? The Opterans themselves would be happy to provide regular deliveries of tetryons if only their Kavian captors let them reopen the spatial tear and return home. This solution will require an away mission to the core facility to shut down the polaron bursts, a possibility discussed in detail later. If the Players propose their own creative solution to the tetryon problem, Gamemasters should use their discretion in whether to allow it. Tetryons are unstable in normal spacetime, so any attempt to produce them artificially should come with some risk and a significant chance of failure.

Players may attempt to intimidate Kaladok or try to deceive her. Kaladok is less likely to respond favorably to those Social Tools and may open fire.

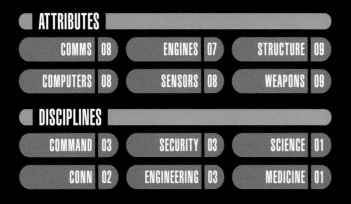

KES KO'FALGRIN

TRAITS: Kavian Collection Barge

ATTRIBUTES

COMMS 08	ENGINES 07	STRUCTURE 09
COMPUTERS 08	SENSORS 08	WEAPONS 09

DISCIPLINES

COMMAND 03	SECURITY 03	SCIENCE 01
CONN 02	ENGINEERING 03	MEDICINE 01

POWER: 7   **SCALE:** 6
SHIELDS: 12   **RESISTANCE:** 6

ATTACKS:
- Tertryon Disruptor Banks (Energy, Range Medium, 10▲, Vicious 1
- Photon Torpedoes (Torpedo, Range Long, 6▲, High Yield
- Tractor Beam (Strength 5)

SPECIAL RULES:
- **Extensive Shuttle Bays:** The vessel's shuttle bays are large, well-supplied and able to support a larger number of active shuttle missions simultaneously. The ship may have twice as many small craft active at any one time as it would normally allow, and it may carry up to two Scale 2 small craft.

Failure to convince Captain Kaladok to abandon her mission will result in open conflict between the Starfleet crew and the Kavians. Combat may erupt between the two starships or on the planet's surface between the Starfleet crew and the Kavian collection teams. Or both combat situations may play out simultaneously, with the Gamemaster cutting regularly between scenes, depending on how the Player Characters respond. In such a situation, the Starfleet ship will have to lower it shields momentarily to allow for an away team to transport. Guidance for each scenario follows below.

SHIP-TO-SHIP COMBAT

There are six potential zones in which the fighting will play out in a starship combat scenario. The first zone is the space immediately surrounding Optera IV. Vessels in this zone gain concealment worth 2▲ Resistance. Three more zones surround each of Optera IV's three moons, which orbit the planet at varying distances. The most distant of the moons is the largest and provides concealment worth 2▲ Resistance for any starships in its zone. The two nearer moons are smaller and provide only 1▲ Resistance. The space beyond the furthest moon that includes the rest of the Opteran system constitutes a fifth zone, and the sixth zone is interstellar space beyond the Opteran system.

Captain Kaladok will position her vessel to take advantage of whatever concealment is available from the planet and its moons and attempt to win a battle of attrition with the Starfleet ship.

The *K.E.S. Ko'Falgrin* is a massive, boxy barge ship designed to transport several decks of detachable cargo holds outfitted as pens for Opterans. Accordingly, the ship lacks the speed and maneuverability of a Starfleet flagship, but it is durable and possesses formidable offensive and defensive systems.

RESOLUTION

If Captain Kaladok feels the tide of battle turning against her, she will surrender under the condition that her personnel on the planet's surface are allowed to return to her vessel. Once that's completed, Kaladok may agree to negotiate with the commanding officer of the Starfleet vessel or the *Ko'Falgrin* may limp out of the system and warp back to Kavia Prime. This would be only a temporary victory for the crew, however. Kaladok intends to return once the Starfleet vessel leaves to mop up any Opterans that remain. And in any case, the Kavians will certainly return in 74 years when the next generation of Opterans surfaces.

The only permanent solution to the Opterans' plight lies in the shielded facility near the planet's core.

Players may be more interested in an engagement with the Kavian collection teams dispatched via shuttle to Optera IV. This section provides such an encounter set in a flat grassland, though the Gamemaster may substitute a different environment of his or her choosing.

A Kavian shuttle sits next to an electronic tower that appears to control spherical force fields dispersed throughout a grassy plain. A team of six Kavian foot soldiers has just finished loading two Opterans into holding cells in the rear of the shuttle. Three more Opterans are trapped inside force fields strewn across the grassland, awaiting transport onto the shuttle.

The standard procedure for gathering the Opterans is for one of the Kavians to drop the force field while the remaining soldiers surround the trapped creature and instantly tranquilize it. Then, they load the Opteran onto an antigrav cart and take it aboard the shuttle.

Any diplomatic attempts to convince the Kavians to release their captives will fail automatically. These soldiers have their orders and will not give up without a fight. Once the fighting breaks out, two of the Kavians will upturn their antigrav cart and use it as cover, granting them 2⚔ Resistance. If the number of Kavians is reduced to two or fewer, the remaining soldiers will attempt to flee in their shuttle.

As in the previous encounter with the Kavian force field lures, Player Characters may overload the force fields with phaser fire to release the captive Opterans. Starfleet characters also may gain access to the Kavian shuttle and release the captive Opterans by unlocking the holding cells. This requires manipulating the control panel for the cells and successfully completing a **Reason or Control + Engineering Task** with a Difficulty of 2. Any released Opterans most likely will take flight away from the battle, but the crew may be able to convince them to stay and fight the Kavians.

Throughout this encounter, Gamemasters may consider using Threat for the following purposes:

- **Summoning reinforcements:** 2 points of Threat will allow an additional shuttle carrying Kavian foot soldiers to arrive from a different location on the planet to join the fight against the Starfleet away team.

- **Tripping force fields:** 1 point of Threat may be spent to entrap one of the Player Characters in a force field, unless the crew manage to shut all the force fields down at their source. This requires one of the Player Characters to access the tower's computer console

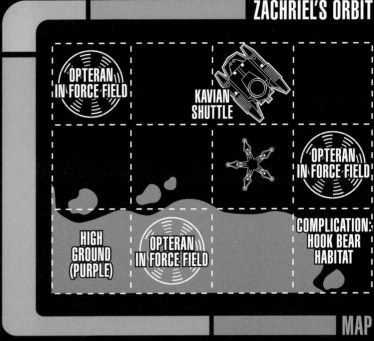

and complete a **Reason + Engineering Task** with a Difficulty of 3.

- **Opteran hook bear:** 2 points of Threat may be spent to summon a huge predator, similar to a grizzly bear, to the battlefield. This creature, protecting its natural habitat from the disturbance of the battle, will indiscriminately attack Kavians, Starfleet personnel or Opterans in the area. This is an opportunity for the Gamemaster to drive the battle to a chaotic climax.

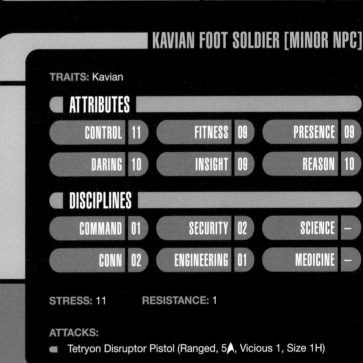

KAVIAN FOOT SOLDIER [MINOR NPC]

TRAITS: Kavian

ATTRIBUTES

CONTROL 11	FITNESS 09	PRESENCE 09
DARING 10	INSIGHT 09	REASON 10

DISCIPLINES

COMMAND 01	SECURITY 02	SCIENCE —
CONN 02	ENGINEERING 01	MEDICINE —

STRESS: 11   **RESISTANCE:** 1

ATTACKS:
- Tetryon Disruptor Pistol (Ranged, 5⚔, Vicious 1, Size 1H)

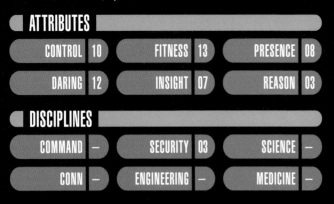

OPTERAN HOOK BEAR [MINOR NPC]

TRAITS: Wild Beast, Apex Predator

ATTRIBUTES

CONTROL	10	FITNESS	13	PRESENCE	08
DARING	12	INSIGHT	07	REASON	03

DISCIPLINES

COMMAND	–	SECURITY	03	SCIENCE	–
CONN	–	ENGINEERING	–	MEDICINE	–

STRESS: 16   **RESISTANCE:** 0

ATTACKS:
- Claws (Melee, 5⚔, Knockdown, Size 1)
- Teeth (Melee, 6⚔, Piercing 2, Size 1)

RESOLUTION

Foiling the Kavian collection team's plans will allow several mature Opterans to lay eggs and fly into space, but more collection teams are gathering Opterans at other locations across the planet's surface. The crew may engage more collection teams at the Gamemasters's discretion. Or a Starfleet victory in this battle may convince Kaladok to recall the other teams and either leave the system or negotiate with the commanding officer of the crew's starship.

SCENE 2: THE SHIELDED CORE FACILITY

The crew should enter the core facility with the knowledge they gathered from investigating the derelict Kavian engineering craft. The only way the Opterans can reopen the spatial tear back to subspace is by shutting down the polaron generator in the center of the installation. They may attempt this with or without the blessing of the Kavians, depending on how they responded to Captain Kaladok's demands. Entering the core facility without Kavian permission will prompt Captain Kaladok to lead a strike force including herself and six foot soldiers into the facility to stop the Starfleet incursion. This may force the crew to attempt the shutdown of the polaron generator in the middle of combat.

You transport into a large rectangular control room filled with alien technology. Narrow windows on one side of the room cast a reddish-orange glow from the planet's molten core. In the center of the room stands the polaron generator, *a formidable metallic apparatus covered in flashing computer consoles. Four thick cables snake outward from the base of the generator and connect to metal boxes in each corner of the room. Every few minutes, the entire facility shudders as the generator whirs to life and injects a burst of polarons directly into the core.*

Inspecting the cables and metalic boxes in the corners reveals them to be crates designed to hold captive Opterans and harvest their tetryons. A single sedated Opteran lies beneath heavy restraints inside each crate, viewable through small slits built into the walls of each device. The exoskeletons of the captive Opterans have faded to a pale yellow color, and their bodies have atrophied over the years. Needles and tubes pierce the exoskeletons of each Opteran, simultaneously keeping the creatures alive while harvesting the tetryons they generate and transferring them to the generator. Any medical or science officer can easily deduce that these are unhealthy and tormented creatures.

The crew, having gained some experience with Kavian technology throughout the mission, may inspect the generator and find that shutting the machine down is a trivial concern and requires no Task. However, doing so will turn off the life support systems sustaining the Opterans. In addition, the shielding that protects the installation will fail once the generator is taken offline, destroying the facility. Anyone remaining in the installation after the shield fails completely will have only moments to escape.

RESOLUTION

The away team may shut down the installation and simply beam out. This would allow the Opterans to reopen the spatial tear and return to subspace, but it also would kill the four Opterans currently powering the polaron generator. To save these captive Opterans, the crew must complete an Extended Task to separate the Opterans from their crates. The Kavian technology has intermingled with the Opterans' biology to such a degree that beaming them away without careful separation would kill them. The Work track for the Extended Task is 19 with a Magnitude and Base Difficulty of 4. The default Task for this is **Daring + Science or Medicine**. If Captain Kaladok is willing to cooperate, she volunteers to Assist.

Each Breakthrough safely frees an Opteran from its prison, while an attempt that doesn't produce a Breakthrough means one of the Opterans didn't survive its separation from the Kavian technology. That means the away team gets a maximum of four attempts. Each attempt, whether or not it yields a Breakthrough, results in one less Opteran providing tetryons to power the installation. This causes escalating malfunctions and allows polaron radiation to leak into the control room as the shield fades.

After the first attempt at the Extended Task, Gamemasters should read the following:

Alarms shriek as the installation's shields weaken due to the sudden drop in available tetryon power. Consoles around the control room flicker and go dark. Without the shields in place, radiation starts to flood the facility. Time is running out.

Everyone in the installation will take 2⚔ damage from the radiation before each subsequent Task to free the Opterans. Additionally, Gamemasters may spend Threat in several ways during the Extended Task. Each spend requires 2 points of Threat:

- A Complication associated with the rapid power loss of the facility imposes 2⚔ Resistance for subsequent attempts to free the Opterans.

- Additional radiation seeps into the control room. Any characters remaining in the control room take 3⚔ radiation damage before each attempt.

- A Complication arises due to the violent shuddering of the installation as its shielding fades. This causes one attempt at the Extended Task to lead to a Dead End, unmarking four points from the Progress Track and killing one of the Opterans.

If the Player Characters succeed at the Extended Task, they manage to free at least some of the Opterans from their technological prison and may safely transport them. If the Player Characters fail the Extended Task, they have mere moments to beam back to their ship before the shields fail entirely and the facility is consumed by the planet's core.

CHAPTER 06.50

BIOLOGICAL CLOCK
CONCLUSION

The conclusion of this mission depends on the fate of the Opterans. If the Player Characters shut down the polaron bursts at the planet's core, any Opterans remaining on the planet or in surrounding space sense the change and return to the largest of the underground caverns. The Opterans will flood the surrounding solanogen crystals with tetryons, causing the spatial tear to ripple open once again. The Opterans will offer their thanks for Starfleet's help before entering the portal. In the process, the solanogen crystals in the chamber become supercharged with enough tetryon energy to last the Kavians for decades. If the Player Characters successfully negotiated a compromise between the two species, the Opterans agree to return to the cavern every 74 years to supercharge additional crystals. Any Opterans rescued from the core facility will invite the Starfleet crew to visit them in the tertiary subspace manifold.

If the crew failed to shut down the polaron generator safely, any surviving Opterans will remain in normal spacetime, longing for an opportunity to return to subspace.

Finally, if the crew never accessed the polaron generator at the planet's core, whether because of the Prime Directive or for other reasons, it's likely the Kavians will continue to exploit the Opterans as an energy source, even if they have to wait another 74 years for another opportunity to collect their "property."

CONTINUING VOYAGES...

This mission offers several hooks for follow-up missions. For instance, Starfleet Command may hold a court-martial to investigate whether the Prime Directive was violated. Or Starfleet may wish to establish normalized diplomatic relations with either or both of the new species introduced in this mission. The Kavians may request help weaning themselves from tetryon-based energy, which would present engineering and science officers with a range of interesting challenges. Or the Opterans may invite the crew into their subspace domain, where the rules of time and physics behave differently than they do in normal space.

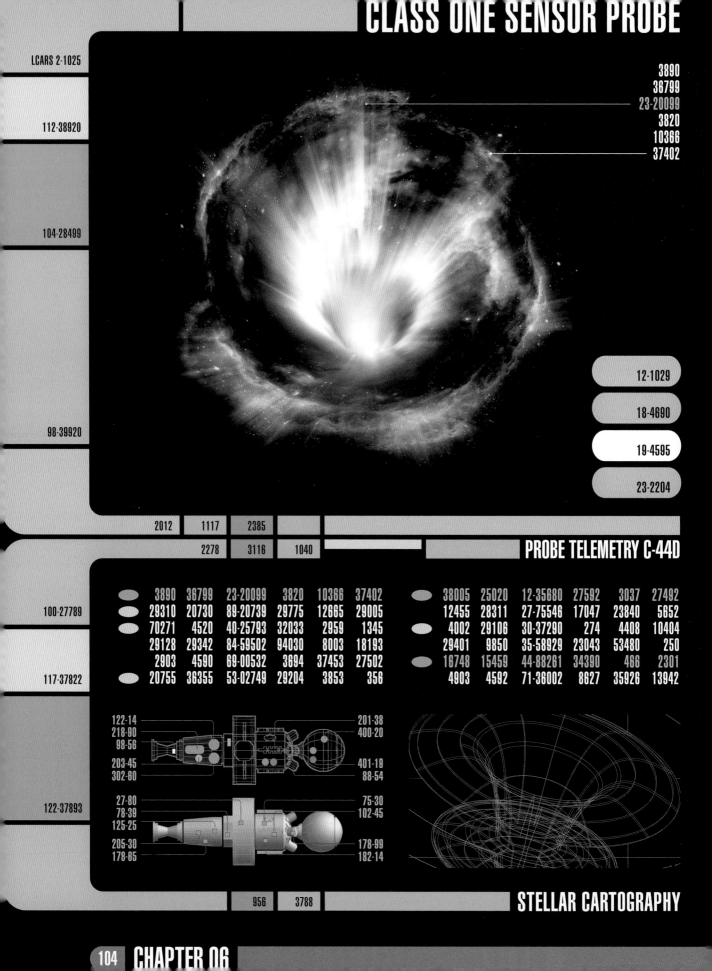

LCARS 2-1025

112-38920

104-28499

98-39920

3890
36799
23-20099
3820
10366
37402

12-1029

18-4690

19-4595

23-2204

| 2012 | 1117 | 2385 | | | |
| 2278 | 3116 | 1040 | | |

PROBE TELEMETRY C-44D

100-27789

117-37822

3890	36799	23-20099	3820	10366	37402		38005	25020	12-35680	27592	3037	27492
29310	20730	89-20739	29775	12665	29005		12455	28311	27-75546	17047	23840	5652
70271	4520	40-25793	32033	2959	1345		4002	29106	30-37290	274	4408	10404
29128	29342	84-59502	94030	8003	18193		29401	9850	35-58929	23043	53480	250
2903	4590	69-00532	3694	37453	27502		16748	15459	44-88261	34390	466	2301
20755	36355	53-02749	29204	3853	356		4903	4592	71-36002	8627	35926	13942

122-14
218-90
98-56
203-45
302-60

201-38
400-20

401-19
88-54

122-37893

27-80
78-39
125-25
205-30
178-65

75-30
102-45

178-99
182-14

STELLAR CARTOGRAPHY

| 956 | 3788 | |

CHAPTER 07.00

A PLAGUE OF ARIAS

BY ALASDAIR STUART

439198365298
91368649816210

A PLAGUE OF ARIAS
SYNOPSIS

Shortly after the recovery of the *U.S.S. Enterprise* from its crash site on Viridian III, the character's ship is dispatched to Starbase Hephaestus, one of Starfleet Medical's primary research centers. The ship is sent there to assist in the anniversary celebrations of Doctor Elizabeth Nostrum's work on Arcturus V curing the 'Aria plague.' A previously unknown disease that spread via involuntary song, the plague devastated the colony world, on the border of Federation and Orion space. She successfully cured it, although not before 153 lives were lost. She went on to be Hephaestus' first CO and her daughter and granddaughter, Doctor Tara Jenner, have continued the tradition.

When the ship arrives, it's greeted by the current CO, Nostrum's granddaughter Captain Tara Jenner. Jenner has been given authority by Starfleet to put the crew to work and she does so. The station is a hive of activity and all hands are needed on deck. The new EMH, based on Nostrum herself, needs refining, the station's communication array is in need of repair and an Orion vessel, *The Solid Bet*, is currently undergoing repairs at Hephaestus.

Tulana Vulko, the Captain of *The Solid Bet*, has faked the damage her ship sustained. In reality, she's at Hephaestus because of what she and Jenner have in common. Vulko's grandparents were Arcturus V colonists. They survived but remained obsessed with what they saw and felt while infected until the day they died.

Vulko has been obsessed with the Aria plague outbreak ever since, and believes that Jenner made the wrong diagnosis. It wasn't a plague; it was an intelligent life form that spread through sound. Jenner, panicking, didn't see this and wiped it out. Vulko's research, and her grandparents' memories, are the core of her beliefs. They were both obsessed with one word 'Zachriel' that they claim they heard repeatedly when infected. Vulko believes this to be the name of the plague's home world.

This is, it turns out, true. And Tara Jenner suspects as much too to the extent that her own research has led her to narrow down the possible locations of Zachriel. She was able to do this thanks in part to the purchase of the remains of an unknown satellite found orbiting Arcturus V's North Pole. Nicknamed Breadcrumb 1, it seems to be the point of

transmission for the plague. Better still it seems to be part of a network. Having discussed the matter with Starfleet Medical, she's been authorized to use the characters' ship to investigate further. This is personal for Jenner. Not only is it her family's reputation on the line but there's a chance the inhabitants of Zachriel can still be saved or, at the very least, understood better.

Following the breadcrumb trail leads the characters to discover a rogue world, reconfigured into a colossal spacecraft. This is Zachriel, the home of the plague. Once they beam down, they discover that the Aria plague was the last attempt of the Zachriel residents, or Zachra, to survive. The characters discover the world is ruined and almost dead, and, if they aren't careful, will also be infected by the Aria plague.

Vulko has tracked them and a standoff ensues in orbit. Unless the characters talk her down, a battle and chase both ensue which lead back to Hephaestus where Vulko has hacked the Nostrum EMH to transmit the sections of the plague it has, causing a second outbreak. The characters must race back there and find a way to not only cure the Aria plague's victims but somehow keep it alive.

The mission concludes with second contact with the Aria plague, Nostrum's mistake revealed and repaired and Vulko either in place as an adversary for future missions, an ally in researching the world, or incarcerated.

DIRECTIVES

In addition to the Prime Directive, the Directives for this mission are:

- Assist Doctor Jenner
- Ensure the Security of Starbase Hephaestus

Gamemasters begin this mission with 2 points of Threat for each Player Character in the group.

My grandma claimed she never got PTSD. All good Doctors pretend they don't get hurt, it's what makes them good. But I remember when she was released on shore leave after Arcturus V. I remember her reading every word intently. I remember her watching our mouths when we talked. I remember finding her, sobbing with relief, a month after she got back because the incubation period was over and she knew she was going to be okay.

– Doctor Tara Jenner, Starfleet Medical

OTHER ERAS OF PLAY

For those Storytellers from the *Enterprise* and Original Series eras, there are a wide variety of options you can use to make your games compatible with *The Next Generation* era game. The important thing to remember is to have fun with it and use whatever options you think will work. Here are a couple of suggestions you can use for your players:

- **For *Enterprise* era players**, the mission remains largely the same, it just springs from different reasons. Instead of the loss of the *Enterprise*-D, the Players' vessel could be an *NX*-class ship designed specifically to educate people. Essentially a ship sized version of the 'classroom' events that NASA have often held.

- This era also allows you to cut out the middle woman. Given how young Starfleet is in this era, it makes sense for Doctor Nostrum herself, not her granddaughter, to be the principle NPC for the module. That in turn adds extra levels of drama. Do the characters assume that one of Starfleet's finest never quite got over her most difficult mission? Or do they believe her and take her off station to discover Zachriel? Better still, Nostrum could be an active antagonist, stealing the ship in a desperate attempt to find the rogue world. That gives your characters even more to do; trying to rescue the ship, stopping Nostrum without killing her, discovering Zachriel and stopping the Orions.

- Alternately you could have Nostrum working with Vulko, and willingly infecting Hephaestus Station in an attempt to find the cure for the plague and redeem what she sees as her past failure.

- The Orions are a relatively unknown quantity in this era. That's actually perfect for Gamemasters and offers you some really fun opportunities. If you set this mission after 'Bound', their primary appearance in *Enterprise*, you can use the *Enterprise* crew's reports as background intelligence.

- Better still, you could even work it so the original advanced civilization the Orions sprung from is known of at this point but hasn't been tied directly to them. That revelation could come from this mission and Vulko's belief that the original Orions knew the inhabitants of Zachriel.

- Alternately, perhaps Arcturus V was originally an Orion colony and Vulko is convinced the plague is a key to the original Orion civilization. That even sets up interesting ethical dilemmas as to how to work against her. Especially if you decide she may be right. Can she be won round? Can you make her an ally or will she commit a terrible crime in the service of knowledge?

- **For Original Series era players**, either Jenner or Nostrum are a good fit for the principle NPC. Better still, Hephaestus Station makes a perfect venue for the first multi-species medical conference. That could give you ample opportunity to have other species' agenda impact on the mission. Perhaps a famous Andorian doctor aboard for the conference is accused of war crimes by the Tellarite delegation? Perhaps the Klingons use the opportunity to grab whatever they can from Starfleet records? Instead of the Nostrum EMH perhaps the Daystrom Institute have installed an experimental diagnostic program (without a holographic body)? One that Vulko has hacked…

- Better still, maybe the mission culminates in a frantic race to Zachriel, the Players' vessel neck and neck with Klingon, Andorian and Vulcan ships? That could lead to a three-way finale where the characters must protect Zachriel, save Hephaestus Station and mediate a major diplomatic incident.

The Aria plague was one of those situations Starfleet Medical train for but hope never to encounter; an endemic plague on an entirely new infection vector. Later research would show that the Aria plague used frequencies below and above human hearing to stimulate structural changes in the chemical levels of the brain. These changes made each host into a better receiver, which in turn accelerated infection, effectively writing new neuron pathways in the brains of its victims.

Each victim sustained long term brain damage in short order and, with the plague spreading via sound, Doctor Nostrum was under huge pressure to find a cure. Finally, she used the deflector dish of the *U.S.S. Pasteur*, her ship, to transmit an ultra-sonic 'wash' through every receiver on the planet. The virus was flushed and the colonists all survived. Due to the acoustic nature of the plague, the records Starfleet have of it are fragmentary but the samples are held in holographic form on Hephaestus, where Jenner continues her grandmother's studies.

A PLAGUE OF ARIAS
ACT 1: ARRIVAL AT HEPHAESTUS

CAPTAIN'S LOG

STARDATE 48650.23

As part of the Escalante's project to educate people about Starfleet's role in the daily running of the Federation, we've been directed to Starbase Hephaestus.

Hephaestus is a Starfleet Medical facility. One part long term convalescence, one part research station. It's also home to Starfleet royalty. Doctor Elizabeth Nostrum was the station's first CO and her daughter Abigail, and granddaughter Captain Tara Jenner have followed in her footsteps. Life savers and risk takers, all. I studied Elizabeth Nostrum at the Academy, can't wait to meet her granddaughter. And my crew can't wait to have a little fun.

a legendary 20th Century Los Angeles teacher, it's intended to be a Starfleet vessel with one hundred percent transparency. Federation citizens on every world, every station, can see where the Players' vessel is and what it's doing at any given time, due to the newly calibrated sensor footprint, that allow interested citizens to establish a subspace link with the ship's public data broadcasting back to the Federation. The command staff have regularly scheduled holodeck 'classrooms' with schools across the Federation and their logs are a matter of public record.

Repurposed and refitted, their job is to do everything Starfleet already does but to do it with transparency. Anyone who wants to can learn about the workings of the organization, or see where the ships are at any time. Starfleet needs a human face and the Players' vessel has been chosen as that face.

NEW MISSION PROFILE

This mission introduces a new Mission Profile (*Star Trek Adventures* core rulebook p. 251) for the Players' vessel to be outfitted with. It grants the following Trait, Departments and Talents. If this mission is the beginning of campaign, or is a desired refit of the ship, then strip the previous Mission Profile from the starship that was given to it at creation and replace it with the following statistics. Otherwise, ignore the Department and Talent changes and just give the Players' vessel the Traits "Expanded sensor footprint," and, "Prototype," for the duration of this mission.

EXPERIMENTAL SYSTEMS

Starfleet needs a win in 2371. With the Fleet reeling from the loss of the *Enterprise*-D, every opportunity for a PR victory or a morale boost is seized on. That's why the Players' ship is dispatched to Starbase Hephaestus.

Onboard, a new experimental system has been installed, named Project Escalante. Named for Jamie Escalante,

TRAITS: Expanded Sensor Footprint, Prototype

DEPARTMENTS

COMMAND	03	SECURITY	01	SCIENCE	03
CONN	01	ENGINEERING	02	MEDICINE	02

TALENTS:

- **Expanded Connectivity:** Extensive user-interface reworking has been done throughout the ship. Due to this any *Override* actions taken, where an action is taken from a different station on the bridge, can be attempted with no penalty.

PROJECT ESCALANTE STAFF

As the Escalante project is in the prototype stage, various staff from Starfleet Operations are here to oversee its first field testing and public debut.

SCIENCE OFFICER KINSKI REID

Kinski Reid likes to describe himself as one-half Russian, one-half Scottish and one-half awesome because he transcends puny three-dimensional science. Kinski has an endlessly dry wit and humor is a part of everything he does. He's far and away the most popular officer in the holodeck classrooms and others have started to hand their assignments to him.

COMMANDER VALNO OKSARI, CORPS OF ENGINEERS

Tellarite engineer Valno Oksari is precise, brilliant and fast. Used to the high gravity of her own world, she zips around the Player vessel like an over-caffeinated puppy. She has a deep, profound love of her projects and other cultures and is constantly working to make the staff of the Escalante project easier.

Statistics for the two characters can be from *Chapter 11: Aliens and Adversaries* from the **Star Trek Adventures** core rulebook (p. 315).

SCENE 1: ARRIVING AT HEPHAESTUS STATION

Starbase Hephaestus is a deceptively small station with a staff of just over 300. Its central section houses the power and computer cores, command decks, crew accommodation and public areas, all based around a single, central multi-story atrium. Three additional modules arranged around it include an isolation and intensive care ward, a full hospital and a lab complex. Up to three ships can dock at any time and the station can take up to 300 extra people. It also does double duty as a field hospital and a secondary archive for Starfleet Medical research. While the primary archive remains part of Memory Alpha, Hephaestus acts as an 'off site backup' of sorts for the latest findings from Starfleet Medical officers in the Quadrant.

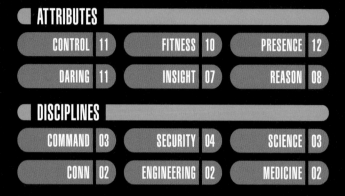

CAPTAIN TULANA VULKO [MAJOR NPC]

TRAITS: Orion

VALUES:
- I'm Orion by Birth, but I'm No Pirate
- An Urge to Find the Truth of the Arian Plague
- Don't Anger Me, Else Feel My Fury
- I Can Turn on the Charm When I Need To

ATTRIBUTES

CONTROL	11	FITNESS	10	PRESENCE	12
DARING	11	INSIGHT	07	REASON	08

DISCIPLINES

COMMAND	03	SECURITY	04	SCIENCE	03
CONN	02	ENGINEERING	02	MEDICINE	02

FOCUSES: Diplomacy, Xeno-Archaeology, Espionage

STRESS: 14   **RESISTANCE:** 1

ATTACKS:
- Knife (Melee, 5⚔, Vicious 1, Size 1H, Hidden 1)
- Disruptor Pistol (Ranged, 7⚔, Vicious 1, Size 1H)
- **Escalation 2:** Pulse Grenade (Ranged, 8⚔ Area, Size 1H, Charge, Grenade)

SPECIAL RULES:
- **Charismatic:** Whenever Tulana buys additional dice, using Threat, for any social Tasks, she may re-roll a single d20.
- **A Nose for Intel:** Whenever attempting a Security Task to gain information, Tulana reduces the Difficulty by 1.
- **Follow my lead:** Once per scene, when Tulana succeeds at a Task during combat or another perilous situation, you may spend two Threat. If you do, choose a single ally. The next Task that ally attempts counts as having assistance from her, using her **Presence + Command.**
- **Furious:** When provoked into combat, for her first Turn, any attacks automatically gain 1d20 to add to the dice pool.

Doctor Jenner is deep in discussions with Starfleet Medical when the Players arrive. The command staff are met by Deck Chief Tomas Dooley and Science Officer T'Vril, who send their CO's apologies and invite them to dinner with her that night. They then give the crew the guided tour and ask for their help on a variety of situations that have come up.

GM Guidance: This leads to the following scenes which can be played through in any order or swapped out as needed. If your characters have friends in Starfleet Medical who are on station, this is a great time to catch up. Likewise, if you have campaign threads you'd like to drop in, this is the place to do them. One last note; these encounters will work just as well with a mixed group as with specialists. Doctors will be able to recognize battle scars on the Orions, security officers will be able to tell if Dooley is hiding something and so on. Laying the mission out this way gives the Players lines of enquiry that don't necessarily fit altogether neatly. That can be frustrating so, if you need to, have Captain Jenner meet them immediately, take them for dinner and explain everything. Then either dive into the individual research projects or head straight for Zachriel.

THE SOLID BET

An Orion ship, *The Solid Bet*, has checked in at the station with some casualties. They were caught by the Nexus during its run through Orion space and were badly damaged. Any security personnel spending time with the Orions will spot straight away that these men and women are career military. In particular, Captain Tulana Vulko, their commanding officer has the look and bearing of a career soldier. That being said, the crew are friendly, helpful and have been assisting around the station. Although, as the characters have the opportunity to find out shortly, there may be ulterior motives for that.

Security on the station has been highly suspicious of the Orions that have docked, and particularly the reports that off-duty Starfleet personnel have been frequenting the vessel, and Chief Dooley asks the Player Characters to report any Starfleet officers going aboard. Any security style investigations by the Players will lead them to discover an Orion sponsored speakeasy being run out of *The Solid Bet*. Players may also be able to find out the names of the Starfleet officers who are frequent visitors. Thorough investigations reveal that they are all members of the communications department of Hephaestus Station.

Talking to any of the officers involved will play out pretty politely, unless you feel like giving your Players a chase scene this early on. Any communications staff they chat to will reveal the following:

- The communications staff were all directly approached by the Orions.

- They're not stupid, however. They know they're being drilled for information and all assure the characters they're being very careful.

- Chief Thomas Dooley, chief of communications, is the only officer to not gamble. When pushed with an Opposed Task for information, he will reveal it's because his father had a gambling problem. Admiral Albert Dooley is a hero of Starfleet so this is pretty surprising news for the players.

Vulko's grandparents were Arcturus V survivors and obsessed over the Aria plague until the day they died. Her grandfather told her stories about the tremendous sense of community and wellbeing he got when he was infected and one word that he doodled endlessly for the rest of his life, 'Zachriel.' He died convinced it was a message, and passed that obsession onto his granddaughter. She's continued his research, monitored Tara Jenner's and is on station to finally make her move.

More specifically, her three moves. Vulko's plan is to locate Zachriel, release the Aria plague on Hephaestus and raid the central data banks in the distraction. Any attention paid to the Orion crew will gain the command staff a visit from Captain Vulko. She is fiercely articulate, very plausible and obviously is playing three or four games at once. The best possible way to run her is through roleplaying the conversation but if you must, use a social conflict of Difficulty 4, to see if she can get her crewmembers released. If your characters win the social conflict, here's what they can find out. Give them the first piece of information for succeeding and the second piece for any *Obtain Information* Momentum spent:

- Vulko is an amateur xeno-archaeologist and has been trying to find time to chat with Doctor Jenner, who she knows is also a fan of the subject.

- Vulko's grandparents were Federation colonists.

SCENE 2: THE SCIENCES DIVISION

Your medical staff will feel right at home on Hephaestus. As well as a chance to catch up on the latest events out in the Quadrant through the on-station archive, Hephaestus is also home to the team developing the Nostrum Emergency Medical Hologram and, through that, conducting further research into the Aria plague.

GM Guidance: It's also a working hospital station and if you're so inclined to introduce them, Player medical officers can get involved in cases to keep them busy. Alternately, this is a great opportunity for the Player medical staff to get caught up on new developments and gossip, as well as potentially run into old mentors or classmates. Also, if you're looking for a place to introduce any famous Starfleet Medical NPCs, this is the place to do it. Jenner is an elite officer in Starfleet Medical, in every sense of the word. She's respected, controversial and has been the subject of debate for decades.

My work at Hephaestus proceeds at the correct pace. The Nostrum EMH is proving an involving project, as well as a stimulating companion. I enjoy debating the ethics of her actions with her…

– Science Officer T'Vril, Starbase Hephaestus

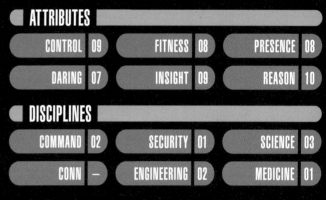

SCIENCE OFFICER T'VRIL [NOTABLE NPC]

TRAITS: Vulcan, Focused, Precise, Cautious

VALUES:
- Precision and Focus Is the Key to Scientific Endeavor

ATTRIBUTES

CONTROL	09	FITNESS	08	PRESENCE	08
DARING	07	INSIGHT	09	REASON	10

DISCIPLINES

COMMAND	02	SECURITY	01	SCIENCE	03
CONN	—	ENGINEERING	02	MEDICINE	01

FOCUSES: Holographic Programming, Psychology, Crisis Management

STRESS: 9   **RESISTANCE:** 0

ATTACKS:
- Unarmed Strike (Melee, 2▲ Knockdown, Size 1H, Non-lethal)
- Phaser type-1 (Ranged, 2▲, Size 1H, Charge, Hidden 1)

SPECIAL RULES:
- Whenever T'Vril is being assisted with any Medicine Tasks by the Norstrum EMH, she may re-roll 1d20 in her dice pool.

Given that, and the ceremony, and Hephaestus' importance for Starfleet Medical it is absolutely understandable if you want to throw some of Starfleet's best Doctors in to help your players out. Doctors Pulaski, Crusher and Bashir could very plausibly be on station for this sort of event. That gives your players the chance to work with one of the all-time greats and you a chance to shore up any holes in their skill set. Maybe having Doctor Pulaski in the Player vessel lab gives the Players a Major NPC as a Supporting Character, allowing her to assist them. Or perhaps Hephaestus' EMH is able, with the

DOCTOR NOSTRUM EMH [MINOR NPC]

TRAITS: Hologram

ATTRIBUTES

CONTROL 10	FITNESS 08	PRESENCE 07
DARING 09	INSIGHT 08	REASON 09

DISCIPLINES

COMMAND 01	SECURITY 01	SCIENCE 03
CONN 02	ENGINEERING 02	MEDICINE 04

FOCUSES: Emergency Medicine, Surgery, Aria Plague

help of your engineering characters, to transmit the complete version of the plague to the Nostrum EMH? Be creative, don't let the NPCs solve the case but be prepared to have them help if needed.

T'Vril is a young Vulcan, a little over 40 years old. She's a psychologist, studying the effect holographic re-enactment has on PTSD sufferers and the potential historical value of using it to consult with long dead individuals. She is nicknamed, although never to her face, 'Doctor Creepy.'

The Elizabeth Nostrum hologram is her dream project. Modeled on Elizabeth Nostrum herself, it's intended to be a tour guide for the station, an interface for the main archive and the go to source for all research on the Aria plague.

When the characters arrive, T'Vril has the EMH singing opera. The sight of Elizabeth Nostrum, in an old-fashioned Starfleet uniform belting out Aida is enough to cause any character to need a **Control + Science Task** with a Difficulty of 1. A failure causes the Complication "Taken aback." Noticing the Player Characters, T'Vril will ask the computer to stop the Opera and introduce herself and the hologram. She asks for their help in chatting with the EMH, to help socialize it. The characters can then assist her by asking the EMH about the station and the events of the Arcturus V plague outbreak. There are Tasks required here but here's what they can find out:

- The holographic audio wave forms of the plague fragments closely resemble human music in some cases and human speech in others. In each case though, the fragments are massive, as though there's a lot of data that isn't being spoken. T'Vril has been using opera as a comparator to see if the plague was a form of music.

- Nostrum never returned to the plague as a research subject, once she eradicated it from Arcturus. Her successors did though and Tara Jenner has run several sections through the universal translator. There's one repeated word which translates out as 'Zachriel.'

- The EMH can play the characters interviews with the survivors of the plague. All of them talk about the euphoric sensation of being connected and all of them, without exception, hum a single bar of music that's bleeped out on the recording. However, T'Vril has a graphical representation of it and has confirmed that, through the universal translator, the phrase comes out as the word 'Zachriel'.

- That a complete roster of the Arcturus V colonists will reveal the names of 100 Orion colonists, including Captain Vulko's grandparents. Any security officer in particular hearing this will almost certainly become suspicious.

- The Nostrum EMH will also happily provide a listing of every crewmember to have worked on it. If this question is asked, any security characters present should attempt an **Insight + Security Task** with a Difficulty of 2. If they succeed, they notice that all the communications staff gambling with the Orions have worked on the EMH. If they mention this to T'Vril, she will become extremely troubled as several of those crewmembers were not assigned to the research. If any of the crew are asked about this, they will explain they were simply checking in to see how the EMH was doing and were listed in error. Anyone attempting an **Insight + Security Task** with a Difficulty of 2 will realize they're lying. If pushed, they will reveal that they were asked to visit the EMH by the Orions.

From here, if the Player Characters decide to investigate the EMH's programming, a **Reason + Science Task** with a Difficulty of 4 will reveal that there is a subroutine hidden deep in the EMH. It's designed to override every communication station and channel on the station and broadcast the plague fragments, triggering a second outbreak. In other words, it turns the EMH and every communications system it can access, into an infection vector.

This changes the mission drastically. Captain Vulko will hand the crewmembers responsible over to Starfleet, apologize unreservedly and lend all available assistance. In public. In reality, she'll abandon the plan to broadcast the plague into Hephaestus and focus on shadowing the Players out to Zachriel.

SCENE 3: ENGINEERING

There's a persistent issue with the station's communication array that needs dealing with. Chief Tomas Dooley has requested any extra staff to go and help.

PERSONAL LOG

There's a fault on the main communication array. Again. I'll take a group out there to fix it. Maybe some fresh eyes will see a way to solve this problem that mine aren't.

– Chief Engineer Tomas Dooley,
Starbase Hephaestus

When the characters arrive, they find Dooley friendly but a little distant. The array itself checks out fine, if a little worn. Anyone conducting EVAs (space walks) to examine it externally will, if they make an **Insight + Engineering Task** with a Difficulty of 3, notice evidence of loosened panels at one particular external network link. Dooley, when asked, will explain he was doing maintenance there last week but he's sure he secured the panel. In reality, this is the location where the Orions hacked the station's internal systems, connecting the subroutine in the Nostrum EMH to their communication system. And Dooley is lying — he was the person who hacked the communication systems. Dooley, conflicted about his role in their plan, has asked for fresh eyes on the scene. His hope is, while he can't risk confessing, they'll spot something that will spark an investigation.

Thomas Dooley is attempting to pay off the debt his father ran up to Vulko's mother's gambling syndicate. His dad is a senior and well-regarded Admiral who fled Orion space in the hopes of leaving the debt behind. Vulko found Dooley and now, that debt has come due. It plays into Dooley's fatalistic view of the universe — that he enlisted and was assigned here to Hephaestus so that his father's gambling debt would come back around.

Dooley is the communications chief for Hephaestus and he's extraordinarily good at his job. A 'student of Miles O'Brien,' Dooley has the same sleeves up, hands on approach to problem solving coupled with the natural compassion of all the staff at Hephaestus. He's also tormented with guilt over what he's doing. Anyone researching the staff who drink with the Orions can discover his father's debt and from there, investigations will lead to Dooley.

SCENE 4: DINNER WITH JENNER

Obviously, the characters may have questions at this stage. At dinner, there is a chance for Doctor Jenner to bring them up to speed with her research and deal with any consequences from their avenues of investigation or interaction with the Hephaestus staff.

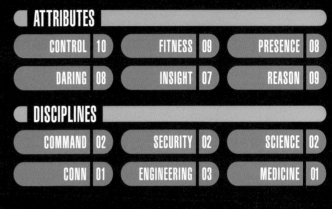

Tara Jenner is a charming, friendly and very over-worked Starfleet doctor. Over dinner she'll chat about the fate of the *Enterprise*-D, other news in the Federation and bond with the characters. She's clearly proud of her station but any insightful characters will notice she's distracted. Anyone pressing her on the issue, or what they found in the individual department tasks above, will get her to open-up about her grandmother:

- She never quite recovered from the Arcturus incident.

- Jenner has never been able to prove it, but she's fairly sure her grandmother lied to Starfleet. Doctor Nostrum claimed that only fragments of the audio patterns that carried the Aria plague were recorded but Jenner's certain the *U.S.S. Pasteur* would have held complete copies. She thinks her grandmother destroyed sections to ensure it could never be fully reassembled. She knows Starfleet Medical believe this and that's why her grandmother retired as a captain, not an admiral.

- She finds it uncomfortable being around the EMH.

- While her grandmother could never bring herself to return to the Aria plague. Tara and her mother have both spent a significant amount of time to it.

TRAITS: Human, Driven, Articulate

FOCUSES: Exo-biology, Exo-medicine, Trauma, Archaeology

ATTRIBUTES

CONTROL	09	FITNESS	08	PRESENCE	07
DARING	08	INSIGHT	09	REASON	10

DISCIPLINES

COMMAND	02	SECURITY	—	SCIENCE	02
CONN	01	ENGINEERING	01	MEDICINE	03

STRESS: 8   **RESISTANCE:** 0

ATTACKS:

- Unarmed attack (Melee, 1▲ Knockdown, Size 1H, Non-lethal)
- Phaser type-1 (Ranged, 2▲, Size 1H, Charge, Hidden 1)

SPECIAL RULES:

- **Authority:** When Tara attempts any Command Tasks in relation to Hephaestus Station and its personnel, she reduces its Difficulty by 1.

She has had several members of her science team working on an alien signal brought to her attention by her research. They have revealed the signal is a set of coordinates. One transmitted on a tight beam in two directions. The first celestial body the signal encounters in one direction is Arcturus V. The other takes it out of the plain of the galactic elliptic.

SCENE 5: BREADCRUMBS

Once they have finished dinner, she invites them down to shuttlebay 1 at the base of Hephaestus. There, the Player Characters find her pride and joy. Contained in the hangar are the remains of what was once a three-meter wide, white metal sphere. It's pitted and scorched, and in three fragments. Any **Science Task** (Difficulty 3) will reveal that it's constructed of a metal similar to durillium, is laced with complex circuits and there's trace evidence of both a fusion power supply and what seems to be some form of robotic manufacturing system. Jenner will tell them the following:

- She refers to it as Breadcrumb 1 or BC 1

- BC 1 was found above Arcturus V.

- BC 1 is made of a durillium alloy that appears to have interstellar hydrogen as its primary component.

- It is at least 1000 years old.

- Starfleet recovered the remains of a device made of the same material on the surface of Arcturus V. She believes this was a lander of some sort.

- BC 1 has taken heavy damage. This was caused by her grandmother's cure for the Aria plague.

The single piece of information she's been able to pull from it was the signal she had the science team working on. Now they have a solid location for that, she's convinced a second satellite, codenamed Breadcrumb 2, is no more than 2 AUs away from the BC 1 site.

When asked where she found it, Jenner explains that she was sold the artifact by an Orion trader. If pressed, she will remember their name as Torian Vosko. A **Presence + Security Task** with a difficulty will reveal Torian Vosko works for the mercantile guild run by Tulana Vulko. A **Presence + Security Task** with a difficulty of 2 will reveal he is presently missing.

Jenner levels with the characters:

- She believes her grandmother, terrified, under incredible pressure and desperate to save the lives of the colony, made a terrible mistake.

- The Aria plague was an intelligence, using BC 1 and the network she believes it to be a part of to travel vast distances.

- Whether it was incompatible with the colonists' DNA or the damage they sustained was intentional isn't something Jenner has been able to find out.

- She believes her grandmother didn't cure a plague, but bungled a first contact.

- She believes the Breadcrumb satellites are proof that the Aria plague's home world is still out there and accessible. If she can find it, and right her grandmother's wrong, she can exonerate her and perhaps provide aid to the Aria plague.

- She was talking to Starfleet Medical earlier to get command authorization to mount an operation following the Breadcrumb's trail. Jenner has been desperate to do this before her grandmother's anniversary and, with the Players' vessel on station and the possibility of an entire world under threat, there's never been a better time.

Jenner will request the Players' vessel to go planet (and plague) hunting. Jenner has narrowed the region that BC 2 is in down to just under 10 Astronomical Units and she needs a ship to take her there. And do so before her Grandmother's centenary. If she can do that, she can turn her grandmother's failure into the first step of a multi-generational research project for her family. It'll save her face, save Starfleet's and everyone goes home happy. Even better, if she can do this before the ceremony, her grandmother's name will have been redeemed before it was ever fully besmirched.

Whether the characters want to do this or not will define where the mission goes from here. While Jenner can force the issue and put them under orders from Starfleet Medical, its possible their investigations on station will take precedent, meaning the planet hunting may be delayed. If this is the case or you give them the option of staying then resolve this as a Social Conflict with Jenner, roleplaying, or a combination of both.

ENCOUNTER: STEALING THE BREADCRUMB

If you wish for Vulko to attempt to steal the Breadcrumb, either by transporting it out or storming the hangar where it's kept, while the characters are there.

ORION COMMANDOS [MINOR NPC]

TRAITS: Orion

ATTRIBUTES

| CONTROL | 10 | FITNESS | 09 | PRESENCE | 08 |
| DARING | 08 | INSIGHT | 07 | REASON | 07 |

DISCIPLINES

| COMMAND | 01 | SECURITY | 02 | SCIENCE | — |
| CONN | 01 | ENGINEERING | 02 | MEDICINE | — |

STRESS: 11   RESISTANCE: 1

WEAPONS:
- Disruptor Pistol (Ranged, 5▲ Vicious 1, Size 1H)
- **Escalation** Disruptor Rifle (Ranged, 6▲ Vicious 1, Size 2H, Accurate)

If you go for this option, then the ship will have to go off in pursuit. A **Reason + Science Task** with a Difficulty of 3 will enable the crew to figure out where the Breadcrumb fits in the trail and once that's achieved, they can race Vulko to Zachriel.

A PLAGUE OF ARIAS
ACT 2: ZACHRIEL

SCENE 1: THE BREADCRUMB TRAIL

The satellites are a vast distance apart, but easily detectable if the characters have researched the signal Jenner had her science team working on. Even if they didn't do that, once the Player vessel reaches the coordinates Jenner deduced

CAPTAIN'S LOG

STARDATE 48650.25

Captain Jenner's findings are eccentric, that's not in any question. But the research she's done…the reasoning behind dispatching us to Hephaestus…It's all solid. Bizarre, certainly. Personal? Definitely, but solid.

So, the Aria plague was transmitted to Arcturus V by an ancient satellite which, itself, was part of a network of those satellites extending back to the home world of a previously unknown alien race.

A home world we are now heading in search of.

Part of me wants to believe that this is not what the Escalante project was intended to do. We're an educational vessel, designed to show the next generation just what Starfleet does. But then, of course, this is what Starfleet does. Leap into the unknown, tricorders and eyes wide open.

The crew are thrilled. And terrified. Me too.

for Breadcrumb 1, **Reason + Science Task** with a Difficulty of 1 will be enough to locate the second satellite or BC 2. Once they have a third Breadcrumb located, engineering or science division characters can then work together on a Difficulty 3 Task (with Astrogation or Orbit Dynamics as example Focuses) to develop a program that will predict the locations of the other satellites. If they succeed with Momentum they can even spend 2 Momentum to *Obtain Information* to predict the endpoint of the path and warp directly there.

ENCOUNTER: CROSSING THE BORDER

The most logical way for the Players' vessel to cross the Orion border is simply to ask. This can be roleplayed, resolved through a Social Conflict with an appropriate Orion NPC, or simply glossed over with the bored Orion traffic controller waving them through. For all the occasional tensions between Starfleet and the Orions, a vessel on medical business as the Players are, is not likely to be held up. However, it is also likely to be reported and Captain Vulko will be alerted if they pass through.

If you opted to have Captain Vulko steal Breadcrumb 1 there are two further ways to play this approach. The first is to have the captain or command staff demand that she be held at the border. That may very well not fly but its proper protocol and if your players have contacts in the Orions, then they may well be able to pull strings to do this. Again, play this either as roleplaying, especially if they have Orion contacts, or as a Social Conflict.

DIPLOMATIC INCIDENTS

If the ship fails, then Orion Naval frigates will be scrambled, the Players will be ordered to heave to for inspection and the confrontation will spiral into a full scale diplomatic incident which will give Vulko all the time she needs to attack Hephaestus and locate Zachriel. This can be resolved via a Social conflict, or the crew just cutting and running but there will be serious long term diplomatic consequences for the region.

The second is to sneak across the border. The area is thick with comets and asteroids so it's possible to hide in their shadow or tail respectively. A **Control + Conn Task** with a Difficulty of 3 will be enough to fly the ship in behind an asteroid, or through other phenomena, and nudge its course across the border using the ship's tractor beam. Alternately, a **Control + Conn Task** with a Difficulty of 4 is required to keep the vessel within a comet's tail to make the crossing. Finally, a **Daring + Science Task** with a Difficulty of 3 will enable the science team aboard to modify the ship's transponder so it doesn't appear to be a Starfleet vessel, though this is strictly against Starfleet protocol.

Finally, the players could ask any Starfleet vessels in the region to be on the lookout for *The Solid Bet* which would increase their likelihood of finding her. This is a Task with a Difficulty of 0, to *Create an Advantage* with two Momentum required to create the Advantage.

SCENE 2: WELCOME TO ZACHRIEL

Zachriel, the world the plague originated from is full of surprises. Not the least of which is that the whole planet is moving at full impulse, in a straight line, in the depths of space outside any charted solar system. A **Control + Conn Task** with a Difficulty of 1 is needed to catch up with it and the same Task with a Difficulty of 2 to enter orbit, to compensate for its traveling speed. Once that's done, the following can be discovered by science and engineering crew with Tasks using those Disciplines.

- The world's surface is at absolute zero.

- It has no atmosphere.

- There is a colossal network of tunnels running all the way through it. The planetary core is very geologically active and seems to be a power plant for the continent sized structures on the world's surface.

- The world has a continent sized engine array at its southern pole. This is clearly badly damaged and sensor readings suggests it has been firing for over 1000 years.

- There is a planetary power grid that is 80% inactive. The remaining 20% is concentrated at a facility on the equator.

- The planet's entire surface is designed to capture energy. Sensors are picking up wave power stations in the frozen oceans, multiple geothermal power plants and evidence of a colossal solar sail array in addition to the geothermal core.

- This is almost unprecedented throughout Starfleet history. An entire world, refitted as a colossal starship. And, apparently, somehow, still active.

SCENE 3: BEAMING DOWN

Establish with the Players that the facility on the equator is the one place where they are most likely to get answers. An away team will need to gear up with Environmental suits, and once they are inside the facility, they are met with a treasure trove of information.

Players interacting with the consoles here will need to attempt a **Reason + Engineering Task** with a Difficulty of 2 to reveal the following:

- A large robotic production facility dedicated to producing the Breadcrumbs. This will yield confirmation they are relay stations. They're also designed to self-replicate if needed.

- A mass driver designed to fire the breadcrumbs into orbit.

- Displays that show the entire planet has been rigged as a storage device. The metal deposits have been reconfigured as circuits and an astronomical amount of data has been stored on them.

THE ZACHRA

The Zachra, the race who created the "plague," knew their world was dying. Some chose to abandon it and set up colonies but many chose to engage in 'The Migration'. They converted their world into a starship and sent it out into space to explore.

Inevitably, after centuries, Zachriel began to fade. As it did, those who remained decided that while they had to leave they weren't ready for the planet to die. Using technology recovered from their many visits to other worlds, they copied and encoded the entire history of their journey, and their own personalities into a single artificial intelligence. Then, they built the Breadcrumb satellites to transmit the AI to any nearby worlds or ships that housed intelligent life.

The Zachra assumed that any race that reached sentience would be able to understand them. They assumed that it would be a simple matter of introducing themselves and conversing with their new 'hosts' before being transferred into a stable computer network or transmitted further away using their host's technology.

The reality proved to be very different. The sheer amount of information overwhelmed the plague's hosts more often than not, and the amount of time it took to be able to communicate was almost always too much. The Aria plague's copies all failed and only the original, still on Zachra, remains. The Zachra just wanted their planet to survive. But now they bring death everywhere they go.

Further investigation around the facility, or by *Obtain Information* Momentum spends will reveal an auditorium, with a breathable atmosphere. The auditorium was intended to be a welcoming location for future voluntary recipients of the Aria plague's information. However, due to the damage the world has taken that's no longer apparent so the Players should draw their own conclusions.

Entering the auditorium will trigger the song, causing the Aria plague, to play. Any character hearing it will automatically be infected — give the Players, secretly or otherwise, a Trait of "Aria infected". Given their knowledge of the Aria plague, it's a fair bet that they'll tread carefully. Infection is purely auditory, so any enterprising character who cuts audio receivers to their helmets or covers their ears immediately will not be infected.

Any character who hears the plague is infected. Being infected is like dealing with a never-ending cacophony of noise as the memories of the personalities in the Aria plague cascade over the characters' own. A **Control + Command**

Task is needed, every so often, starting at Difficulty 4. Success means the character can compose themselves, while a failure means the character sings what they are perceiving, transmitting the activation signal for the plague itself or the Zachra's own language.

Untreated, within 24 hours the memories and personalities of the Zachra, within the plague, consists of begin to overwrite the victim's own. Inside 48 hours the brain chemistry of a victim is permanently altered and inside 72, the systems are so damaged by the strain of carrying this information that they collapse and die inside a further 12 hours.

ENCOUNTER: THE SOLID BET PAYS OFF

And then, Captain Vulko arrives. Or, if she stole Breadcrumb 1 and ran for it, she's already there. That's a great opportunity to have the characters beam down to the surface to try and stop her team (using her and the commandos, p.110 and p.115) as the crew aboard the Player ship tries to de-escalate the starship conflict in orbit.

There are three ways you can play Captain Vulko, depending on how obvious you want her to be about her plans, in this encounter.

EVIDENCE
Captain Vulko's plan is simple; she wants Zachriel. The Breadcrumb trail, and what the Aria plague and Nostrum did to her grandparents mean she views it as her birth right. She plans to claim the world as a technological refuge for the Orion Syndicates, and sell it to the highest bidder.

If the Starfleet personnel oppose her on this, and they will, she'll remind them they have under a day to get back to Hephaestus, because she has just triggered the EMH to broadcast the plague throughout the station (see her plans at the beginning of Act 3). And with only a fragmentary recording of it, who knows what extra damage the victims will cause to each other?

DECEPTION
While all Hell breaks loose on Hephaestus (if the Players haven't foiled the broadcast of the Aria plague through the communications systems), her team will raid the central computer there, pick it clean of anything of value and then 'ride to the rescue'. She could offer to cut the characters in, or she could simply be telling them this before attacking the Player ship and leaving them there.

STARSHIP CONFLICT
Vulko appears, targets the auditorium and initiates a standoff with the Player vessel, threatening them. If they

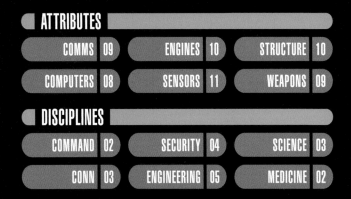

THE SOLID BET

TRAITS: Orion

ATTRIBUTES
COMMS 09	ENGINES 10	STRUCTURE 10
COMPUTERS 08	SENSORS 11	WEAPONS 09

DISCIPLINES
COMMAND 02	SECURITY 04	SCIENCE 03
CONN 03	ENGINEERING 05	MEDICINE 02

POWER: 10   **SCALE:** 3

SHIELDS: 14   **RESISTANCE:** 4

WEAPONS:
- Phaser Arrays (Energy, Range M, 7▲ Area 1 or Spread 1, Versatile 2)
- Tractor Beam (Strength 7)

SPECIAL RULES:
- Hull Plating: +1 Resistance
- Aliases: *The Solid Bet* can be configured to appear as a Federation vessel or a much smaller Orion vessel.

LAUNCH BAY:
- 1 Shuttlepod

move to destroy her, she can attempt to destroy the auditorium before anyone can be beamed out. Resolving this starts with a Social Conflict to get Vulko to bargain her way into letting the characters free. Perhaps she comes clean, blames a crewmember for the Outbreak. Perhaps she helps them in exchange for Orion Archaeology Syndicates to be given first rights to Zachriel. Perhaps she simply tries to kill them, cover it up and run.

If defeated, or talked down, Captain Vulko will make a run for it back to Hephaestus to try and salvage something of her plan from the data on the Aria plague maintained at the station. Alternately, the characters could have her and *The Solid Bet* on the ropes when she reveals she's already attacked Hephaestus. Either way, the characters must race back to the station… if they need an extra push then a distress call from Doctor Jenner will oblige the Players to assist the station.

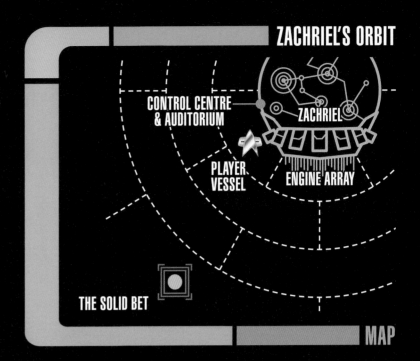

ZACHRIEL'S ORBIT

CONTROL CENTRE
& AUDITORIUM

ZACHRIEL

PLAYER
VESSEL

ENGINE ARRAY

THE SOLID BET

MAP

CHAPTER
07.40

A PLAGUE OF ARIAS
ACT 3: THE PLAGUE

CAPTAIN VULKO'S PLANS

Vulko's plan to raid the station plays out like this:

Captain Vulko bribed several officers and blackmails Chief Dooley to get access to the Hephaestus communications array. She used a combination of Dooley's access, and a program uploaded via the bribed officers' communicator badges to download a new subroutine into the Nostrum EMH. At her command, the Nostrum hologram appears on every screen, station wide and broadcasts the fragments of the Aria plague it has on file. This causes the infected to become actively violent and confused.

A concealed group of Orion commandoes, wearing ear protection, will attempt to break into the station data core and download the entirety of its contents. They will leave in a stolen shuttle and Vulko plans to picks them up at the edge of the system on her way back from Zachriel. Once she has what

CAPTAIN'S LOG

SUPPLEMENTAL

Captain Vulko's attempts to extort Starfleet Medical have failed. Her attempt to release The Aria plague has not. We are at full warp, heading back to Hephaestus to render all assistance possible. I have sent messages to every other Starfleet vessel in the area to render aid and my medical teams are prepping now.

We're going to save the people on that station. We have to. They'd do the same for us.

she wants, Vulko pulls *The Solid Bet* outside sensor range and sends a distress signal on the station's behalf. Once the heat has died down, she will sell the information she's stolen.

SCENE 1: APPROACH

When the Player vessel makes it back to Hephaestus, the station is quiet and running lights are off in several sections. Sensors show the crew scattered across the station, all alive. Any open audio channel to the station will reveal the Aria plague being played over every speaker, infecting anyone who listens. Any visual communication will reveal the Nostrum EMH on every screen, singing the plague.

As a result, the ship is running, if not blind, then deaf. An **Insight + Conn Task** with a Difficulty of 2 will reveal that a single crewmember is currently in a station airlock. They can't be hailed, and sensors show they don't have a suit. Their comm badge identifies them as Chief Dooley, and he is about to open the outer airlock, blasting himself into space. To transport him to a transporter room aboard the Player vessel requires a **Control + Engineering Task** with a Difficulty of 2 if attempting the Task from a transporter room, or Difficulty 3 if initiating transport from a bridge position.

If Dooley is beamed aboard, he'll confess everything; that Vulko blackmailed crewmembers into gaining access to the communications system, that she triggered the outbreak, is planning on robbing the station, even the truth about his father. He's distraught and clearly needs medical attention but gives them one chilling piece of information; the plague victims are frantic, even violent. The fragment they've been exposed to is making them desperate for the whole thing and they're actively dangerous to anyone not infected.

That leaves the characters with two challenges: curing the plague, and stopping the Orions. Both will involve them going aboard the station and dealing with the infected station staff.

SCENE 2: SAVING THE DAY

The crew are faced with a major challenge; how do you cure a plague that wants to be cured, but whose very survival tactics are stopping you from doing so? The information the Players collected at Zachriel, or any infected crewmembers, will be the key to finding the cure, but where to start?

This is a chance for your medical, science and engineering staff to get creative and there are several possibilities, all of which allow for each type of character to get in on the action.

- Have a character volunteer to be infected. If none of the characters do, Jenner is the logical choice for this.

- Attempt a **Reason + Engineering Task** with a Difficulty of 4 to transmit the Aria plague directly to the Escalante project's holo-classrooms. There, downloaded into one of the educational programs, the Player Characters can

safely try to work through the artificial aural intelliegnece, exploring the truth about itself through safe, verbal, communication.

- Use a Basic Challenge to download the auditorium's computers information into a tricorder. This would be a **Reason + Engineering Task** with a Difficulty of 2 to download the data intact, followed by an **Insight + Medicine Task** with a Difficulty of 4 to safely analyze its programming to ensure the full structure of the Aria plague can be uploaded to the Escalante project's computer systems without infection.

A Complication for the Player Characters is:

- **"Acoustic infection"**: The Aria plague spreads acoustically, but contains a vast amount of information that needs to be extracted and given somewhere stable to exist. The infected are so desperate to vocalize and to infect others because that way the information can be passed on faster and the damage minimized. As a result, the Aria plague's own infection tactics will hamper the characters.

In other words, the disease is now also a patient. At this point the Players face a challenge, composed of several key Tasks.

- A complete sample of the virus' musical structure needs to be assembled, whether through scans or infection.

- Retrofit a transmission medium, either the station's communications array or the Players' starship's array.

- Find an information buffer big enough to hold all the information in the Aria plague, the Hephaestus central computer, and prepare it for receiving the plague.

- Broadcast the complete musical structure to cure its victims.

CHALLENGE: PLEASE STATE THE NATURE OF THE MEDICAL EMERGENCY

An **Insight + Medicine Task** with a Difficulty of 3 will reveal that because the EMH is transmitting an incomplete version of the plague its victims are desperate to fill the gaps through communicating with other infected, via song, to complete the musical structure. Alternately, a **Reason + Security Task** with a Difficulty of 1 will reveal that an unusual number of victims are fixated on the screens where the Nostrum EMH appears. As the point of infection, they think it will sing them the rest of the Aria.

There is one staff member on station uniquely equipped to survive exposure to the Aria plague; the Nostrum

Nostrum's old cure, the ultrasonic 'wash' will still work. But doing so permanently destroys an element of the plague's intelligence. By curing Arcturus V, Nostrum indirectly damaged an entire culture, and victims were left with permanent mental scarring.

Creating the ultrasonic wash is a Challenge, with 3 key tasks:

- Access the information from the Hephaestus computer.
- Retrofit the communications systems to broadcast the ultrasonic wash.
- Broadcast.

EMH. Already home to a fragment of the Aria plague, its combination of Nostrum's personality, the information already encoded into it and the huge memory banks of the holodeck make it the perfect choice. All they have to do is get every plague victim on station to sing to the EMH at once and for long enough for it to get a complete structure.

Treat this approach as a Linear Challenge, which breaks down into the following Tasks:

- Transmit the complete version of the Aria plague the Players' have assembled station wide. This is a **Control + Engineering Task** with a Difficulty of 2. This will instantly quell the violent tendencies of the outbreak victims.

- Use the station computer to override every screen or holo array outside the main atrium by making a **Reason + Engineering Task** with a Difficulty 2.

- Raise internal forcefields to create 'rabbit runs', set routes that can only lead to the main atrium by making a **Reason + Security Task**, assisted by the ship's **Structure + Security,** with a Difficulty of 3 from the internal systems station aboard the bridge of the Hephaestus.

- Seal the doors to the atrium once everyone's inside by making a **Control + Security Task** with a Difficulty of 2.)

- Activate the Nostrum EMH by making a **Reason + Engineering Task** with a Difficulty 1.

Every living soul on the station will sing to anyone they can, including any characters who've been infected. Anyone monitoring on sensors will see a massive amount of information transmitted to the EMH which, due to its programming, is able to parse it and convert it into non-acoustic energy. Once the information download is complete, the EMH will go offline and the plague Victims will collapse. Anyone checking their vitals will see they've returned to normal, and anyone checking sensors will see that the plague is no longer being transmitted. They're cured.

ENCOUNTER: STOPPING VULKO

Vulko tasked an Orion commando unit to empty the central core of Hephaestus, setting Starfleet Medical research back years. The commando team will attempt to gain access to the computer core, take the information and then beam back to Vulko's ship.

If the Player Characters attempt to stop the commandos, use the following map, with Captain Vulko and five commando minor NPCs.

HEPHAESTUS COMPUTER CORE

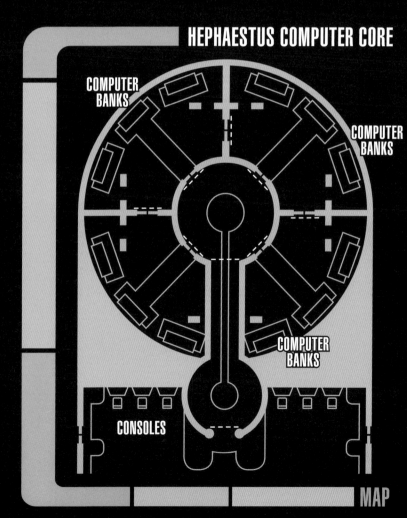

COMPUTER BANKS

COMPUTER BANKS

COMPUTER BANKS

CONSOLES

MAP

Once the plague is 'cured' and Vulko is either captured or fled, the characters will be asked to stay on to help with repairs. The Nostrum EMH must be repaired for one and once brought back online, it will explain that it now contains the sum total of all the Zachra information in the Aria plague. It's still cataloguing the information but it assures the characters that the Zachra want to help and they wish to talk to the Federation about possible relocation. A diplomatic and science team are both en route to the station to begin second contact protocols. Elizabeth Nostrum, and her granddaughter, both have the answers, and the exoneration, they craved and the Zachra finally have a home they won't destroy simply by existing within it.

If Vulko was apprehended by the characters she'll want to cut a deal. She knows a lot about how the Orions operate and will cheerfully plea bargain her way to freedom if given half a chance. If she escaped then the characters will run into her again further down the line. Or perhaps back on Zachriel...

Speaking of Zachriel, Starfleet assemble a multi-ship task force to begin research into the rogue world. The initiative will stage out of Hephaestus as the nearest Starfleet facility and the Player vessel and her crew will be welcome to be a part of it. Otherwise, there are plenty of other strange new worlds to find. Regardless with second contact achieved, a new world discovered, Nostrum and Jenner's reputations both saved and Vulko seen off, the Player's ship and her crew have had a very good week. So good, they'll have plenty to talk about in their next holo-classrooms.

CONTINUING VOYAGES...

The events of this module can be plugged into any number of follow ups. Here are several possibilities.

DIXON HILL...?
The Player Characters vessel is invited back to Hephaestus for the Zachra's official 'moving day.' They're being relocated to a specially designed Starfleet facility nearer the centre of the Quadrant. Nicknamed 'Memory Sigma' it's a combination of a huge holographic array, a data vault and a laboratory complex. There, the Zachra will work to apply their knowledge to making life better for everyone in the Alpha Quadrant.

Except, when the characters arrive at Memory Sigma, the facility appears to be a district of old New York, floating in space. Beaming aboard, they find that the holo emitters have gone wild, and the entire station looks like something out of a Dixon Hill novel. So do the Zachra and the Starfleet personnel aboard. One of whom has just been murdered.

The hard-bitten investigators must play by the rules of the story to discover what happened to Memory Sigma, why the Zachra have no memory of who they really are and just who killed Captain Duffy. If he's even dead. After all, Dead Men Don't Command Starbases.

THE AESCHALUS
A distress signal is received from the Zachriel task force and the Players Characters' vessel is one of those scrambled to assist. When they get there, they discover everything seemingly fine. The crew of the Aeschalus, the lead vessel explain that they were accessing some of Zachriel's databanks and triggered a system shutdown but all's well. Then, the bridge crew are kidnapped by the Aeschalus. The task force inadvertently activated a sleeper program within Zachriel's memory. One built to defend the world at all costs. One that, with four Starfleet vessels in its grasp, is preparing to start a war. Trapped on different ships, the Player Characters must work together to purge the Aeschalaus and her crew of the sleeper program and stop Zachriel going to war with the rest of the Galaxy.

TOXICOLOGY

SON 256
EXO 10
RAD 21
ORG 02

1004-44 1768   1137
2216 1720-23 8225
2180-19 0098   37789
117-04 1002   20010
72-71 2911   32891
                 998

CHAPTER 08.00

THAT WHICH IS UNKNOWN

BY JOE RIXMAN

2565734745768356823124122221

THAT WHICH IS UNKNOWN
SYNOPSIS

The Player Characters are on routine patrol when they receive orders to travel to the Takara system, where they will observe and provide security for the field testing of a new and improved high-yield quantum torpedo. They are to cooperate with the Takarans and assist them with whatever they need to conduct the field test safely. They arrive at Takara and are invited down by Dr. Ja'Brenn, who requests detailed schematics of the crew's ship to help him in determining the safest, yet best possible distance in which to observe the field test. After viewing the destructive power of the torpedo in a simulation, the torpedo is transported to the ship for delivery to the testing location, where it will be activated.

The prototype is delivered to a derelict craft, activated, and, before it can be tested, Klingon birds-of-prey attack the ship, steal the prototype, and destroy the derelict ship before breaking off and fleeing under cloak. The attacking ships are

identified as older models purchased by the Klingon House of Duras and scans confirm Klingons crew the vessels. Questioning Ja'Brenn confirms his torpedo is powered by a quantum singularity which can be tracked. The Player Characters determine the Klingons are on course for the Romulan Neutral Zone and, if lucky, can be caught before reaching it. Starfleet Command orders the Player Characters to track the Klingons and retrieve the torpedo before they enter the Neutral Zone.

An accident occurs on the bird-of-prey carrying the torpedo, apparently killing all on board. The torpedo can't be beamed out and the time it would take to get over to the ship, retrieve the weapon and return to one of the other ships would allow Starfleet to be on top of them. The only choice, then, is to destroy the Federation ship following them and then take the time to retrieve the weapon. Once the remaining birds-of-prey

OTHER ERAS OF PLAY

For those Gamemasters from the *Enterprise* and *Orginal Series* eras, there are a wide variety of options you can use to make your games compatible with the *Next Generation* era game. The important thing to remember is to have fun with it and use whatever options you think will work. Here are a couple of suggestions you can use for your Players:

◀ For *Enterprise* era Players, replace the Takarans with the Antarans. Antarans are a militant race that has been "at war" with the Denobulans on numerous occasions and may attempt to gain Starfleet's favor. As such, the Klingon House of Duras can be replaced by the Orions, who may be attempting to profit from the stealing of military secrets. They have been hired by an anti-Antaran faction of Denobulans who want the weapon, a new and improved version of Starfleet's photonic torpedo. Now, the Players must retrieve the device from the Orions, who no doubt wish to double-cross the Denobulans for their own power-hungry, nefarious reasons, as well as avert another war between two long-time adversaries, whose populations still feel a deep-seeded hatred for each other. This, of course,

provides any Denobulan characters with moral choices of their own throughout the scenario, as well as advancing the duplicitous nature of the Orion Syndicate for further play in games of that era.

◀ For Original Series era Players, the obvious choice to play the antagonists are the Klingons. However, it might be just as fun, if not more so, to use other races. One such suggestion may be to have the Tellarites play as the Takarans and using their age-old adversaries (and fellow Federation allies), the Andorians, in place of the Romulans (used in the *Next Generation* era setting of this game). The Tellarites raid an outlying Andorian research base and steal plans for an upgraded photon torpedo. Why would they do that? Perhaps an insecure faction with the Tellarite government, or a rogue scientist with a particular grudge against the Andorians. Our blue-skinned friends would have no problem taking back what they believe is theirs and, suddenly, the Players must fight to keep a civil war from igniting between two of its founding members.

realize they aren't going to make it to the Neutral Zone before being caught, they engage the ship, bent on destroying it.

With luck, and skill, the Klingon ships are defeated. Now, the Federation crew has to find a way to retrieve the torpedo. Upon doing so, however, they find themselves suddenly surrounded by a trio of Romulan warbirds, who demand the return of their property, allegedly stolen by the Takarans, who violated their space and murdered dozens of Romulan scientists in order to claim the weapon for themselves and the Federation.

Starfleet orders the crew to avoid an interstellar incident with the Romulans at all costs, even if it means returning the torpedo. The crew learns that Takaran Intelligence operatives, in association with their military, captured a Romulan ship, used it to raid a Romulan research facility, and stole the plans for a Romulan version of a quantum torpedo, which uses a micro-singularity for its power source. The Player Characters must decide what to do with Ja'Brenn and find a way to avoid a confrontation between the Takarans and the Romulans.

DIRECTIVES

In addition to the Prime Directive, the Directives for this mission are:

- Protect the Secrecy of this Test

The Gamemaster begins this mission with 2 points of Threat for every Player Character in the group.

THAT WHICH IS UNKNOWN
ACT 1: TAKARANS

SCENE 1: SURPRISE REQUESTS

When the Player Characters are ready, give the log opposite to the captain to read.

The mission begins with the Player Characters arriving at Takara, where they receive word that Dr. Ja'Brenn is awaiting their arrival. He requests an away team transport down to the planet, where he will demonstrate a simulated test of the device prior to delivering it to the vessel for field-testing.

Upon the crew's arrival planet-side, Dr. Ja'Brenn requests detailed schematics of the Player Character's ship, telling them that it is to help him provide the safest, yet closest, distance in which to observe the field test and obtain the best data for further development of the weapon. Afterwards, Dr. Ja'Brenn will instruct the Players to begin preparations for transfer of the quantum torpedo prototype to the Starfleet ship for travel to a designated site deeper in the Takara star system, where the actual field test will take place. Once there, the torpedo will be placed on board a derelict freighter

CAPTAINS LOG

STARDATE 48635.1

We have just received orders to head to the Takara system. This mission is delicate enough to be classified as TOP SECRET — COMMAND EYES ONLY. What I can say is, we are to meet with Dr. Ja'Brenn. He is the lead scientist we'll be working with. Our orders are to help supervise the field test of a new, improved quantum torpedo that Ja'Brenn and his team are currently developing. Starfleet Intelligence has concerns that, with the Romulan border less than twenty light years from Takara, they may know about and intend to steal the device. The crew is expected to be on alert and to provide whatever security measures are needed to ensure no one gains access to the potential weapon, especially the Romulans. It can't be stressed enough that the Federation doesn't want them to have access to something that could conceivably affect the balance of power in the quadrant.

DOCTOR JA'BRENN [MAJOR NPC]

Ja'Brenn is the lead scientist of the quantum torpedo program. He was given the schematics for the torpedo from a friend of his in the military. Ja'Brenn thought nothing of it, until he realized the only way for the torpedo to reach its maximum potential was to power it with a micro-singularity. This connection made him realize that, somehow, the military had stolen the schematics. Quietly investigating, he found proof that his friend had been involved in a military attack on a Romulan research station in disputed space. Scientists had been killed by Takaran military personnel on a raid. At that moment, Ja'Brenn decided to somehow return the torpedo to the Romulans. He began corresponding with them surreptitiously and his contact in the Romulan government agreed to assist him. However, his own government, proud of his "accomplishments" invited the Federation to witness "their success" at creating a new, prototype weapon. His Romulan contact found a way to make that work. Ja'Brenn is a scientist, first and foremost, but he can't let the military get away with what they've done and is just vain enough to not want his government to know he is betraying them.

TRAITS: Takaran

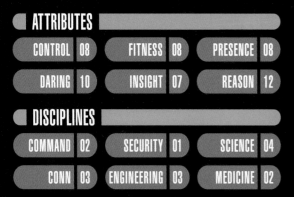

ATTRIBUTES

CONTROL	08	FITNESS	08	PRESENCE	08
DARING	10	INSIGHT	07	REASON	12

DISCIPLINES

COMMAND	02	SECURITY	01	SCIENCE	04
CONN	03	ENGINEERING	03	MEDICINE	02

FOCUSES: Quantum Mechanics, Singularity Physics

STRESS: 9 (12)   **RESISTANCE:** 0

ATTACKS:
- Unarmed Strike (Melee, 2▲ Knockdown, Size 1H, Non-lethal)
- Phaser type-1 (Ranged, 3▲, Hidden 1, Size 1H, Charge)

SPECIAL RULES:
- Immune to Pain

SUBCOMMANDER VORIS [NOTABLE NPC]

The commander of the Romulan fleet knows he is in the wrong by violating the Neutral Zone treaty with the Federation. However, he can't allow what he believes was the wanton theft and murder of Romulan citizens to go unchallenged. Not wanting to get the Romulans directly involved, Voris hired the services of the Duras Family, Klingons seeking power within their own government and willing to assist the Romulans in exchange for back-up and support during their attempts to gain leadership of the Klingon Empire. Once the Klingons failed in their task, he felt he had no choice but to violate treaty and take back what was stolen from the Takarans and the Federation. He believes he is in the right overall and will do what he needs to do to ensure the Federation and its allies don't gain any further from the quantum torpedo program.

TRAITS: Romulan

VALUE: I Will Not Fail in My Duty to the Empire

ATTRIBUTES

CONTROL	08	FITNESS	09	PRESENCE	11
DARING	09	INSIGHT	07	REASON	11

DISCIPLINES

COMMAND	04	SECURITY	03	SCIENCE	02
CONN	03	ENGINEERING	02	MEDICINE	01

STRESS: 12   **RESISTANCE:** 0

ATTACKS:
- Unarmed Strike (Melee, 4▲ Knockdown, Size 1H, Non-lethal)
- Disruptor Pistol (Ranged, 6▲, Vicious 1, Size 1H)

ramifications later, as the Klingons won't simply target engines and shields when they attack, but will target the ship's weapons and warp core. An **Insight + Command Task** with a Difficulty of 3 for detecting some form of subterfuge, although Dr. Ja'Brenn will maintain his story at all times that his concern is for the safety and welfare of your ship during the test (which is, in essence, true).

The Player Characters view the simulated test. A **Reason + Science** or **Reason + Engineering Task** with a difficulty of 4 provides information regarding the simulated test data that only specialists in quantum physics might understand. Dr. Ja'Brenn appears extremely nervous and defensive throughout the test.

and detonated, hence the request for schematics to ensure the safety of the Starfleet vessel.

GM Guidance: *The Captain's choice of whether or not to provide the information Dr. Ja'Brenn requests could have*

GM Guidance: Success of their respective Tasks will provide information regarding the active power source of the torpedo as a micro-singularity, providing a constant supply of almost unlimited power. The detonation of the torpedo implodes the singularity, causing damage to physical structures and to subspace in the vicinity of the implosion, essentially creating a rupture in subspace that prevents a stable warp field. Failure of this Task means that a science observer realizes there are strange readings regarding the power signature of the torpedo without revealing the source as being a micro-singularity.

The simulation goes perfectly and Dr. Ja'Brenn requests the Player Characters transport the prototype aboard their ship and prepare to travel to the coordinates of the actual field test.

A **Control + Engineering Task** with a Difficulty of 1 gets the prototype safely aboard the vessel.

ENCOUNTER: SURPRISE GUESTS

With the success of the simulated testing, you've been asked to safely transport the prototype torpedo to a secret location deeper into the Takaran solar system. Dr. Ja'Brenn is accompanying you, and his torpedo, to the coordinates of a derelict freighter that will be used as the actual site of the field test. Now, you just have to take the torpedo over in a shuttlecraft, place it onboard the derelict freighter, and get far enough away so that you can view the test and record the data real-time in the relative safety of your vessel.

Once the Player Characters deliver the torpedo (**Daring** or **Control + Conn Task** with a Difficulty of 1) and safely place it in the hold of the freighter (**Daring** or **Control + Engineering**, Difficulty of 1), they can return to the ship (**Control + Conn**, Difficulty of 1). From there, the ship can travel to a safe viewing distance (approximately 100,000 kilometers) to observe the detonation and the impact on surrounding space.

Upon reaching safe distance, sensors pick up three Klingon birds-of-prey decloaking near the ship. They immediately open fire. One of the three breaks off its attack and races toward the freighter while the other two attack the Players' ship.

GM Guidance: Depending upon the Captain's earlier choice, the surprise attack allows the Klingons to target either ship's engines or her shield generators. Once the engines are

SHUTTLECRAFT

Based upon the mission at hand, the ship's shuttlecraft are currently designed to move small numbers of personnel or small quantities of cargo over short to medium distances only. They are unarmed, and while they can be refitted with a small phaser banks, they are not configured to do so at this time. Shuttlecraft (of *The Next Generation* era, not the Original Series time) can travel at low Warp.

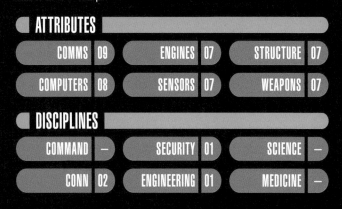

ATTRIBUTES

COMMS	09	ENGINES	07	STRUCTURE	07
COMPUTERS	08	SENSORS	07	WEAPONS	07

DISCIPLINES

COMMAND	—	SECURITY	01	SCIENCE	—
CONN	02	ENGINEERING	01	MEDICINE	—

POWER: 4   **SCALE:** 1
SHIELDS: 4   **RESISTANCE:** 1

CREW COMPLEMENT: 1 or 2, plus 6 passengers

---

damaged, the weapons will become their secondary target. However, if the schematics were not provided earlier, the Klingons will target first the ship's shields and then her warp core in an attempt to destroy the ship. Once the freighter is destroyed, all Klingon ships will immediately cloak and retreat in the direction of Romulan space.

RESOLUTION

Once the ship is disabled and the derelict freighter is destroyed, the Klingons will cloak and leave the field of battle. A sharp-eyed operations officer might notice their last reported heading was toward Romulan space rolling a **Control + Conn Task** with a difficulty of 1.

The Takaran Security Fleet will respond to the battle, too little, too late, but they will be furious and demand the Starfleet Captain's head. A **Presence + Command Task**, with a difficulty of 2, gives the Captain time to formulate the questions that need to be asked here.

GM Guidance: Questions to be asked include, but are not limited to:

- *What are Klingon birds-of-prey doing in Federation space?*

- *Who were in those birds-of-prey? Klingons? Romulans? Another species altogether?*

B'REL-CLASS BIRD-OF-PREY

A light scout vessel, the *B'rel*-class bird-of-prey is used on long-ranged forays into enemy territory, and to raid poorly-defended outposts and vessels. In larger battles, they are used as escorts and grouped into squadrons.

TRAITS: Klingon bird-of-prey

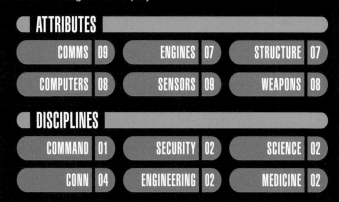

ATTRIBUTES

COMMS	09	ENGINES	07	STRUCTURE	07
COMPUTERS	08	SENSORS	09	WEAPONS	08

DISCIPLINES

COMMAND	01	SECURITY	02	SCIENCE	02
CONN	04	ENGINEERING	02	MEDICINE	02

POWER: 7   **SCALE:** 3
SHIELDS: 9   **RESISTANCE:** 3

CREW: Talented (Attribute 10, Discipline 3)

ATTACKS:
- Disruptor Cannons (Energy, Range Close, 7▲, Vicious 1)
- Photon Torpedoes (Torpedo, Range Long, 5▲, High Yield)
- Tractor Beam (Strength 2)

SPECIAL RULES:
- **Improved Reaction Control System** (Talent)
- **Cloaking Devices** (see p.259 of the core rulebook)

- *Assuming they are Klingons, why are they breaking treaty by using their cloaks in Federation space and attacking a Federation Starship?*

- *How did they know about the torpedo in the first place, as this was supposed to be a top-secret mission?*

- *What happened to the torpedo (was it destroyed along with the derelict ship or stolen by the Klingons)?*

- *Why are the Klingon ships heading toward Romulan space?*

- *How do you track the Klingon ships and find the torpedo so you can retrieve it before they are gone for good?*

Encourage active debate and questioning, with the caveat that time is now of the essence if you wish to locate and catch up to the Klingons. Also, plans for retrieving the torpedo will need to be made and what to do with the Klingons after the fact.

When the Players are ready, read this:

The Takaran fleet has raced off in pursuit of the Klingons. Six ships prepared to go to war and drag the Federation in with them, although it is clear that, even if they were fast enough to catch them, they don't have the firepower to take on three birds-of-prey. Starfleet Command has responded with what can only be described as a terse note: Find out what's going on and, under no circumstances, are you to allow the Klingons to leave Federation space with the Takaran torpedo, especially if they are delivering it to the Romulans, who, we suspect, covet the weapon to use for their own nefarious designs.

GM Guidance: *A couple more questions may be added to the list:*

- *Suspecting the Romulans want the torpedo, did they actually hire Klingons to steal it?*

- *If so, they still needed to know about the test. Do they have an operative on Takara, or worse, have they co-opted the Takaran government? But then, why would the government invite the Federation?*

- *Do either the Klingons or the Romulans have operatives working within the Federation itself?*

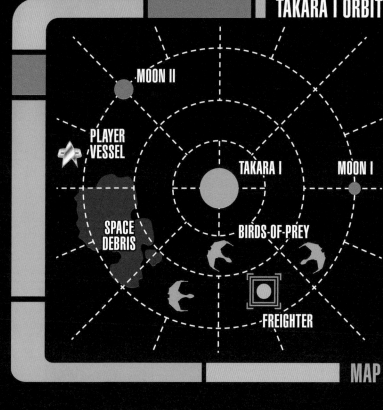

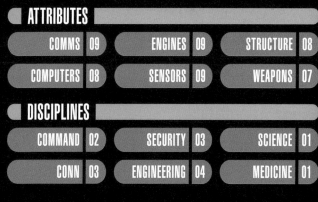

TAKARAN FAST-ATTACK SHIP

Takaran Fast-Attack Ships are built for speed and maneuverability and are intended more to swarm their targets than overwhelm them with superior firepower.

TRAITS: Takaran Small Warship

ATTRIBUTES

COMMS	09	ENGINES	09	STRUCTURE	08
COMPUTERS	08	SENSORS	09	WEAPONS	07

DISCIPLINES

COMMAND	02	SECURITY	03	SCIENCE	01
CONN	03	ENGINEERING	04	MEDICINE	01

POWER: 9   **SCALE:** 3
SHIELDS: 11   **RESISTANCE:** 3

CREW: Proficient (Attribute 9, Discipline 2)

ATTACKS:
- Phaser Arrays (Energy, Range Medium, 6⚔, Versatile 2)
- Photon Torpedoes (Torpedo, Range Long, 6⚔, High Yield)
- Tractor Beam (Strength 2)

THAT WHICH IS UNKNOWN
ACT 2: THE KLINGONS

SCENE 1: QUESTIONS AND ANSWERS

Give this to the Player captain to read:

CAPTAIN'S LOG
SUPPLEMENTAL

The Klingons have brazenly attacked a Federation starship and destroyed the Takaran freighter which apparently still contained the prototype torpedo. Once destroying the freighter, they broke off their attack, cloaked, and fled the scene of the unprovoked attack, believed to be heading toward Romulan space. There are too many questions and not enough time for straight answers, even if Dr. Ja'Brenn was interested in giving them to us. Why is he being so evasive? Our orders from Starfleet were clear: provide whatever assistance was needed from the Takarans and ensure the successful completion of the field test, ensuring no other powers, specifically the Romulans, involved themselves. Those orders didn't include allowing the Klingons to crash the party and end the test before it began. We need some answers and we need them fast.

GM Guidance: This scene sets up the political ramifications of allowing the prototype to be destroyed (or stolen), as well as presenting Challenges and Obstacles to discovering what really happened on the testing range and locating the Klingon ships that have disappeared after attacking your ship. Play up Dr. Ja'Brenn's annoyance that Starfleet allowed the torpedo to be stolen from under their very noses and his reluctance to provide any useful information about the torpedo itself.

CHALLENGE: FINDING ANSWERS TO IMPORTANT QUESTIONS

The answer to one question leads to two more. Most importantly, why would the Klingons risk a war with the Federation by attacking them? Also, what happened to the torpedo? Was it destroyed or stolen? Why wasn't the implosion of the torpedo as powerful as Ja'Brenn had indicated it would be if it had been detonated? Also, sensor readings indicate only radiation from Klingon disruptor fire present and no radiation or subspace damage indicating the destruction of the torpedo. Success with **Reason + Science Task**, with a Difficulty of 3, may provide the answers.

About the Klingons: they're not currently at war with the Federation and are, in fact, on friendly terms, if anyone can be on friendly terms with the Klingons. So why risk it? The Romulans are not so far away that their involvement can be ignored, especially as the Klingon ships are headed toward Romulan space. How might they be involved in this? Was it possible they, or someone else, appropriated three Klingon warships and used them for this act of war, or theft? A **Reason + Command Task**, with a Difficulty of 3, could provide insights into possible motivations.

Why is Dr. Ja'Brenn suddenly being so evasive? Sure, he's angry. His work has been interrupted and possibly derailed by the Klingon attack. And yet, he doesn't seem interested in cooperating with the investigation. In fact, if the Player Characters bring up talk of Romulans and conspiracy, he becomes angry. An **Insight + Security Task**, with a Difficulty of 4, might provide a clue to Dr. Ja'Brenn's nervousness. Upon detailed questioning, success with **Presence** or **Reason + Security**, with a Difficulty of 2, should provide an explanation.

Dr. Ja'Brenn will remind the Player Characters that the Romulans have no reason to be interested in his people, aside from the fact that the Takarans are developing a weapon for possible use by the Federation. Dr. Ja'Brenn argues that the Romulans wouldn't risk violating Federation space and committing an act of war for a simple torpedo. He assures the Players that the Klingons must be responsible and are simply trying to make it look like the Romulans are involved. He refuses to speculate further on conspiracies.

The Klingons could possibly travel by cloak, as could the Romulans. But, again, the question is why. Is the reward worth that level of risk? Who hired the Klingons to steal/destroy the weapon? Or have they chosen to go to war?

GM Guidance: *A review of the ship's sensor logs and the warp signatures of the Klingon vessels will reveal the identification of the ships.* **Reason + Engineering** *or* **Security**, *with a Difficulty of 3, provides history of the ships as being purchased by the Duras Family, who are believed to have associations with the Romulans. That which is unknown is beginning to come into focus.*

Then, there are the questions of how the Klingons knew about the weapon's existence and where the testing was to take place. A **Reason + Security Task**, with a Difficulty of 3, may provide answers when backtracking and searching for some kind of sensor data that shows they were being followed.

GM Guidance: *By now, the Player Characters should have determined that the torpedo was stolen and is currently in Klingon hands, with their ships making good progress toward Romulan space at last report. Characters should begin looking into ways of tracking the birds-of-prey and intercepting them.* **Reason + Conn**, *with a Difficulty of 2, should provide an appropriate challenge to Player Characters attempting to locate the Klingons and follow their trail.*

SCENE 2: SEARCH AND RETRIEVE

When the Players have made their decision, read the following:

Your new orders have been received. Starfleet needs your ship to find that stolen torpedo and ensure the Romulans don't get it, or the Klingons don't KEEP it! Such firepower might give the Romulans an upper hand in the ever-increasing arm's race between the two powers. It can also move the Klingons toward a civil war if it's ever discovered they violated treaty, or joined with the Romulans. However, an interstellar incident with the either the Klingons or Romulans is to be avoided at all costs.

GM Guidance: *It's time to find out what Dr. Ja'Brenn knows, or doesn't know. A* **Presence + Command Task** *can give your ship's Captain the ability to persuade or intimidate Dr. Ja'Brenn into providing more information into what's happening. Options to consider:*

- *Obtaining the correct wavelength of the quantum torpedo's radiation signature;*

- *Was Dr. Ja'Brenn a conspirator in allowing the torpedo to be taken, and;*

- *How to gain this information without creating a diplomatic rift with the Takarans.*

A **Reason + Science Task**, with a Difficulty of 3, will allow the Player Character to locate a faint radiation trail that could be emitted by an operational quantum torpedo.

CHALLENGE: INTERROGATING DR. JA'BRENN

GM Guidance: Questioning Dr. Ja'Brenn should be quite difficult and will eventually provoke a violent, physical response. He appears to be doing everything possible to stall the search for his torpedo, making him an obvious suspect. If the crew begin to doubt his story, Dr. Ja'Brenn will shut down and refuse to cooperate further. If the Takaran government is notified of his behavior and lack of cooperation, it will demand the return of their citizen for questioning in an act of treason.

As a Starfleet vessel was attacked, the Captain has authority over this matter, should he choose to ignore or negotiate with the Takaran government. Should the Players be unable to obtain the information from the Takarans or Dr. Ja'Brenn, there is always the chance they can get the information on their own. **Reason + Science** is the primary combination here.

To locate and track the correct wavelength from the radiation trail without knowing what you are even looking for, you will need to succeed on an Extended Task, with a Work track of 12, a Magnitude of 4, and a base difficulty of 4, with each successful Breakthrough reducing the Difficulty by 1. This will provide the information needed to track the radiation trail. Time is of the essence here, as you need to find the Klingon ships before they successfully enter Romulan space and the sooner this is done, the quicker your ship can respond and retrieve the stolen prototype, so track how many Intervals the Extended Task takes (with each Interval being 10 minutes) but don't give the Players a time limit, only let it inform the following scenes.

GM Guidance: Once Ja'Brenn is identified as a suspect, he will absolutely refuse to cooperate. If he is taken into custody, or learns he is being handed back to the Takaran government, he will attempt to flee and hide somewhere on board the ship. Due to the extremely high Fitness of Takarans, stopping him initially will prove impossible and he will find a way of escaping into one of the Jefferies tubes, where he will wait until he gets his chance to escape.

TAKARAN PHYSIOLOGY

Takarans have the ability to slow their metabolism at a cellular level, allowing them to take massive amounts of damage with little discernible effect. It takes decapitation or complete disruption to actually kill a Takaran, thus their high Fitness and resistance to phaser fire or melee damage. Takarans are immune to pain.

Locating Dr. Ja'Brenn won't be that difficult by using the ship's internal sensors. Subduing the Takaran is another matter altogether. He will fight to the death and will seemingly attempt to commit suicide rather than be caught.

GM Guidance: Once Ja'Brenn is located, he will attack from range at first, then begin melee attacks. He can sustain a great deal of damage, but at the point he realizes he cannot escape, he will attempt to "play dead". A **Reason + Medicine Task**, with a Difficulty of 5, will determine whether or not he is truly alive. Even a success will show only that parts of his unique metabolism remain functioning, but at a very slow rate and only at the cellular level. At some point in the struggle, he will "die" and the Players will have to deal with the ramifications of their actions.

The Takarans will be unhappy when they hear that Dr. Ja'Brenn has died and demand the immediate return of his body to one of the Takaran Security vessels in the area. An autopsy will not be allowed, as it is a matter of profound religious and cultural beliefs that a Takaran body is a sacred temple, not to be "dissected" by outsiders. His body must be turned over to a Takaran military vessel immediately.

At this point, an astute medical officer may recall a previous incident regarding a Takaran's involvement in a possible theft aboard a Federation Starship. An **Insight + Medicine Task**, with a Difficulty of 2, will be enough for the doctor to recall and investigate the situation via medical records from that time.

GM Guidance: Again, the need for diplomacy is required, with **Insight** or **Presence + Command** and a Difficulty of 3, as an avenue to follow to ensure Dr. Ja'Brenn remains on your Player's ship, rather than be handed back over to the Takarans. Should the ship's medical officer recall the nature of Takaran physiology, the Difficulty level can then be reduced by 1 to allow for a continued investigation into the alleged death. If the roll is a failure, Dr. Ja'Brenn must be returned to his people and a nearby Takaran ship will accept his body via transport.

At this point, The Takarans will no longer respond to hails or any form of communication. They will be following and will be at red alert the entire time, but will take no hostile actions against the Player Character's ship.

SCENE 3: UNFORESEEN CIRCUMSTANCES

GM Guidance: Take some time here to encourage your Player Characters to plan a course of action. How are they going to approach this puzzle?

Attempting a **Control + Security Task** with a Difficulty of 1, the Player Characters notice that their ship's sensor are picking up some wild energy fluctuations aboard one of the Klingon

Following the degrading radiation trail of the prototype torpedo, our sensors have finally picked up something, but not what we expected. The Klingon ships have, for some reason, decloaked and stopped on the edge of Romulan space. Sensors indicate they've sent out a distress signal. But to whom? One thing is for certain, if time was a factor before, it's become even more of an urgency now.

vessels. None of the ships are cloaked and two of them appear to have taken defensive positions around the third one. Once your ship gets within Medium range, the Klingon ships will break formation and attack the Player Character's ship at will. The Player Characters will also notice that there are no power readings emanating from the third vessel.

GM Guidance: *The Klingon ships will target the shields of the Player's ship and, if they can break them, will transport boarding parties over. Those Klingons will use both phasers and bat'leths, while the ship continues to target the Player's ship's weapons systems. Meanwhile, the third ship appears dead in space and is emitting high levels of tachyon radiation. It's likely the Player Characters will have to end this with the destruction of the two attacking vessels, but you should encourage the Players to discover an alternative to wanton destruction.*

Once the attack has been repelled, get the Player captain to read the following:

CAPTAIN'S LOG

SUPPLEMENTAL

We've rid our ship of the Klingon intrusion and dispatched their ships, but repairing the ship will take time, but should be manageable. And, of course, more questions have emerged from this engagement. What happened to the third Klingon ship, sitting powerless and, now, flooded with tachyon radiation? Why didn't the Takarans assist and why do they remain just within sensor range, but not communicating?

A **Reason + Science Task** with a Difficulty of 2, allows the Players to determine that the prototype's power source reacted with the Klingon ship's cloaking system, which caused a massive release of tachyon radiation from the prototype that affected the entire Klingon ship.

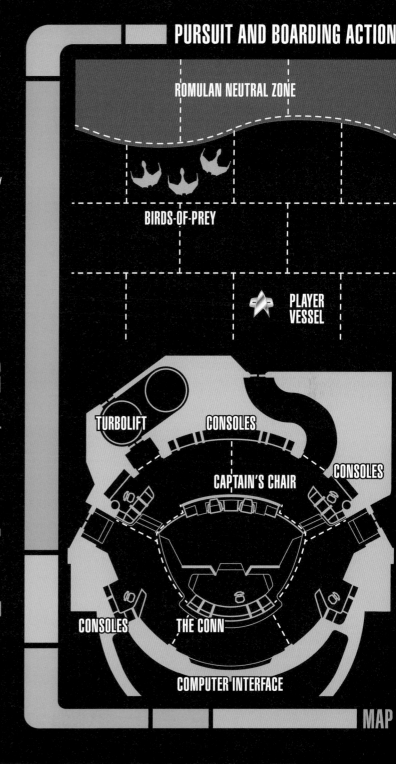

PURSUIT AND BOARDING ACTION

ROMULAN NEUTRAL ZONE

BIRDS-OF-PREY

PLAYER VESSEL

TURBOLIFT   CONSOLES

CONSOLES

CAPTAIN'S CHAIR

CONSOLES   THE CONN

COMPUTER INTERFACE

MAP

OBSTACLE: TACHYON RADIATION

Ship's sensors can determine if the tachyon radiation is lethal and if there are any other power signatures on board the Klingon ship. You can also tell if there are any life signs aboard, however, if the sensors were damaged in the attack, they would have to be repaired first. A series of Challenges can be created, with simple repair tasks, such as identifying the damaged circuits, replacing those circuits with new ones, etc., with a **Reason + Engineering Task** and a Difficulty of 2.

A **Reason + Science Task** with a Difficulty of 1, provides the information that the transporter, even if undamaged, would be unable to penetrate the radiation without transport enhancers. As it is, transporting the prototype over could cause the same effects on the Player's ship as it did on the Klingon ship.

A **Reason + Medicine Task** with a Difficulty of 1, answers any questions regarding the toxicity of the radiation on biomatter (flesh). The concentration of tachyon particles is so dense, that even environmental suits won't protect anyone who goes over there for very long before cellular decay begins to affect everyone.

Either way, Players need to get over to the Klingon ship if they want to retrieve the torpedo. The easiest way to do that would be by shuttlecraft.

An added complication to this option is that environmental suits won't protect Players from tachyon radiation of this magnitude for long and cellular decay will began fairly rapidly, so this option adds yet another time component. There is no known way of blocking the radiation, which means that prolonged exposure will force the irradiated characters to be treated in sickbay until the effects can be reversed.

The Player Characters have no choice but to risk exposing themselves to tachyon radiation poisoning by infiltrating the Klingon ship. Once there, they need to locate the prototype, procure it, and return to the shuttle for travel back to your ship, as the risk of transporting the weapon is too great, even if they can get a lock through the intense field of radiation.

Somehow, the Player Characters need to find a way to disperse the tachyon radiation first, which can only be done locally, on board the Klingon ship itself, or the task of finding the weapon becomes much more difficult. Since transporting the prototype is out of the question, it will need to be carried, which means the away team will need to have a minimum of four characters.

A simple matter of a **Control + Conn Task** with a Difficulty of 1, gets the away team over to the Klingon ship in a shuttlecraft, where the real work begins.

HAZARD: RADIATION EXPOSURE

As the away team enters the Klingon ship, they notice there is no power; this includes lights, gravity and life-support. The radiation will begin to affect them almost immediately. Now, they have to locate the ship's engineering section, or bridge, give it some juice and disperse the radiation as quickly as possible.

The following can be read in increments, allowing the characters to know what's happening to them at each point in the process. If they succeed in ridding the ship of radiation before any severe effects of radiation poisoning manifest, they won't have to know the pain of exposure.

When the Player Characters board the Klingon bird-of-prey, read them the following:

Within moments, you begin to feel a tingle in your extremities.

Then, in short time increments, as the Gamemaster sees fit, read them the following:

After ten minutes, the tingling gives way to numbness and you begin to feel nauseous. You are losing the ability to hold and grasp things, like your phaser or tricorder.

After fifteen minutes, you are unable to walk.

After twenty minutes, you find yourself becoming delirious, unable to reason or think.

After thirty minutes, you will be dead.

A **Daring + Command Task** with a Difficulty of 2 must be attempted in order to remain composed once crewmembers pass the ten-minute mark. Success means that the character remains calm and Momentum can be spent to assist other characters in remaining composed, otherwise, they lose their nerve and flee back toward the shuttle (where the effects will stop accumulating).

Even with success, a **Fitness + Medicine Task** with a Difficulty of 2, must be rolled the next turn or another **Daring + Command Task** with Difficulty of 2 must be made. Each subsequent failure of Fitness makes the difficulty of the next Daring roll one point higher.

CHALLENGE: TACHYON RADIATION DISPERSAL

To quote a famous captain of engineering, "Damage control is easy; reading Klingon, that's hard." The first challenge is finding a way to restore power to a console. Finding the correct engineering console requires a **Reason + Engineering Task**.

Once you find the correct console, characters can attempt to transfer power from their tricorders (or phasers) to power the console, another **Reason + Engineering Task** with a Difficulty of 1.

There will only be a limited amount of power in your tricorder, enough for one attempt at locating the correct sequence of buttons that will purge the tachyon radiation from the ship. This should be a difficult, but not impossible challenge.

Control or **Reason + Security Task** with a Difficulty of 4 and characters bypass the security protocols on the console. Failing the security task means the console is locked out and the characters will need to locate another one (there are a total of four such consoles in the engineering section of the Klingon ship). Remeber, each time a console is approached, another tricorder needs to give up its power to operate it.

Locating the correct seuqence of buttons on that console that will purge the enironmental control systems requires

a **Reason + Engineering** Task, with a Difficulty of 3. Complications that may arise include the possibility of accidentally ejecting the ship's warp core, setting off the auto-destruct sequence or perhaps powering up the ship's tactical systems.

The problems are time and the number of tricorders and phasers available to power up the consoles and succeed at the task.

GM Guidance: This is a good time to remind the Players that they can use the Improving the Odds options of buying extra dice by spending saved Momentum, adding to Threat, spending Determination, etc.

Once the radiation is dispersed into space, locate the prototype (in a nearby cargo bay). A **Reason + Security Task**, with a Difficulty of 1, locates the cargo bay in question. Carrying it will require at least four characters. A **Fitness + Command Task**, with a Difficulty of 1, gets it back to the shuttlecraft. A **Control + Conn Task**, with a Difficulty of 1, gets you back to the ship.

THAT WHICH IS UNKNOWN
ACT 3: THE ROMULANS

SCENE 1: SUBTERFUGE

When the Player Characters return to the ship, read:

CAPTAIN'S LOG

SUPPLEMENTAL

The prototype quantum torpedo is back in Federation hands and the away team is none the worse for wear…

When the Player Characters reach the bridge, they find the view screen filled with three decloaked Romulan Warbirds and the bridge officers on duty called for red alert. The Player's ship is surrounded. Read the following:

The Romulans are hailing. They demand the return of their stolen property immediately or they will open fire and destroy your ship.

The Romulans are not in the mood to talk. A **Control + Command Task** with a Difficulty of 2 will give your Captain time to consult with his crew on a plan of action. The Romulans give the Players a maximum of five minutes to comply. They know they are in violation of the Neutral Zone treaty by crossing into Federation space unannounced.

TRAITS: Romulan Warbird

POWER: 10 **SCALE:** 6
SHIELDS: 14 **RESISTANCE:** 6

ATTRIBUTES

| COMMS | 09 | ENGINES | 10 | STRUCTURE | 11 |
| COMPUTERS | 10 | SENSORS | 10 | WEAPONS | 09 |

DISCIPLINES

| COMMAND | 02 | SECURITY | 03 | SCIENCE | 02 |
| CONN | 02 | ENGINEERING | 03 | MEDICINE | 02 |

CREW: Talented (Attribute 10, Discipline 3)

ATTACKS:
- Disruptor Banks (Energy, Range Medium, 10▲ Vicious 1)
- Plasma Torpedoes (Torpedo, Range Long, 6▲ Persistent, Calibration)
- Tractor Beam (Strength 5)

SPECIAL RULES:
- **Cloaking Devices** (see p.259 of the core rulebook)

GM Guidance: *Again, encourage debate and discussion on a plan of action as to how to deal with the Romulans. One thing for certain is that the Player's ship won't survive long against three powerful warbirds, so an all-out assault won't do them any good. A reminder of Starfleet's orders might help them understand their situation and formulate a plan.*

After the Players have decided on a course of action, read this:

Ship's sensors show a fleet of six Takaran fast-attack ships approaching at high warp. The Romulans have armed their weapons and targeted your ship. You receive a hail from the Romulans. They say your time is up and they are again demanding that which was stolen from them. They are also suggesting that you order the Takarans to power down or face repercussions.

At this point, the Player Characters have a few options:

- **The High Road:** The main objective is to avoid an interstellar incident that could lead to war between the two galactic powers. In the interest of peace, request a summit to discuss the issues. This would include ordering the Takarans to back down.

- **The Low Road:** The objective here is to obfuscate, intimidate, or even threaten the Romulans to disengage and return to their side of the Takaran border. This position is tricky to pull off, but the Players have something the Romulans want.

- **Submission:** Irreparably damage the prototype before giving it back to the Romulans, ensuring neither side has the weapon and must begin from scratch.

Each of these options is covered in more detail below. Note that they are not mutually exclusive. Beginning one course of action does not mean the others will be automatically ignored.

PLOT COMPLICATIONS

Star Trek is about moral dilemmas, the struggle to understand and accept other cultural belief systems and morals, and to look at issues from the often difficult or near-impossible perspectives of other, alien cultures. Consider adding the following two plot complications:

- Dr. Ja'Brenn, thought to be dead (if he is still aboard your vessel), awakens. He quietly takes out a security guard and, locating the prototype, steals it, commandeering a shuttlecraft and leaving the Player's ship. He is taking the torpedo directly to the Romulans. How can you stop him from reaching his goal?

- The Takarans ignore your requests to back down and attack the Romulan forces, leaving the Player Characters with a decision to make regarding which side to back. The Player Characters can attempt to reach out to the Romulans, but the Takarans will need to be dealt with somehow.

GM Guidance: *This section really does focus primarily on diplomacy and the Player Character's abilities to avert an all-out conflict between multiple opposing forces. The Romulans want their property, which they believe was stolen from them by the Takarans; the Takarans want to destroy the Romulans before it can proven to the Federation that they*

them of; Dr. Ja'Brenn wants to return the prototype to the Romulans in an effort to avoid open hostilities between their two governments; and the Federation wants the quantum torpedo, but will they keep it at the cost of war with the Romulans, or will they alienate the Takarans by handing over the prototype and accusing their erstwhile partners of attempting to incite a war?

OPTION 1: THE HIGH ROAD

The United Federation of Planets is known for taking this option more often than not. The challenge here is to address the Romulan accusations of theft and murder by the Takarans, as well as the Federation's need to keep the balance of power from tipping over. The only real way to ensure this happens is to sit down at a table and discuss it.

Obviously, **Presence + Command** would be the default method of getting the two sides to power down and talk. However, one could argue for **Reason** or **Insight + Security** as being just as helpful. The Player Characters can come up with many other plausible ways of talking down the Romulans and threatening away the Takaran fleet before it can attack.

A **Insight + Security Task**, with a Difficulty of 3, could very well provide the Player Characters with the reasons as to why the Takaran military wants to attack, but the Takaran government disavows any knowledge of a theft. It might also explain why Dr. Ja'Brenn appeared to be sabotaging his own program, or at least resisting Federation attempts at retrieving the stolen torpedo.

GM Guidance: Intense roleplaying here, with lots of diplomacy, explanation and discovery. The potential rift between the Takaran government and its own military, the possibility that the Federation has no moral high ground regarding the development of the quantum torpedo and the outside chance the Romulans will take revenge on those involved in the attack in Federation space all ups the ante in terms of tension.

OPTION 2: THE LOW ROAD

The interpretation of Starfleet's orders here skew on the side of ensuring the weapon, regardless of how it was obtained by the Takarans, remains in the hands of the Federation. The Romulans are in Federation space, in direct violation of Neutral Zone treaty, and the Takarans will stand as witness to their transgressions.

Here, the Player Characters have multiple options to explore, including the destruction of the prototype (if we can't have it, neither can you), aiding the Takaran fleet in the attack and potential destruction of the Romulan fleet (in Federation space) or using threats, intimidation, persuasion, and subterfuge in forcing the Romulans to admit defeat and head back to their space.

GM Guidance: This option does not play well in regards to how Starfleet usually operates. However, in keeping with the best traditions of allowing beings to be beings, this possibility must be considered. It is a short-term solution with long-term drawbacks, and a Player Character who insists that she was ordered to maintain the peace at all costs will have a tough time talking her way through this, but could use the letter of the law to justify her decisions.

OPTION 3: SUBMISSION

Again, the Player Character has several options here:

- Simply acquiesce to the Romulan demands and turn over the torpedo, at which point, Dr. Ja'Brenn immediately requests Federation asylum from his government.

- Damage or destroy the prototype and advise the Romulans that such damage occurred while on the Klingon vessel and this was how you discovered it. Players can add that the Klingon cloaking device interfered with the power source of the prototype, creating a deadly flood of tachyon radiation that killed the entire Klingon crew, which their scans will corroborate. Dr. Ja'Brenn will then immediately request Federation asylum.

GM Guidance: This option is the quickest and easiest way of settling the conflict. It avoids all the diplomatic overtures for resolving the situation and yet, in the best traditions of diplomacy, ensures that neither side gets everything it wants. Again, there is some trickiness for the Player Characters in adopting this option, as it does tend to go against Federation principles. However, as with Option #2, the choice must be made available for the Player Characters who sees this as the best way to solve a problem that stems from orders coming down from way above their rank and position.

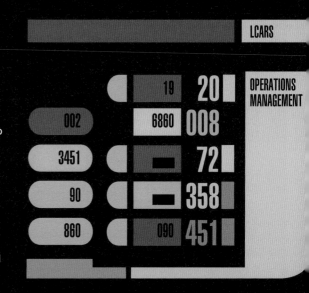

LCARS

OPERATIONS
MANAGEMENT

19   20

002   6860   008

3451   72

90   358

860   090   451

THAT WHICH IS UNKNOWN
CONCLUSION

Consider the following options as you bring this mission to a close:

- The Romulans agree to return to their space without the torpedo but will file a formal grievance against the Federation and will name the Players as directly involved. This will necessitate a review of the Player's performances by Starfleet Command. However, in the end, war was averted, for the time being, and Starfleet is aware of the Romulans' research into higher-powered weapons, as well as Romulan involvement in Klingon internal affairs.

- The Romulans are given the torpedo, with apologies and assurances that Starfleet had no knowledge of the Takaran theft prior to their involvement in the testing stage: The Takarans are incensed and mortified that their subterfuge has been discovered. They attempt to lay blame on a militant faction within their government. Dr. Ja'Brenn will request political asylum in the Federation due to his fear of retaliation by his own government for attempting to return the stolen weapon to the Romulans and fear that the Romulans will assassinate him for knowing their secrets. As far as Starfleet is concerned, the Players succeeded in averting a confrontation with the Romulans and have retained the scientist involved in the weapon's research, ensuring the Romulans do not tip the balance of power with their new weapon and allowing the Federation to continue researching weapons using a micro-singularity as a source of power. Also, the Players might be able to obtain more information from the Romulans regarding their Klingon "allies" as a "favor" for returning their prototype back to them.

- The Romulans attempt to take back the torpedo by force, creating a confrontation that could lead to more deaths and destruction and possible war between the super powers of the Alpha Quadrant: This is, obviously, the least desirable course of action and goes directly against Starfleet orders. Should the Players survive this action, they will have to justify their choices with Starfleet and may not have a career to continue, should they be unable to adequately articulate the decisions they chose

to make. While this could be uncomfortable, it would also make for, arguably, the most dramatic ending, especially if the characters are able to defend their actions for the betterment of the Federation.

CONTINUING VOYAGES...

If you wish to expand this mission into the starting point of a new campaign, or as part of an existing campaign, consider the following questions to continue the story.

- Will the Romulans go home empty handed, but having averted a war?

- Will they go home victorious?

- Will Ja'Brenn be given sanctuary, or will he be handed over to the Takarans as a traitor?

- Will the Takaran military establishment be held accountable by their own government for their actions against the Romulans and how will that affect future relations with the Federation

- What of the Klingon connection to Romulus?

- What happens to the research and science of the quantum torpedo?

CHAPTER 09.00

THE SHEPHERD

BY OLI PALMER

572821400412
3985104697936745

THE SHEPHERD
SYNOPSIS

Most conflict in *Star Trek* comes externally, but how will your crew react when they unknowingly invite the threat on board? In *The Shepherd*, your crew will respond to a distress signal from a planet where there has been a revolt. Details are sparse but either way your orders are clear: journey to Stallas II, rescue the civilians who sent the distress signal, and get them to safety while you investigate what's happened.

The crew was recently on Stallas II, where they assisted in the discovery of a new type of mineral while excavating. Unbeknownst to the colony or the crew, this new mineral was in fact a new lifeform. This lifeform communicates by 'singing', a process where they move the minerals in each other's structure. Humans of course do not talk like this, resulting in a form of mania developing in some of the populace as these new lifeforms try to move minerals around in their brains. The colonists have taken one of these lifeforms and fashioned it into a centerpiece for a statue; free of the earth, the lifeform is now shouting to be heard, amplifying the danger to the humans.

The evacuated survivors have managed to bring this creature with them. They have taken to worshipping it, believing it to be a deity of some sort that will guide them to a better life, a being called the Shepherd.

OTHER ERAS OF PLAY

While The Shepherd is written to work in any era, you can change it up a bit by adjusting the race on Stallas II to the Klingons. Obviously in an Original Series or *Enterprise* era the opening prelude wouldn't work but the trade-off would be the heightened tensions of coming to the Klingon's rescue and having them welcomed on board your ship only for the chaos to ensue!

Alternatively, you could have the planet recently colonized by Andorians who perhaps are a bit more neutral to Starfleet's presence but still welcoming of the assistance. If you chose to switch the race in this style, it would be good to include an appropriate Directive, "Learn more about this race", or "Be on your guard"

DIRECTIVES

In addition to the Prime Directive, the Directives for this mission are:

- Rescue the Colonists
- Preserve the Colony

The Gamemaster begins each session with 2 Threat for each Player in the group.

PRELUDE: DEEP IN THE CAVERNS

Before you get into the meat of this mission, have your Players participate in a flashback scene, when they first uncovered the Shepherd with the colony engineers.

FINDING THE PERFECT GEM
It's been a long shift. The engineers have been working tirelessly to work their way deeper into the mountains; the surface of Stallas II is habitable but it's far more pleasant underground and the decision was made recently to expand their colony into the mountain. The engineers' current goal is to excavate more space to continue the colony expansion.

This is a new colony that is not yet a part of the Federation, but hopefully will be in the future. To strengthen relations, the crew have recently delivered a batch of phaser-based excavators to assist in the colony's expansion. The crew are assisting in the initial deployment of this new machinery to replace the mechanical bores the engineers were using initially.

The mines are well lit, the air adequately circulated and breathable, but this doesn't stop the conditions being fierce. Despite the new equipment and the expertise of the crew to hand its still time consuming work.

At least a third of your Players will be actively excavating the cavern walls, another third will be monitoring the system readings, while the remainder will be taking a break. Those excavating will be operating the excavation equipment; these units are about half the size of a shuttlepod and fire in bursts for several minutes before pausing to cool down and transporting the debris behind it to be cleared away.

The monitoring equipment will be checking a few feet ahead at any given moment for irregularities while also monitoring the geological structure of the material the units are breaking down. It will also be checking for the common issues such as gas pockets and unstable rock types that might lead to a potential cave-in.

One of your Players currently doing the monitoring will receive some very strange readings just as one of those manning a unit will panic as it suffers an electrical breakdown and emits a shower of sparks — something has caused the phaser beam to reflect back. The readings will show a strange material that seemed to change density briefly as the beam first encountered it. They've just found a stone that looks like a crystal, almost glowing with a range of colours as the light catches it. It's an odd, lumpy shape, like two irregular baseballs merged together. It has a vague purple hue and seems to catch the light in interesting ways.

As they look at this delightful stone, your Player Characters will feel different things. Explain that the engineers all appear to be experiencing a range of similar emotions, though one in particular appears to be completely enamored with it, eager to hold the stone in their hands.

- An overriding feeling of bliss and happiness.

- An uncomfortable anger that such a beautiful thing is trapped beneath the stone.

- A sense that this thing is the most precious thing ever to exist.

The main bore of the drill has cracked and broken as it encountered this new stone and work cannot continue.

CHAPTER
09.20

THE SHEPHERD

ACT 1: UNRAVELING THE MESS

SCENE 1: THE BRIEFING ROOM

Starfleet received the distress signal and immediately instructed the Players' crew as the nearest vessel to urgently attend. The briefing will begin with the showing of the distress signal from Stallas II.

THEY'VE GONE MAD!

The person recording the distress signal appears to be crouched down behind an overturned table. Phaser bursts explode over her head as she desperately alternates between talking to the camera, and briefly peering over her cover to return fire. She passes on the following information:

"Please, you need to come back and help us! Something has turned some of the colonists mad, they attacked us in our sleep! We've managed to make our way to the surface, we've managed to barricade ourselves into the

CAPTAIN'S LOG

STARDATE 48425.4

We recently assisted the colonists of Stallas II by supplying a range of new excavation equipment, allowing them to greatly speed up their expansion underground. While demonstrating the new technology, a new type of mineral was discovered that displayed some unusual properties. We relayed our findings to Starfleet Command, who dispatched a science ship to Stallas II to conduct further tests, but before we had left the system we received a distress call from the colony.

arrival center planetside but I don't know how long we can hold out! We have many wounded and we urgently need assistance, please!"

ORDERS, SIR?

The crew are to beam down, round up the survivors and evacuate them back to the ship. They are then to try and peacefully defuse the situation and ascertain what has happened now the two groups are separated. Starfleet advise that the crew are to remain unbiased until they have all the information and have completed a full investigation.

STELLAS II

On the surface, Stellas II is a desolate, harsh planet; a grey mountainous landscape, with a cold wind tearing through the canyons and across the barren surface, and lacking vegetation of any kind. It's little wonder that the colonists here have decided to move underground. Surface side there are a few buildings of standard civilian design; a landing pad for shuttlecraft, an arrivals center to greet visitors, a monitoring outpost, and a large complex that houses the entrance into the underground settlement.

Underground, it's a far more welcoming environment. The colonists have done a very good job of creating a habitable environment and indeed throughout much of the town there is very little rock face on display with most the walls covered in beautiful murals of modern art. High ceilings are bathed in bright light during the day and shrouded in darkness at night to keep its citizens comfortable. There are numerous statues on each street intersection, sitting atop little islands of grass and flowers.

The registered population of Stallas II, according to records, sits at 137 governed by a small council (of which Anthony Simmons is the only remaining live member after the revolt). Security is handled by a local militia, with most of the adult colonists armed to some extent. As they have encountered no other lifeforms on the planet, and live in the relative security of being underground, combat is something the colonists are not used to. The colony has been there for coming close to 5 years, in which time they have made remarkable progress in developing their civilization underground.

The survivors who sent the distress signal are barricaded in the arrivals center. A corridor leads from the center to a large building that houses the entrance to the colony underground. Another corridor leads away from the center to the landing pad for shuttlecraft. There still seems to be some combat but sensors show that it's not as chaotic as it was when the signal was originally sent. It looks like the attackers have briefly fallen back underground to recuperate before launching a new assault.

It's possible to talk to the survivors, as they have control of the communications equipment. They will advise the crew that they have roughly 40 people to evacuate, ten of which are wounded and need urgent medical attention. Unfortunately, there have been several deaths since the distress signal was first sent, and the atmospheric conditions are worsening.

The recommendation would be to take a shuttle down to the planet surface and begin to evacuate the colonists but someone from the crew may wish to attempt to beam them directly on board. Any transportation attempts are at a Difficulty of 4, due to atmospheric conditions. Suggested Complications that might arise would include the worsening of the weather, the attackers deciding to make a renewed assault on the survivors, or even the death of some of the colonists in transport.

Piloting down via shuttle is also made more difficult by the atmospheric conditions, increasing any piloting and navigation Tasks by 1.

SCENE 2: THE ARRIVALS CENTER

The Arrivals Center is reminiscent of a terminal lounge. There's a small display with a little about the history of the planet and its colonization. There are several screens set up to show environmental statistics and scheduled shuttlecraft information — these all currently show error messages or wildly inaccurate information. Comfortable plush seats have been torn free from their mounts and stacked up against the doors and windows leading towards the shuttle docks and the colony entrance respectively. In the corridor leading to the colony entrance, a barricade of destroyed tables lie scattered. It appears the survivors fell back to the center completely and sealed themselves in.

There are two main doors to the center. One set opens into a large corridor which leads to a giant door fixed into the ground, this leads to the main colony. The other set of doors lead to the shuttle landing pads outside, via a long corridor that has artistic murals adorning the walls. The shuttle landing pads themselves are little more than flat areas for craft to safely touch down, and offer little in the way of defense from the weather. The attackers have retreated underground now but peering down the corridor its evident that the entrance is still open and another attack could be launched at any moment.

A NOTE ON TERMINOLOGY

The new lifeform has not yet been named, and instead is colloquially referred to as the Shepherd throughout. Later in the mission, all those affected by the Shepherd are referred to as Followers regardless of if they are from Stallas II or from Starfleet. This is purely to assist you in keeping track of the NPCs quickly.

The dead have been laid respectfully to one side, the wounded are currently being tended to by other colonists, a few children sit in a state of tearful subdued silence while someone tries to comfort and reassure them. The remaining colonists not occupied are armed and keeping watch through the windows of the center; the corridors themselves are mainly glass and so the survivors are able to keep an eye for an impending attack.

If the crew didn't warn the colonists they were beaming down, they're going to get a surprised reception; the children will scream, and a few of the colonists will open fire. The combat should realistically only last one round before one of the colonists manages to take control of the situation when they see the Starfleet uniform, though its assumed that your crew will attempt to defuse the situation first.

SARAH SHIPLEY [NOTABLE NPC]

TRAITS: Human

VALUE: The Shepherd Must be Saved

FOCUSES: Belief in the Shepherd, Diplomacy.

STRESS: 10   **RESISTANCE:** 0

ATTRIBUTES

CONTROL 09	FITNESS 08	PRESENCE 10
DARING 09	INSIGHT 09	REASON 09

DISCIPLINES

COMMAND 04	SECURITY 02	SCIENCE 03
CONN 01	ENGINEERING 05	MEDICINE 01

ATTACKS:
- Unarmed Strike (Melee, 3▲ Knockdown, Size 1H, Non-lethal)
- Phaser Type-1 (Ranged, 4▲, Size 1H, Charge, Hidden 1)
- **Escalation** Phaser Type-2 (Ranged, 5▲, Size 1H, Charge)

SPECIAL RULES:
- **Devoted to the Shepherd:** The worshipper may spend 2 Threat to immediately gain a single Focus for the remainder of the scene.

Alternatively, if the crew take the shuttlecraft down, the survivors will open the doors allowing the crew entrance.

Sarah Shipley is the most organized of the colonists, and the crew will recognize her as the one who sent the distress signal. She will greet the crew with relief before she updates the crew on everything that has happened.

It was the morning after they had opened the newest section of the colony, a botanical area. There had been a party and

an unveiling of a new statue the night before, but many had turned in early. The first dangers she encountered were when the colony alarms burst into life and she opened her door to see fighting in the streets. Those unwilling to get caught up in this made their way to the Arrivals Center, picking up others on the way. As they progressed, the fighters soon turned on them. During the conversations, the following may come up:

- Sarah is legitimately unaware of what has started the fighting at this point.

- She believes in the Shepherd, and is sure it is the Shepherd's intervention that brought the crew to Stallas II so quickly.

If a crew member wishes to press Sarah for more information on the Shepherd at this point, it will be a **Presence + Command Task** with a Difficulty of 3; Sarah is not ashamed of her current belief in the Shepherd but she's going to be reluctant to begin a theological discussion when they could be attacked at any minute. Should the Player succeed, she will explain that the Shepherd is a god, in any real sense that can exist in the Galaxy, that looks after her and the colonists. That Player can *Obtain Information* by spending Momentum to learn from Sarah that she has the Shepherd in her possession.

- Sarah has the Shepherd in her possession, tucked away in a satchel.

All the other survivors know that Sarah has the stone. They will defer to her as the leader of the group, which won't seem unusual to the crew, but in reality, the other colonists see her as some sort of religious leader.

GM Guidance: Don't be tempted to drop any subtle hints here to the nature of the stone! If you ran the Prelude, your Players

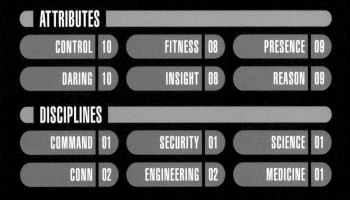

COLONISTS

TRAITS: Human

ATTRIBUTES

CONTROL 10	FITNESS 08	PRESENCE 09
DARING 10	INSIGHT 08	REASON 09

DISCIPLINES

COMMAND 01	SECURITY 01	SCIENCE 01
CONN 02	ENGINEERING 02	MEDICINE 01

STRESS: 9   **RESISTANCE:** 0

ATTACKS:
- Unarmed Strike (Melee, 2▲ Knockdown, Size 1H, Non-lethal)
- Phaser Type-1 (Ranged, 3▲, Size 1H, Charge, Hidden 1)
- **Escalation** Phaser Type-2 (Ranged, 4▲, Size 1H, Charge)

THE STONE

There is no logical reason as to why the crew would even know of the Shepherd but it could be discovered. The crew may insist on searching all the colonists who are beamed aboard, despite the urgency of the evacuation, and they may question why she seems to think this is an important object to take with her.

In this instance, try different options with Sarah. She may try and deceive the crew by saying it's simply an item of great personal importance to her, or perhaps its critical to her studies. Her goal is to get the Shepherd off the planet with her.

Either way, if the crew succeed in convincing or pressuring Sarah into giving it over, let Sarah relinquish the stone if she knows that the crew are still planning to take it off-world. She can think

about how she plans to get reunited with the stone once she's aboard the ship, for now though she and the other colonists are still in danger and she needs to get everyone to safety.

If one of the Players takes possession of the stone, please see Act 3, Scene 2 for information on what should happen to them if they hold onto the stone for any length of time.

If the Shepherd does end up staying on the planet, relocate the future acts on the planet in scene appropriate to places on the planet. Once the colonists are evacuated, it's unlikely that the crew would opt to leave without investigating just what has been going on.

will already be formulating some ideas and do not need fuel for those concerns at this stage – you want the dangerous reveal to occur later on when it is, effectively, too late.

ENCOUNTER: EVACUATION

Evacuating the survivors will need to be done in groups, presumably sending up the wounded first. Some of the colonists may insist on the dead being transported as well as they believe they will never be returning to the planet, a logical reason not to would be that the crew plan to defuse the situation anyway at which point the dead can be properly buried in accordance with any requirements each colonist may have. This will require a convincing social Task however if the crew don't want to delay the evacuation in any way.

Evacuation will take the form of a linear Challenge, as five groups need to be evacuated. Either a **Control + Conn Task** with a Difficulty of 3 to make a journey via shuttle, or a **Control + Engineering Task** with a Difficulty of 4, assisted by the ship's **Sensors + Engineering** to attempt the evacuation of a group via the transporters. The Players may wish to *Create Advantage* with Momentum generated from getting down to the colony, in order to reduce this Difficulty.

The survivors have very little in the way of personal belongings, most are barely dressed considering how the fighting broke out. It's important to take time to highlight how harmless these people look, even those who've been defending the building. There should be no fear that these colonists are dangerous in anyway, one of the children for

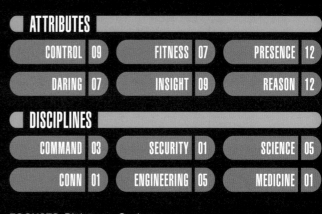

TRAITS: Human

VALUE: We Don't Need to Fight

ATTRIBUTES

CONTROL 09	FITNESS 07	PRESENCE 12
DARING 07	INSIGHT 09	REASON 12

DISCIPLINES

COMMAND 03	SECURITY 01	SCIENCE 05
CONN 01	ENGINEERING 05	MEDICINE 01

FOCUSES: Diplomacy, Geology

STRESS: 8   **RESISTANCE:** 0

ATTACKS:
- Unarmed Strike (Melee, 2⚔ Knockdown, Size 1H, Non-lethal)
- Phaser Type-1 (Ranged, 3⚔, Size 1H, Charge, Hidden 1)
- **Escalation** Phaser Type-2 (Ranged, 4⚔, Size 1H, Charge)

SPECIAL RULES:
- **Devoted to the Shepherd:** The worshipper may spend 2 Threat to immediately gain a single Focus for the remainder of the scene.

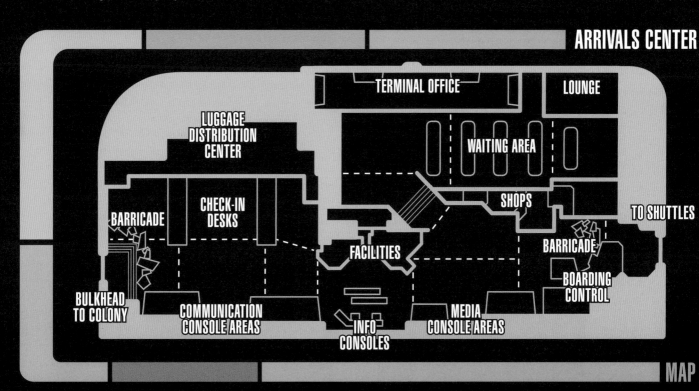

ARRIVALS CENTER

TERMINAL OFFICE

LOUNGE

LUGGAGE DISTRIBUTION CENTER

WAITING AREA

CHECK-IN DESKS

SHOPS

TO SHUTTLES

BARRICADE

FACILITIES

BARRICADE

BOARDING CONTROL

BULKHEAD TO COLONY

COMMUNICATION CONSOLE AREAS

INFO CONSOLES

MEDIA CONSOLE AREAS

MAP

TELEPATHY

Some Betazoid Player Characters may possess the ability to either read a subject empathically or delve into their minds telepathically. For the former, the character senses something else inside the minds of the colonists — a collective belief, a devotion to something. They'll also be in a heightened state of underlying panic, not just from the attacks and the fighting but from a deeper worry from within.

Telepathy may glean more informed results — concentrate here on the belief in a deity. The Shepherd the name in the colonist's mind. Don't mention the stone at this point, instead focusing on their belief that the Shepherd is watching over them and the opinion of the colonist on Anthony Simmons or Sarah Shipley.

example should be clutching a teddy bear and looking lost. It is however an entirely reasonable request to disarm the colonists before beaming aboard but if the crew neglect this fact then make a note for later — this will increase the amount of destruction they find on the ship when the colonists try to seize control of the ship.

As the survivors are being evacuated, the colonists still outside the center will make a renewed assault on the building. At this point it's up to the crew as to whether they try to negotiate from the planet side or regroup on the ship and communicate from there. The Player crew need to desperately beam up survivors, or transport them via shuttle, as phasers erupt in the air around them; the attackers breeching the entrance and pouring through the entrance.

The attackers will quickly stop fighting when they see the last of the survivors have left. They've only been attacking because they were concerned that the survivors were going to seal the colony or destroy the landing port in some manner, but seeing Starfleet officers should mollify them sufficiently to stop attacking.

WHO IS ATTACKING WHO?

At some point the crew will be speaking to the remaining colonists on the planet, either in person if they stayed behind or via a comlink. The remaining colonists will be grateful for the Federation's assistance in ending the fighting. Their spokesperson, one Anthony Simmons, will explain that the group the crew now have on board their ship were in fact the ones who started the fighting. He'll ask for medical assistance to help their injured, and invite the crew to meet so this can be discussed.

An **Insight + Security** or **Command Task** with a Difficulty of 3 will show that Anthony is telling the truth, or at least what he believes. The *Obtain Information* Momentum spend will

reveal that he's maybe hesitant, and not entirely sure of the facts. Spending additional Momentum will reveal that he knows a bit more about the reason the fighting broke out: he believes that Sarah's group were trying to harm the Shepherd in some way. Anthony is as fanatical as Sarah.

Of course, Sarah Shipley will vehemently deny this and beg the crew not to fall for Anthony's lies. If Players try to ascertain if either side is lying, they'll find that both sides believe they did not instigate the fighting but both sides are hiding something.

The problem is that the fighting started out like all good brawls — with little coordination or planning. The two sides formed after the fighting started, each believing the other side were trying to harm the Shepherd in some way. It just happened to be that Sarah's group were the weaker of the two and forced to fall back, but fortunately for her she managed to collect the Shepherd on route.

Both sides believe they are innocent and that the other is dangerous. The majority of the colonists have developed some level of fanatical devotion to the Shepherd by this stage, though the ones who are still on the planet will slowly start to regain a little composure the longer the Shepherd is away from them.

THE SHEPHERD

The Shepherd is in fact a new lifeform, one of many that live within the terrain of Stallas II. Silicon based, these lifeforms communicate by magnetically pulling the minerals around each other. They have been dimly aware of the arrival of the colonists but unsure of what to make of them. They perceive their surroundings through magnetic energy, and feeling the vibrations and movements around it. The colonists however found one of their kind, and it tried its best to communicate in the only way it knew. It tugged and pressed the minerals around in the colonists' minds, trying to persuade the humans to return it to the rocks and leave it alone.

The attempts at communication resulted in the colonists experiencing temporary bouts of mental instability. They became easily influenced, developing a strong affection for the stone they had found. It was decided that this beautiful stone would make a fine centerpiece for a statue, so it was handed to one of the artists to work their magic.

The sculptor began carving the lifeform into the shape of an eye, driving it to incredible pain and causing it to cry out to its kind in the surrounding caverns. The lifeforms worked together to try and make their presence known to the colonists, but this just boosted the mild lunacy that had been developing in the town.

During the celebration of the new sector and the statue, as the alcohol had loosened up some thoughts, the colonists began to voice to each other the belief that been developing amongst them — the stone was in fact a god, something that was guiding them and keeping them safe. Those who actively prayed to the stone directly experienced surreal visions, a fantastical display of colors, an array of pleasing emotions — while they believed this to be a direct will of the Shepherd, it was in fact down to their closer proximity and increased suggestibility. These were all effects of the lifeform trying to communicate.

The fighting started over a misunderstanding, but the end result was that both sides believed the other was seeking to destroy the Shepherd. Sarah's goal is to get the Shepherd to safety, while Anthony has taken control of the other side and managed to persuade them that the Shepherd will still be watching out for them regardless of where it is. While some of the remaining colonists don't believe Anthony and at present still cling to the notion that it is a godlike being, they recognize the sense in Anthony's commands and comply for the benefit and safety of everyone.

The longer the Shepherd remains among the colonists, the further into mania they sink. Even when the stone is safely concealed away from the group, they colonists still believe in the Shepherd. Given time away from the influence of the lifeform, and extensive therapy, the colonists can be cured. For now, however, that stone is now aboard your Players' ship and it is still trying desperately to communicate with those around it.

THE SHEPHERD
ACT 2: THE SHEPHERD

CAPTAINS LOG

SUPPLEMENTAL

It's unclear at this stage where this sudden aggression has originated from but we intend to get to the bottom of the matter quickly. While we have stopped the fighting for now, we need to investigate both sides to determine what has caused the matter and how to resolve it — its apparent at this stage that we are not being told the full story.

SCENE 1: THE INJURED

Whether the crew are actively checking on the colonists in the ship's sickbay or planetside, the results will be the same — while the wounds are for the most part treatable, the readings will show unusual brain activity in the colonists. Aside from the injuries and the odd readings, there appears to be strange disruptions around their bodies; parts of muscle seem to have warped, internal scarring seems to have formed in some extreme cases, organs too have suffered a similar kind of manipulation. More tests can be run of course but they won't highlight too much this early on beyond the fact that mild trauma seems to have occurred across the body.

If any of the crew wish to pursue studies on the colonists, they can do so with a **Reason + Science** or **Medicine Task** with a Difficulty of 2. A success will highlight that the damage has been caused recently by something manipulating the minerals in the subject's brain. This is explaining the odd behavior of the colonists (and any crew subsequently affected by the Shepherd going forward), and any Momentum spent here could *Create an Advantage* to assist in Act 3 when the crew are attempting to construct something to thwart the Shepherd.

Sarah and the colonists will be grateful for the assistance but oddly secretive. Regardless of if they are assigned quarters, they will group somewhere and talk quietly amongst themselves. If anyone actively tries to befriend the colonists, they'll start to pick up snippets about how they believe in the Shepherd. Any Tasks to decipher more information from the colonists regarding the Shepherd will be made, at this stage, with reasonable Difficulty.

THE EFFECTS ON THE REST OF THE CREW

After a few hours on board, the Shepherd's influence will already be felt by those around it (whether it's still in Sarah's possession or somewhere else in the ship). The Shepherd now recognizes it's in an entirely alien environment and is panicking. The NPC crew or Supporting Characters near the colonists will begin to experience visions (sped up if any of them have been able to see the Shepherd physically).

This can be introduced subtly at first. For example, if you're about to beam back down to the surface, it's clear the transport operator looks a bit dazed and hesitant. While speaking to the doctors in sickbay, they might seem a bit emotional, giggling or becoming distressed inappropriately.

SCENE 2: INVESTIGATING THE STATUE

There is a chance that by this stage the Players still aren't aware of the significance of the stone, or the statue it was originally fashioned into. The wounded on the planet side have been gathered around the statue however because it was where the initial largest number of causalities occurred, and there's also the belief that the statue itself may still bring good fortune despite its defilement.

This is a great chance to give the Player's the first piece of the puzzle. As they enter the area, the dominating feature should be the statue itself. It depicts a stylized figure standing tall with its hands stretched upwards and it's clear that it used to be holding something in its grasp. The statue now however is twisted and buckled, almost melted in appearance, its form both sickening and alien to behold.

If a Player scans the statue with a tricorder, attempting an **Insight + Science Task** with a Difficulty of 1, they will learn that the statue's structure has been oddly manipulated at a Molecular level, its fabric twisted and pulled in a unusual formations. The tricorder essentially picks up many different elements in the statue — magnesium, iron, zinc, copper as well as glass, many different stones and other minerals.

They'll also notice hairline cracks in the rock, as if a force of some kind of wave has been affecting it. *Obtain Information* Momentum spends will show that the center of the statue where the Shepherd stone resided was the source of this unusual tampering, or that the hairline tears are similar to those seen in the colonists, linking them to the phenomenon affecting the statue.

If approached, Anthony will explain that the colonists who revolted did this damage as they stole the stone. The reality is that this was caused by the lifeform initially as it tried to free itself — as the statue warped before the eyes of the remaining colonists earlier that morning, some took it as a sign that the stone should be taken upwards so others may learn of the Shepherd, others believed it should be kept close to them, remaining with the devout.

If the Players take a moment to read the mood of the area with the Insight Attribute, they'll be able to pick up on the fact that people seem more upset than expected for a simple stone being removed. Anthony will also betray the occasional flicker of distress, especially if he thinks there's a chance that the stone won't come back. While he's one of the least affected, he's aware that the colonists seem to have some unnatural affection for it and he's not sure of how long he can keep order at present.

If the Players ask about the stone itself, Anthony will lead them to Jasmine Belfont, the sculptor who originally worked on the stone. She has a wealth of information regarding the compound of the stone. She'll happily discuss the information but it's clear that something isn't right, and a few times she should slip up that she in fact believes the stone to be a supreme being of great power and importance.

SPREADING THE WORD OF THE SHEPHERD

Meanwhile, back on the ship, the influence of the Shepherd's Eye is taking root in the ship's crew. If the Players come back to the ship, or try to communicate to someone on the ship, they'll find there's a 1 in 6 chance that the person has become unstable and is sharing the colonist's religious propaganda.

WHY SCULPT THEIR GOD?

Two key facts to remember when revealing information about the colonists' belief to your Players. First of all, when they initially uncovered the stone, they predominantly believed it was simply a very beautiful stone. Some of them may have admitted that it made them feel good but that's as far as it went.

By the time Jasmine had completed her statue, the mania had taken a stronger hold in the colonists, with the initial outburst

from the lifeform when Jasmine began working causing this development to speed up considerably.

At its completion, some may believe that Jasmine has given an immortal life a beautiful form. Others may believe that the stone is simply a device to communicate with their new god. Either way, no one believes Jasmine has caused harm to the Shepherd with her work.

Like the colonists however this doesn't turn the crew members into zealots. Instead they are simply more favorable to the idea that the survivors should be escorted promptly to the nearest starbase. The more outspoken of the survivors will be talking about finding a new planet to colonize, already dismissing Stallas II. Some will even be caught suggesting that the remaining colonists are sinners, unworthy of the Shepherd.

This will affect the Players if they try to do anything to help the colonists down on the planet, such as providing supplies or medical assistance.

If the Players are able to persuade the colonists to let them study the Stone, this will speed up the process of understanding that the Shepherd is indeed a lifeform. If not, this realization won't potentially be confirmed till the crew explore the dig site later in Act 2.

SCENE 3: JASMINE'S OFFICE

Jasmine's office looks like it started out as a professional studio but has given way to a chaos of paper diagrams, rock samples, various tools, and old coffee cups. A table in the center of the room holds a scale model of what the statue that housed the Shepherd looked like initially: it truly is a work of art, and it's clear that Jasmine is talented.

Jasmine will be welcoming to her guests though a bit distracted. She was caught up in the fighting and boasts a few grazes and bruises, and she's also distressed at the destruction of the statue. She will give the crew full access to her notes and geological study reports but if the crew at any point appear to mock her or look to be actively trying to disprove the existence of the Shepherd then she will get very defensive. Jasmine is one of the most strongly affected by the Shepherd having worked with it extensively, and she wants nothing more than for the Shepherd to be returned.

If the crew upset her, she will not restrict access to the files, but she may insist on the crew leaving and taking a copy of the files back to their ship for study.

THE FILE CONTENTS
The files will dictate the reports of the miners from the Prelude, explaining what happened. They will also share the geological findings, highlighting the sudden inexplicable change in density as the drill encountered the new stone, as well as scans of the surrounding area.

Attempting a **Reason + Science Task** or similar roll with a Difficulty of 2, a crew member will notice that the readings show the same ripple effect witnessed on the statue in the rock around where the Shepherd was found, and that this actually reveals the locations of several other similar geodes in the area.

JASMINE BELFONT [NOTABLE NPC]

TRAITS: Human

VALUE: My Work is Important

ATTRIBUTES
CONTROL 08	FITNESS 11	PRESENCE 07
DARING 09	INSIGHT 10	REASON 11

DISCIPLINES
COMMAND 03	SECURITY 01	SCIENCE 05
CONN 01	ENGINEERING 05	MEDICINE 01

FOCUSES: Sculpting, Geology

STRESS: 12   **RESISTANCE:** 0

ATTACKS:
- Unarmed Strike (Melee, 2🗡 Knockdown, Size 1H, Non-lethal)
- **Escalation** Phaser Type-1 (Ranged, 3🗡, Size 1H, Charge, Hidden 1)

SPECIAL RULES:
- **Devoted to the Shepherd:** The worshipper may spend 2 Threat to immediately gain a single Focus for the remainder of the scene.

A SECOND SHEPHERD

How would the colonists react if they uncovered another stone? They will default to believing it's a part of the Shepherd, convincing themselves that seeing as the Shepherd is a god then it is capable of existing in two places at once. With that in mind, they will not be willing for the crew to take this one off the planet surface as well and brute force attempts to do so will result in fighting. Finding another one of these lifeforms however will allow the crew to conduct tests on how to deflect its attempts to communicate with greater success.

Having a second Shepherd should reduce the Difficulty of creating a solution to combatting the Shepherd's attempts at communication in Act 3.

SCENE 4: THE DIG SITE

It's possible the crew may ask to see the dig site, a request that won't be considered abnormal but Anthony (or any of the other colonists on the planet who are asked to take the crew there) may seem a bit surprised that the crew are showing an interest in something so mundane.

Since the day they found the Shepherd, digging had been progressing at a more controlled pace. While the colonists may be currently under the effects of the Shepherd's attempts to communicate they still recognize that there may be more unknown geodes sealed in the cavern walls. There's also the issue that they didn't know they had come across the Shepherd till they were right on top of it — the equipment has since been recalibrated to run deeper penetration tests as the equipment digs.

It will be possible for the crew to boost the equipment with their own advanced tools from the ship to find more 'Shepherds' if they were to choose to do so. If they were to find another one of these lifeforms, they'd have the upper hand in the next Act as they'd be able to study an undamaged one without too much interference.

If a crew member successfully learned about how to find other Shepherd's in the previous scene, this will lower the Difficulty of finding another geode.

THE SHEPHERD
ACT 3: GOD IS IN HEAVEN

STARFLEET CREW [MINOR NPCS]

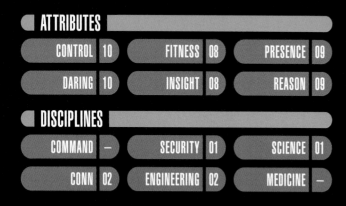

TRAITS: Starfleet

ATTRIBUTES

CONTROL	10	FITNESS	08	PRESENCE	09
DARING	10	INSIGHT	08	REASON	09

DISCIPLINES

COMMAND	—	SECURITY	01	SCIENCE	01
CONN	02	ENGINEERING	02	MEDICINE	—

STRESS: 9   **RESISTANCE:** 0

ATTACKS:
- Unarmed Strike (Melee, 2▲ Knockdown, Size 1H, Non-lethal)
- **Escalation 1** Phaser Type-1 (Ranged, 3▲, Size 1H, Charge, Hidden 1)
- **Escalation 2** Phaser Type-2 (Ranged, 4▲, Size 1H, Charge)

SCENE 1: THE BRAWL IN THE MESS HALL

The crew will be interrupted with news that a full-blown fight has erupted in the mess hall on-board their ship. By this stage, the effects of the Shepherd will have spread around the ship partially, and while minor disputes have been flaring up for the past hour it's turned into a full-on brawl in the mess hall. Tables have been tipped over, punches are being thrown, drinks being smashed — it's a chaotic mess.

By the time the crew make it there however things will have escalated. Security will have tried to defuse the brawl, but unfortunately by this stage some of the security staff will be under the effects of the Shepherd (particularly the ones that have been guarding the colonists on board, who will have also been listening to the colonists' story). This has resulted in the use of phasers in the fight, albeit set to stun.

It will take a calm, commanding voice to stop this fight from carrying on further. Alternatively, the crew may think of a way to incapacitate the occupants of the room with noise or similar. Suggested Tasks include **Presence + Command,** or **Insight + Security**. If you feel your Players have been

CAPTAIN'S LOG

SUPPLEMENTAL

Our investigations remain ongoing but it is becoming apparent that the trouble the colonists are in involves the new mineral discovered on Stallas II. The colonists have, seemingly overnight, developed a form of religious zeal for the stone which has caused a split in their society. More alarming however are the reports I've begun receiving that this zealous nature has spread to my own crew. Time has become critical now in resolving this matter.

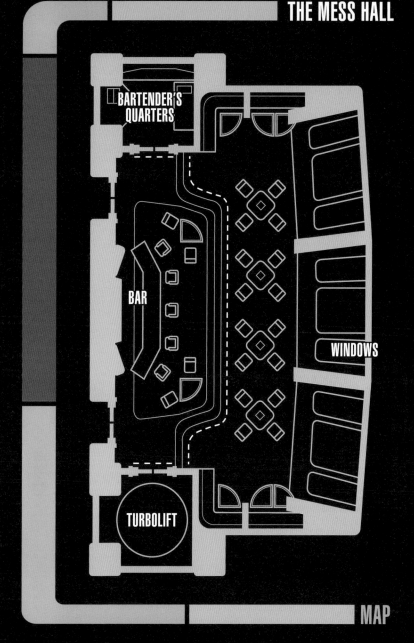

BARTENDER'S QUARTERS

BAR

WINDOWS

TURBOLIFT

MAP

unchallenged up to this point, this could be a good time to resolve this as a Challenge and require instead at least 3 successes from around the group to bring the mess hall under control.

If combat breaks out, assume there are 12 active combatants (6 per 'side'). The aggressors nearest the entrance give your Players an edge to resolve the situation.

SCENE 2: CONFERENCE ROOM

Things are getting worse. Regardless of the outcome of the brawl, there will be reports coming in from all areas of the ship. Ranging from simple arguments through to physical fighting, things are quickly getting out of hand. If the crew try to track where the colonists are they will find they've gone missing: in reality, most of them are currently en route to main engineering where they plan to take control of the ship. A third of them however have spread out around the ship, lost but still preaching the word of the Shepherd.

The crew will need to formulate a plan to deal with this quickly. The remaining sane top ranking officers have congregated in the conference room with the crew while they try to take back control of the situation. A status report along with suggestions will be presented:

- A rough estimation suggests that by now at least half the crew are acting under the control of the Shepherd.

- If the crew haven't already uncovered this information directly, it should be confirmed that the Shepherd is in fact the source of all the problems and that it's not a disease or something contagious.

- If the crew have learned that the Shepherd is trying to communicate based off of their findings at the dig site, and share this information with those in attendance, an idea may be suggested to combat the communication attempts through either an engineering based method or a medical solution. An appropriate roll will be required by the crew members to see if this can be done successfully.

- Someone will suggest sending an alert to the nearest starbase, appraising them of the issue, and going to red alert.

If your crew show no interest in developing a solution or remotely investigating what could be the cause of this chaos, skip to Scene 4 and raise awareness that the Followers have secured control of main engineering.

SCENE 3: MOVING AROUND THE SHIP

It's assumed that the discussion in the conference room will see the crew trying to come up with a way to prevent the effects of the Shepherd. This scene will take place in a suitable location: if for example they're pursuing the idea of a medical solution then logically they'll be in either sickbay, or a suitable science lab.

Moving around the ship is going to be difficult at this stage. The crew will come across pockets of other officers fighting each other, there will be wounded trying to make their way to safety. Moving between locations will trigger a small scene, with one of these options of a combination of them:

- **The crew come across the aftermath of a battle.** Phaser burns mark the walls, an injured Starfleet officer lies slumped against the wall while someone

ARE THE CREW AFFECTED?

If the crew have been around the Shepherd for extended periods of time, it'd be reasonable to assume that they too would fall under the effects. In the event that a crew member does spend prolonged time with the stone, have them attempt a **Control + Command Task** (including any relevant Focuses or Traits) with a Difficulty of 4. If they succeed, the Shepherd fails in its attempts to communicate. If they fail, the Shepherd succeeds in its mineral manipulation.

While the crew member is now a lot more impressionable, they will exhibit a certain amount of irrational behavior (how this is portrayed is down to the individual Player) and

they will be favorable to the colonists on the ship. This doesn't mean that they are suddenly willing to give in and try and take control of the ship — they are still trained members of Starfleet who will be logically wanting to prevent any harm befalling the ship.

Most Players will likely revel a little in being able to play their characters as mildly unhinged, but some will try and ignore their new mental state. In this instance, whenever they make any kind of decisive roll whisper to that Player, "Is this what the Shepherd would want? Maybe the colonists are on to something…"

It's your job to fill that Player with doubts about everything they've uncovered so far. The longer they're around the Shepherd, the more you should ramp up those doubts. When the Player comes into contact with the Shepherd towards the end of the Act, increase the Difficulty to any rolls that would see the Player try and harm the Shepherd in anyway by 1.

tries to administer their wound as best as they can. If questioned, the crew will learn that a small team made up of both colonists and Starfleet officers opened fire on them, and succeeded in taking a few prisoners. They overheard that they were on their way to engineering.

- **The crew stumble into an active battle.** The colonists are now armed and are fighting off a security team. It's clear that the colonists are trying to encourage the opposite force to throw down their weapons and let the Shepherd guide them. There will be an equal number of colonists to Players and at this stage they are not interested in giving up themselves easily.

- **A lone colonist child of about 8 is wandering the corridor, looking for their mother.** The child is not actively affected by the Shepherd, having never been near enough the stone, and doesn't quite understand what's going on. They will have mixed reactions to the crew, a combination of fear and desperation — they just want to go home.

- **A corpse will be lying in the middle of the corridor, either Starfleet or a colonist.** This can serve to highlight the severity of what is currently unfolding around the ship and increase the urgency to resolve it quickly.

SCENE 4: THE LAB

The crew will hopefully have made it to somewhere equipped with the tools they need to create their solution — this will likely be a lab, or at least somewhere where they are capable of accessing the equipment they'd need. For example, a shuttlebay may have the basic tools needed to construct something that would insulate humans from the effects of the Shepherd. Try to be flexible with your Players — the final scene of this Act should be quite intense and dramatic, and right now your goal is to build the pressure without boxing your Players into a place of frustration that "kill everyone" becomes the only desperate resolution left.

You should present this as a Group Challenge, with Players trying to successfully complete the following tasks:

- **Establish the manner in which the Shepherd is affecting people.** This should be, initially, a Difficulty of 4 but lower the Difficulty based on the crews' success so far. If they've already learned how the Shepherd acts based on their findings at the dig site for example then this should be lowered accordingly. The Difficulty should also be lowered if they took time to analyze those affected by the Shepherds at the beginning of Act 2 (or since then).

- **Come up with a suitable theory in which to negate that process.** The crew will likely have a few ideas that they wish to run with, create suitable rolls to have them explore each hypothesis, and then choosing their most successful one to run with.

- **Build a solution that enacts the theory.** You may wish to break this up into smaller tasks depending on the complexity of their solution. The more powerful their solution appears to be, the harder it will be to create. For example, a solution that will only work by placing the Shepherd inside a container will be relatively easy compared to a program that will generate enough static in the whole room to cancel out the Shepherd's attempts at communication. See *The Scientific Method* in the **Star Trek Adventures** core rulebook (p. 157)

Upon completing the Group Challenge (or after failure), the lights will dim and the computer will announce that emergency life support has been engaged. Checking with the computer, the crew will learn that control of the ship has been successfully diverted to engineering. The followers of the Shepherd are now in control.

GM Guidance: If the crew had decided to go to engineering to build their solution, they will find the fighting in full action there, and they're going to struggle to get close. This should be an encouragement to fall back and develop the solution in safety for now, but if not then proceed onto Scene 4.

ENCOUNTER: MAIN ENGINEERING

By this stage, the corridors are mostly deserted: the ship's crew that aren't affected by the Shepherd are safely secured in their quarters, or have retreated to sickbay. Otherwise, those that can fight are currently trying to get into engineering where the colonists and the affected star fleet officers have barricaded themselves in.

The wounded and dead will litter the hallways, more scenes of destruction and confrontation will greet the crew as they get closer to main engineering. Some of the dead Followers will have scrawled messages on the walls in their own blood, begging for the Shepherd to guide them to safety. The occasional surviving Follower will be struggling as crew members try to get them to sickbay, crying out that the Shepherd will save them and to let them go. It should be possible to move around now without encountering combat but there should be enough chaos to suitable unnerve your Players.

The corridors leading directly to engineering will have force fields set up to prevent access and the actual doors have been locked shut. Inside, the followers of the Shepherd are actively rerouting various system functions to prevent

THE WARP CORE

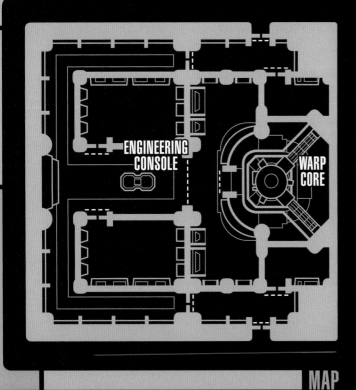

ENGINEERING CONSOLE

WARP CORE

MAP

FOLLOWER [MINOR NPC]

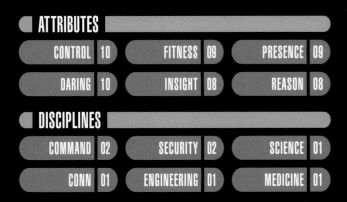

TRAITS: Human

ATTRIBUTES

CONTROL 10	FITNESS 09	PRESENCE 09
DARING 10	INSIGHT 08	REASON 08

DISCIPLINES

COMMAND 02	SECURITY 02	SCIENCE 01
CONN 01	ENGINEERING 01	MEDICINE 01

STRESS: 11   **RESISTANCE:** 0

ATTACKS:

- Unarmed Strike (Melee, 3▲ Knockdown, Size 1H, Non-lethal)
- **Escalation** Phaser Type-2 (Ranged, 5▲, Size 1H, Charge, Hidden 1)

SPECIAL RULES:

- **Devoted to the Shepherd:** The worshippers may ignore the cost to *Keep the Initiative* for their first Round of combat.

external control but there is also dispute amongst the followers themselves: some wish to proceed to the starbase as planned, some wish to find another habitable planet, while some wish to open fire on Stallas II and kill the 'sinners.'

To add further chaos, the Shepherd has found what it thinks is a lifeform closer to its own kind — the warp core dilthium crystals. It's trying to communicate with the warp core now, sending it into erratic behaviour and causing random power fluctuations.

When describing this scene, ensure that you keep the energy high. You need to impress upon your Players the pressure of this situation, and encourage them to react fast. This shouldn't be a moment to sit down and calmly review their options — everyone on board the ship is at risk now and the crew are going to likely end up dead if they don't act quickly.

Upon opening the doors, it's clear that the colonists are doing the following:

- Sarah, whose mind is now a jumble of disconnected thoughts, is on her knees before the warp core, holding up the Shepherd towards it. She is sure this is a way for the Shepherd to control the ship directly (of course it's not, unless the Shepherd's will is to blow up the ship). Some other followers are surrounding Sarah, also on their knees in a state of worship as Sarah speaks out barely coherent prayers.

- Initially there is a group guarding the entrances and a group working at the various consoles doing whatever they can to allow the Shepherd to access the dilithium crystals.

- The computer will announce a critical warp core failure is imminent.

This combat encounter takes place alongside an Extended Task to repair the warp core. Typical Tasks involve **Control + Engineering**, **Daring + Science**, or even **Insight + Conn**. The Extended Task has a Work track of 15, a Difficulty of 3, and Magnitude of 3, with the following special rules:

- While the Shepherd is in Close range to the warp core it imposes a Complication, raising the Difficulty of Tasks in the Extended Task by 1.

- Player Characters applying the solution created in the previous scene, then the Shepherd's Complication is removed. If this solution requires access to the Shepherd, at Engaged or Close range, then this Task will of course be locked until in range.

- Complications during the Extended Task reduce Power to the ship. Threat spent here can reduce Power points further, point for point.

- This is a Timed Task, with intervals equaling the number of Power points the Player's vessel creates at the beginning of the encounter, each Interval equating to 1 Round of combat.

- If the Player Characters don't complete the Extended Task in time, then the warp core shuts down, no Power is generated by the ship, and main systems will begin to fail (with back-up systems coming online.)

During combat, Sarah will be ignorant of what's happening and instead maintain her prayers to the Shepherd. Sarah will not give up the Shepherd willingly at this stage and will need to be subdued in some manner.

Once the crew have applied their solution to silence the Shepherd, they can look to restoring some semblance of order aboard the ship.

CHAPTER 09.50

THE SHEPHERD
CONCLUSION

WHAT HAPPENS TO THE SHEPHERD?

With the Shepherd safely contained either with the solution the crew initially came up if it was sufficiently sustainable, or in a more sophisticated manner now they've been able to get their bearings.

The Followers will be receiving medical attention. It's going to take some time for the psychological damage to completely heal but they are at least on the road to recovery. They can't simply be dropped back on to Stallas II with the other colonists instantly, and there's still the consideration of the Shepherd and its fellow lifeforms that live on the planet.

Communication with the lifeform may be achieved through an extended scientific study but for now the colonists will either have to abandon Stallas II or at least try and set up safe zones away from the lifeforms. As for the Shepherd itself, it and the rest of its kind just want to be left alone. They have little in the way of needs.

If you've found that your Players during the mission have viewed the Shepherd as a malevolent force, then the above ending can be a nice twist. However, if they've formulated the opinion that the Shepherd has been acting out of self-defense then it could be an equally fun twist to have them now hostile to all intruders on Stallas II.

The Starfleet solution would be to return the Shepherd to the dig site and collapse the tunnel. It's clear that this is certainly where it originated but it may be suggested that it's taken to a starbase initially for study. Let your Players debate this and if they can come up with a logical argument one way or another then run with that idea. Destroying the Shepherd should certainly not be an option but it's possible.

CONTINUING VOYAGES...

If this mission has been run as a part of a series, consider the implications going forward on board the ship. A lot of the crew will require medical review and therapy for a few weeks at least, and this may also present an opportunity for the Players to reassess their Values. Perhaps one of the Players wishes to study the new lifeform further, even perhaps take a role in naming it. As for Stallas II, what happens there? While mentally and physically the colonists can recover, it may take time before they function successfully as a community — there were quite a few deaths and injuries caused by the conflict, people aren't going to forgive as quickly as they heal.